HV
5816
.M34
2002

D0861084

The Fall of
the God of Money

SOCIAL & BEHAVIORAL SCIENCES History, Geography & Area Studies Asia & Oceania

40-4773   HV5816   2002-1882 CIP
McMahon, Keith. **The fall of the god of money: opium smoking in nine-teenth-century China.** Rowman & Littlefield, 2002. 247p bibl index afp ISBN 0-7425-1802-7, $70.00; ISBN 0-7425-1803-5 pbk, $24.95

McMahon (Univ. of Kansas) offers a cross-cultural study of opium, examining Chinese and Western attitudes toward the drug (both societies associated it with the worst features of the other) and the way it was consumed in China and the West. Taking a largely cultural and heavily theoretical approach, the author relies heavily on literary sources, including an 1878 account by a Chinese opium smoker, which is translated fully in an appendix. McMahon also considers the different experiences and images of male and female smokers and demonstrates how cultural norms in China and the West shaped laws against addictive drugs. He suggests that opium smoking was a reasonable choice in a time of cultural conflict and argues that the physical and social costs of opium consumption have been greatly exaggerated. "Opium may be an addiction, but so are steamships, guns, oil, or cars." Readers may disagree. This study contributes to the cultural history of late imperial China and the contemporaneous West, but less to the social and political history of the drug. **Summing Up:** Recommended. Upper-division undergraduates and above.— *R. E. Entenmann, St. Olaf College*

JACKSON LIBRARY
LANDER UNIVERSITY
GREENWOOD, SC 29649

The Fall of
the God of Money

Opium Smoking in
Nineteenth-Century China

Keith McMahon

ROWMAN & LITTLEFIELD PUBLISHERS, INC.
Lanham · Boulder · New York · Oxford

JACKSON LIBRARY
LANDER UNIVERSITY
GREENWOOD, SC 29649

ROWMAN & LITTLEFIELD PUBLISHERS, INC.

Published in the United States of America
by Rowman & Littlefield Publishers, Inc.
An Imprint of the Rowman & Littlefield Publishing Group
4720 Boston Way, Lanham, Maryland 20706
www.rowmanlittlefield.com

12 Hid's Copse Road Cumnor Hill, Oxford OX2 9JJ, England

Copyright © 2002 by Rowman & Littlefield Publishers, Inc.

All rights reserved. No part of this publication may be reproduced, stored
in a retrieval system, or transmitted in any form or by any means, electronic,
mechanical, photocopying, recording, or otherwise, without the prior permission
of the publisher.

British Library Cataloguing in Publication Information Available

Library of Congress Cataloging-in-Publication Data
McMahon, Keith.
    The fall of the god of money : opium smoking in nineteenth-century
China / Keith McMahon.
        p. cm.
Includes bibliographical references and index.
    ISBN 0-7425-1802-7 (alk. paper) – ISBN 0-7425-1803-5 (pbk. : alk.
paper)
    1. Opium habit–China. 2. China–History–19th century. I. Title:
Opium smoking in nineteenth-century China. II. Title.
    HV5816 .M34 2002
    394.1'4–dc21

2002001882

Printed in the United States of America

♾™ The paper used in this publication meets the minimum requirements of
American National Standard for Information Sciences–Permanence of Paper for
Printed Library Materials, ANSI/NISO Z39.48-1992.

Contents

List of Illustrations   vii

Preface   ix

1   Introduction to "Western Smoke"   1

2   A Short History of Opium Smoking in China   33

3   Westerners' Intercourse with China   45

4   Westerners on Opium and the Chinese   69

5   Zhang Changjia's *Yanhua*, "Opium Talk" (1878)   105

6   Eaten by Wild Dogs: Opium in Late Qing Fiction   139

7   "Why the Chinese Smoked Opium"   175

Appendix: *Yanhua*, "Opium Talk," by Zhang Changjia of Jinshan County, Jiangsu Province   193

List of Characters   217

Bibliography   225

Index   235

About the Author   249

Illustrations

Duncan MacPherson, M.D., in the costume of a mandarin,
from the frontispiece of his book, *The War in China*   84

Robert Fortune's illustration of an opium pipe and
paraphernalia from his book, *Three Years' Wanderings in the
Northern Provinces of China*   85

Francis H. Nichols's photo "An Opium Beggar"
from his book, *Through Hidden Shensi*   100

Preface

This study of opium smoking in nineteenth-century China mingles sources from China, Britain, the United States, and France. My premise is that opium is so basic to both the intimacy and the alienation between China and these Western cultures that we must think of it only through this intermingling of sources. In carrying out such a cross-cultural approach, I am assuming that just because opium has certain predictable effects on the person who consumes it, this does not mean that all addicts are alike, all people get equally addicted, or that all people are equally (if at all) attracted to opium. Opium addiction in China was not simply a case of many people consuming a drug and having what a medical expert would classify as a standard range of so-called addictive reactions. Opium was intricately involved with the unfathomable interaction between China, India, Britain, the United States, France, and other European nations, no nation of which was one solid front.

A study like this should ideally take into account the early use of cinnabar and other minerals (including arsenic and mercury), hemp, datura, aconite, poppy, and numerous substances taken throughout Chinese history for various shamanic, euphoric, or other mind-altering purposes. Knowledge of this early history is still in a preliminary state.[1] Lu Xun, Wang Yao, and Yu Jiaxi, among others in this century, have mostly written of mineral-based substances from the Han, Six Dynasties, and after. We would be hard put to find a general term for what are now labeled narcotics, much less for the uses and effects of such substances. "Shamanic" and "euphoric" only roughly capture some of their past uses (which also included rendering victims unconscious in order to rob them). I have started this study at a relatively late date in Chinese history, the middle to late Qing dynasty, when smoking opium is much more familiar to us, since it closely precedes the type of narcotic drug use prevalent all over the world from the nineteenth century on. Opium is also

more familiar to us because Euro-Western imperialism has tied these countries to one another in newly extended ways. Numerous studies exist concerning the early history of such drugs, tracing their use among relatively
isolated groups of indigenous peoples (e.g., datura or coca in the Americas
before the arrival of Europeans) down to the chemically refined drugs of
consumers in the contemporary capitalist world. The location of this study
in both time and place focuses on the beginning of the more global uses of
drugs like opium. The historical result of this transition from more isolated
and local uses is that intoxicants like opium have been condemned and
banned. Why this banning has occurred is a question that still needs addressing, and thus the writing of this book. The poppy has gone from being
a minor but valuable item in the panoply of age-old drugs to one of the most
moneymaking substances sold today and one of the most attractive drugs
ever to exist.

Since I hope this book will be of use not only to scholars but also to students reading about early modern China, I have given substantial attention
to an area that is of inherent importance to these students: the framing itself
of knowledge about China by the Euro-West. I thus devote a complete chapter to this topic in which opium, though always in the background, is hardly
discussed. Since opium is of such fundamental significance in the way China
and the Euro-West began to interact and characterize each other in the nineteenth century, I have also concentrated on the ways in which this framing
of knowledge about China overlaps with perceptions of opium smoking and
drug addiction in general. The message should be clear, therefore, that it is
impossible to write about Chinese opium smoking without considering how
opium traveled and how much it both joined and divided so-called East and
West. We find elementary etymological examples of such cross-traveling in
the fact that the Chinese word for opium, *yapian*, is a loanword (possibly
Arabic or Persian), as is the English word "yen," as in "to have a yen for
something," which derives from the Chinese word *yin* for addiction (and
probably also *yan* for smoke).

Finally, writing about such a sensational issue as drugs, I have tried to
avoid overarching and melodramatic statements. But a few are irresistible.
When there are other problems (social, personal, ecological, etc.), the drug
problem will be worse. Drugs, however, will not "solve" those problems.
What it means either to outlaw drugs or to go off them, then, should be obvious: minor solutions for major problems. It is also true that drugs are not
trivial. The need for them will overwhelm, outrun, and out-invent all attempts to control them. Anything that is taken too seriously—and here I
mean things like sobriety, private property, right to own guns, right to consume expendable resources of any type—will induce a parody of itself. The
role that drugs have been given is precisely to parody these various types of
sobriety. Parodying also means being a parasite on or doubling and replac-

ing the original in a maddening way. If it is a question of the right to own or to consume, drugs will outdo anyone in owning and consuming. These statements were not thinkable prior to the drug era that we have now lived in for two centuries. So, to put it simply, why have drugs come to mean so much and to be so difficult to deal with in these times?

Many friends have helped with advice and information about sources in the early stages of this study, especially Roger Bradshaw, Chris Connery, Ken Irby, and Simon Schuchat. My colleague at the University of Kansas, Feng Shengli, gave me much needed help with my translation of "Opium Talk." Michael Nylan devoted many hours to a careful editing of the manuscript and provided an extremely helpful critical commentary. Students in my classes at the University of Kansas aided me as well, especially Brian Baker, whose collection of antique drug paraphernalia was inspiring and instructive. Anonymous readers have helped along the way, especially the latest and most generous from Rowman & Littlefield, whose editors and production staff have also been very kind and supportive. My family, Maija, Teija, and my wife, Deborah Peterson, have helped the most, especially in converting me from the addiction to being single. This book is dedicated to Deborah Peterson.

NOTE

1. Datura stramonium is known by several names, including *yangjinhua* and *mantuoluohua*; aconitum carmichaeli is known as *wuhui* (see Li Ling 1993, 306–9).

Chapter One

Introduction to "Western Smoke"

THE ARRIVAL OF OPIUM

As the black sheep sibling of Coca-Cola and other consumer stimulants, opium opens up one of the first truly global crises of identity. By global I mean the new world that is joined by the opium trade between Britain and China beginning in the early nineteenth century and by the exponential growth of the phenomenon of addiction during and after the same period. The issue I want to explore is the difficulty that arises when cultural identity—in this case, Chinese, British, American, and other Asian and European Western—is no longer secure because of the formation of this new world. Opium is one of the primary carriers of this transformation.

What unique qualities enabled opium to exert such a radical effect in the nineteenth century? Opium creates in the addict its own unshakable and self-justifying world, one that might seem to differ little from that of any people who are certain of their needs, or of the god or scientology they believe in. The nineteenth-century appearance of science fiction and the idea of people from alternate worlds strangely coincide with the appearance of the use of opium and other mind-altering drugs on a mass scale. Before that time there had only been adultery of a sexual sort. Now alternate worlds suggested adultery of another sort altogether. The Oriental dope fiend loved the opium way of life, not "our" way of living. The demonization of the Orient that appears in many nineteenth-century writings (Thomas De Quincey's in particular)[1] signals this fear of an alien other who defies being converted and assimilated to "monogamy." The awesomeness of China was threatening in a most fundamental way, no matter how superior Euro-American weapons, religion, or forms of government might seem to be. However heathen or sottish, the Chinese appeared to live in certainty of their eternal superiority and invincibility. Such extreme contradictions produce extreme solutions: go to war or smoke opium; either way, global identity crisis.

I center my account of this confrontation on an otherwise unknown writer named Zhang Changjia, who in 1878 published "Opium Talk," a collection of comments and short narratives about his experience of opium addiction. Like many other works of its time, it firmly embeds the phenomenon of addiction in the cross-cultural history of the nineteenth century. The intrusion of Westerners into China coincides with the arrival of opium, both of which signal irreversible transformation. As Zhang writes, "The rise of the opium demon has led to the fall of the god of money," meaning that no one can love money more than opium. The fall of money–Chinese money–in turn parallels the fall of Confucius, for "it is impossible for the way of Confucius to take effect in the foreign lands. Christianity, however, is surely on its way to transforming China."[2]

Although Zhang never questions the one-way nature of this transformation from "west" to "east," our extension of his words should be that a new global space immediately formed for everyone when opium became a main medium of exchange between China and Britain. From this we should also ask, If opium so fundamentally hinged the early relationship between Chinese and Euro-Westerners, and if it was such a solid generator of wealth, then to what extent does opium still underlie these relations and the situations of modernity itself? How has addiction shadowed the formation of a global symbolic order? How have opium and its addictive demands affected cultural and national loyalties of any sort, whether "Eastern" or "Western," to God or gods, to formerly hallowed values, laws, or pleasures? In posing such questions, I am taking into account the role of opium in the economic and administrative functioning of European colonialism and the late Chinese empire. Smoking itself as a way of life has not been questioned adequately. The fundamental issue is how opium the drug symbolically marks a man, a woman, or a nation as a whole. Likewise, the historical conditions in which opium smoking as a way of life became possible have not been thoroughly questioned. How did opium smoking and addiction appear on a mass scale in world history when they did?

In answering these questions, I address a series of points, starting with the idea of opium as a key agent in the formation of the concept of the global. Opium is central in the world commodity trade system from the early nineteenth century on, in a distinctively different way from other major commodities such as tea, coffee, sugar, or silk. First, opium's distinction lies in its central role in the defining processes of the imperial, colonial project, processes that were grounded in the postulation of the incommensurable difference between the cultures of Europe and China.

Second, there is an overlap between the idea of incommensurable difference between Europe and China with the two main discursive realms of culture and gender. The question here becomes, How have cultural and gender differences defined addiction and the use of drugs like opium? In other words, how do we compare drug use among different drug users? Cultural and gender differences among individual smokers, both male and female, and on a broader level between the masses of Chinese opium "sots" and European "drunkards" are central to my analysis of both Western and Chinese texts on opium smoking. The debate that pitted opium against alcohol, in short, tied in with the debate that distinguished the remote and self-satisfied Chinese—who are "effeminate"—from the outgoing and progressive Europeans—marked as masculine.

The image of the remote, self-satisfied Chinese leads to a third essential point: the idea of opium as signifier of an uncanny otherness. Opium euphoria exposes a new form of insatiability—a monstrous type of enjoyment that appears profoundly narcissistic to the sober subject. In terms of culturally defined entities, the effeminate "Asiatic" acquires a strange fullness that in turn threatens to envelope and consume the sober, masculine "European." In gendered terms, opium phallicizes the inferior while emasculating the superior. Opium exerts a doubling effect, moreover, in its parasitism on the capital market as a commodity that outdoes all other commodities. It is the commodity par excellence, functioning in a way that apes the capital market by channeling all demand to itself and sapping the demand for anything else. As this uncanny other, opium creates a parody of sober society, mirroring the supposed narcissism of the addict back onto the narcissistically protected center of the capital system.

The idea of opium parody leads to my fourth point, namely, the necessity of challenging the conventional rhetoric of drug use and addiction. I incorporate the thoughts of numerous writers, including (besides Zhang Changjia) Avital Ronell, Jean Cocteau, and William Burroughs, to make the general statement that smoking opium and becoming addicted to it are entirely relevant ways of living both the disruptions and the daily life of what we may call the opium era in China. In the preface to "Opium Talk," the writer throws open the definition of addiction by asserting that it is not only the smokers who are addicted: "What finally is today's greatest addiction?" the preface writer asks as he mocks the overly ambitious plans of inept rulers. "How can it only be opium?" The common definitions of addiction refer to a minor and very specific form of addiction—an individual addict's dependence on opium. The legal and moral pronouncements on addiction amount to paranoic delimitations of forms of consciousness: straight consciousness ardently defends itself against supposedly dangerous forms of altered consciousness.

All such notions about addiction developed over time, and the conditions for their formation were already in place at the beginning of the opium era. I use the following allegory (the first of several in this book) to describe opium's historical effects. The history of the opium interaction between Britain and China is a story of seduction and estrangement. For British merchants, opium was a commercial panacea that opened a Chinese market that had stubbornly remained closed until seduced by opium. But China was seduced by opium only. Nothing else British was attractive to the Chinese, though all came along anyway. Meanwhile, China entered a giant opium present that, if we use Zhang Changjia's words to portray it, was characterized by the repetitive cycle of the opium high and the opium crash. The coolie on opium was one of the most visible figures of this cycle. He was a human beast in repetitive motion, back and forth from point to point, traveling with enormous burdens and fueled by meager rations and opium dross (cheaper opium already smoked by wealthier smokers). This opium present was a void, a place with no future or past. To nonsmokers, especially the Euro-Westerners, this void was a menace, something they faced the possibility of being sucked into. To the Westerner, the opium smoker became a threatening monster that represented absolute lack of forward realistic drive. The opium sot was the quintessential image of the Chinese, even to the progressive Chinese elite. By the 1890s and early 1900s, state, medical, and moral-religious alliances were formed in an international effort to discharge opium addiction from the planet.

For the telling of this history, Zhang Changjia's "Opium Talk" has been my main inspiration. Using his and other works, I foreground the convergence of Chinese and British history on the phenomena of opium and addiction. In numerous Chinese renditions, opium, Christianity, and Westerners made up an integral threesome that was "transforming China," as Zhang Changjia said. But in the dominant European rendition, opium was the perfect drug for the Chinese, who were seen to be sottish and addicted to pleasure by nature. Opium smoking thus proved either that the Chinese were indeed heathens who needed the Western Christian to save them or that the Western merchant selling opium to the Chinese was not introducing something new and unnatural.

The other literary sources that I use include poetry and a number of nineteenth-century novels. All of these help show how opium served in relationships among addicts: for example, between men in opium dens, men and prostitutes in brothels, and husbands and wives at home. The relations between addicts and nonaddicts are crucial as well. Novels are the main source for the portrayal of female addicts. These women include the opportunistic prostitute whose opium smoking is part of her working survival and the spoiled daughter who demands the finest opium before setting off for her marriage and life in the home of her parents-in-law. The prostitute takes or rejects men depending on their ability to support her. Male wastrels who ruin themselves pursuing their fascination with opium and prostitutes are easily replaced by other men. The addicted prostitute's eventual ruination comes with the loss of health and looks that is hastened by opium smoking. The married woman addict is destroyed by her infertility and jealousy over her husband's prettier (not yet opium-emaciated) concubine. These women and their addicted babies (or the babies they don't have) represent a symbolic culmination of the spread of opium smoking. If addicted men and women pass their addiction on to their children, then the proverbial "everyone" becomes addicted. As we will see, the totalizing spread of opium is one of the strongest assertions of the prohibitionist argument against opium, in China and in Europe.

THEORIZING OPIUM

Opium as "Eyesore"

In regard to opium as a way of life, it is not enough to simply report the experiences of opium smoking from the various perspectives I have named. The definition of addiction and the emblematic difference between the Chinese who smoke opium and the Westerners who do not also take on meaning in the symbolic cross-cultural order that encompasses all subjects involved. In this order subjects assume roles according to both conscious and unconscious cultural heritages that govern everyday life. Once the two great orders of "China" and the "Euro-West" began to interact (trying to pinpoint exactly when that began is impossible), a new global space constituting another symbolic order automatically took shape then and there. The new symbolic order was characterized by unresolvable questions of inclusion and exclusion, continuity and discontinuity, and symmetry and asymmetry. In material terms, the question came down to assigning and distributing symbolic value that could also be translated into actual wealth.

The difficulty of this interaction is signaled by the confusion and disruption that occur when different cultural heritages, which a priori are unevenly matched, come into confrontation. Of these two competing cultures, one inevitably assumes the offensive mode, that of the exclusivist and discriminating Master. It generates a fashionable crowd that overwhelms the unfashionable with shame and loss. Specifically, the symbols of what it is to be Western and modern begin to take the form of a kind of pedagogy that has to be persistently translated and retranslated into an ostensibly international language. This language has to be inclusive of and persuasive to the symbolically alien Chinese, that is, the non-Western and nonmodern but the supposedly "also human." In Homi Bhabha's rendition, the dominating force of the colonial sword displaces the native "superego" but cannot replace it with anything, leaving the native in a state of loss: "a melancholia in revolt" (Bhabha 1992, 65). Displacing the Chinese superego is like Zhang Changjia's

Christianity transforming China and driving Confucianism off the stage. But the so-called exchange does not necessarily imply that what is introduced or exchanged remains identical to itself. Christianity, for example, does not stand only for itself but also transposes with—or comes along in the same breath as—opium. That is, Christian transformation also becomes opium transformation; Christianity is consumed as opium; one becomes Christian-Western Chinese by smoking opium, which comes from the "West." The unabashed smoking of opium is an "incorpora[tion] of loss or lack" in the Chinese addict's own body, which is also an "act of 'disincorporating' the authority of the Master" (Bhabha 1992, 65). "The native wears his psychic wounds on the surface of his skin like an open sore—an eyesore to the colonizer"—as Bhabha further explains (referring to Frantz Fanon). In other words, opium smoking is guaranteed to be distasteful to the Master's eye.

This is the symbolic framework in which I place opium. One of the main terms for opium in the nineteenth century was *yangyan*, "Western-sea smoke." The word *yang* is also one of the main terms for Western foreigner, *yangren*, "people of the Western seas."[3] My point in signaling these terms is that whatever was Western, whether smoke or Christianity, never made its way to China simply as a refulfilling displacement of Chineseness. The effect of that displacement brought a chaos of cross-categorization as opium and Christianity left the hands of Western purveyors and recombined in unpredictable ways (the Chinese-Christian Taiping Rebellion being one of the most outstanding examples). Opium as commercial panacea opened up China and generated good business. But it also became the open sore that scandalized the colonizer, who then began to fear for his own "disincorporation" by teeming Asiatics. The late Victorian specter (c. 1890s) was the revenge of the colonial world on the colonizer. The Asiatic and his opium were already speeding toward England and America and threatening to cross and confuse boundary lines of race and gender.

Opium smoking signified in both shared and unshared symbolic orders of China and the Euro-West certain binaries that occupied the lenses of mutual recognition and misrecognition in those times. The Chinese smoked opium; the British "ate" (actually drank) it in the form of laudanum. Smoking was a "luxuriant" use; drinking was for the sake of curing ailments. The Chinese smoked in company; the laudanum drinker like De Quincey proudly kept his solitude.[4] The Chinese reclined; the European was upright. De Quincey had horrific nightmares, which after the publication of *Confessions of an English Opium Eater* in 1821 became a trope of British-American opium discourse. The nightmare is not a theme in Zhang Changjia's "Opium Talk" and other nineteenth-century Chinese sources. The term "opium sot" is an English locution that usually refers to a male Asiatic who is stupefied by opium. From a Chinese perspective we should refer to the opium wastrel, who was a member of a family that he was potentially ruining through his expenditures on opium. The "opium sot" was someone incapable of articulation. But Zhang Changjia the opium addict spoke as a hero of opium smoking, using language and style that assumed an elite understanding of classical Chinese texts. Contrasts such as these—especially smoking versus eating, company versus solitude, reclining versus standing—must make us suspicious of any universalizing assumptions about the experience of opium or other psychotropic substances. All such experiences must be attended to in terms of their historical and cultural conditions of possibility. Even such particulars as reading De Quincey, or not, influenced the way persons wrote about and consumed opium.

The Conflation of China and Opium

I start my investigation with a conflation of nineteenth-century British-American characterizations of Chinese in general and of opium smokers in particular. This conflation was a central trope of both Euro-Western strategies in China and the major defining constructs of opium, other narcotics, and addiction itself. In nineteenth-century Britain and North America, the Chinese were not only Chinese but also "Asiatic" and "Oriental," not to mention heathen. Opium smoking, as already noted, was a quintessentially "Oriental" activity. By late century, opium was thought to suck the brain dry, deprive the person of will, strip men of their virility, and turn women into sexual demons. Opium threatened to usurp all human and divine sovereignty and, as late nineteenth-century prohibitionists warned, would succeed in counterabsorbing the Euro-American unless "stern" measures were taken.

What opium did to the Chinese or anyone who smoked it was not the only issue. The institutionalized selling of it was also a topic of intense debate. Opium was *the* commodity in that critical period of the so-called opening of China. At the same time, opium commerce already exposed too baldly the capitalist system of opening up and channeling consumption for the capitalist to accrue the most profit to himself. In other words, it was too easy a sell and brought too easy a profit.[5] Such accusations were made throughout the nineteenth century but became especially vociferous after the 1860s in Britain and the United States.[6] By that time foreign traders had made tremendous fortunes. The unmistakable attributes of modern capitalism—its creative and destructive energies, its cycles of production and consumption, and the phenomenal accumulation of capital—that Marx described so vividly in *Das Kapital* and other works—had become fully established. Indeed, the commercialization of opium was vital not only to the British colony of India and numerous individual traders, but also to the formation of modern capitalism itself.[7] Once they were well organized and financed, capitalists could afford to begin distancing themselves from the opium trade. Although

Britain (in India) and other colonial powers (France in Cochin China and Holland in the Netherland Indies) continued to derive substantial revenues from their opium monopolies for the rest of the century, the days were soon approaching when respectable capitalists and capitalist nations would no longer deal directly in such a thing as opium.[8]

In the history of economic and commercial relations between China and Britain, opium played a privileged but also unwieldy role. The most succinct example of opium's unwieldiness, and the unwieldiness of relations with China in general, is the fact that the British and American hold on opium was not invincible. Instead, it had to yield to participation by the Chinese themselves. As J. Y. Wong shows, after the legalization of the opium trade, which Britain forced on China in the Tianjin Treaty (1858–1859), China began growing its own opium on a large scale (the previous Nanking Treaty of 1842 had the de facto result of unstopping the opium trade, but it did not actually specify the legalization of opium).[9] Soon Chinese production exceeded the foreign import at cheaper prices (later the Japanese entered the market with their importation of morphine into China). What this competition shows in general is that the Chinese, however disadvantaged they were, found ways to customize both their participation in and evasion of cooperative relations with powers that were monopolizing stunningly increasing amounts of capital and resources.[10]

The conflation between China and opium smoking was a strongly contributing factor in the production of knowledge about both China and opium the narcotic. Although my purpose in this book is to describe opium smoking in the cross-cultural context, I also want to challenge the dominant political rhetoric about drugs in the twentieth century.[11] In the next few pages I lay the groundwork for this message, which will weave through the presentation in later chapters of sources from both China and the Euro-West. The basic tenets of the prevailing rhetoric about drugs were in existence from the early days of interaction between British and Chinese in the late eighteenth and the nineteenth centuries. In those times opium smoking was already becoming defined as an activity performed by unfit humans, the Chinese being one major illustration of that theorem. They were soon becoming a generalized figure of stagnation, underdevelopment, and irrationality. The definition of addiction and the vilification and suppression of opium as opposed to alcohol or cigarettes have everything to do with drawing lines between fit and unfit states of being.

In framing these and earlier points theoretically, I rely on two types of thinking, those having to do with colonialism and Orientalism and those concerning drug addiction, both of which rely heavily on the theories of psychoanalysis. The primary sources of this book, however, are nontheorists from diverse times and places like the late Qing Zhang Changjia, the early twentieth-century Jean Cocteau, the late Qing novelist Peng Yang'ou, or the mid–nineteenth century British physician Duncan MacPherson. I have drawn them together as if in a dialogue about the significance of opium smoking in the cross-cultural context of what amounts to the first period of addiction on a mass scale in world history. Fictional, autobiographical, and various other types of accounts represent opium smoking as a specific Chinese problem and as an issue assuming significance across both largely defined cultures. The questions to ask include the following: Who is the Chinese opium smoker? How does he function in Chinese society and in the cross-cultural society? What kind of humans are opium smokers seen to be? Why do so many of them appear in China in these times? Why is Western attention so riveted on Chinese opium smokers? The central and highly rhetorical question is, Why do Chinese smoke but not Euro-Westerners? All such questions can be summed up as a quest to identify the opium smoker as a character type in the grand scenario of China, Europe, and America from the 1830s to the end of the Qing in 1911.

The Totalizing Allegory of Opium Addiction

In describing the symbolic role of opium in the Chinese social order, I find it useful to refer to allegorical frameworks suggested by Qing narrative fiction. Character types in these works such as misers, shrews, and polygamists (as well as wastrels, beauties, and scholars) define gender hierarchies, family relationships, and sexual economies, symbolizing conscious and unconscious positions in a grand social order.[12] At the apex of this society is the polygamist, whose fantasy of unlimited access to as many women as possible is the most authoritative and commanding of all. All other characters have to arrange themselves or be arranged around this centering model of desire and its assumption of the primacy of the male cycle of energy. Subordinates destroy each other but also form alliances through which they support each other and achieve some measure of control over superiors. Novels of the nineteenth century inherit the character types of earlier fiction but are written in a time when the Chinese male primacy is disturbed by the intruding primacy of the "Western" cycle of energy. The profligate wastrel of earlier fiction also enters a qualitatively new realm as he now ruins himself and family with the help of opium.

Much of this fiction is heavily focused on the erotic. One of the main uses of opium is as an aphrodisiac. I expand on this use to read erotic elements into a variety of opium interactions, whether attraction or repulsion, whether between man and prostitute or British observer and Chinese smoker. Zhang Changjia's "Opium Talk" can be thought of as an erotics of opium smoking, an activity that he and others commonly refer to as inducing "lovesickness," with opium assuming the role of unrequiting lover. The pleasure of opium, as Zhang writes, supersedes all others, especially that of sex. Thus opium severely challenges the normative categories of sex in the service of social and sexual reproduction. Radically unfamiliar boundary crossings suddenly appear as floods to those who at this point become guardian officials of sobriety. This threat of flood comes into play in the turn-of-the-century attempt by numerous nations to control states of consciousness by designating the manner in which certain substances can and cannot be consumed.

Before going into theoretical reasons and examples for why opium is condemned, I set two brief allegories side by side—one Chinese, one Western—to demonstrate how each culture arrived at the conclusion by which opium was totalized into an ultimate menace to social order and stability.

The polygamist, so common in earlier fiction, returns in a new guise as the wealthy male smoker who goes from experiencing opium as aphrodisiac to suffering emasculation at the hands of what turns into an insatiable and fixating lovesickness. In what I call the core opium allegory of the late imperial fantasmatic, this male smoker takes the form of the wastrel son whose father purposely indulges this addiction as a method of pacification. In one famous version of this story, the father is a rich miser who deliberately addicts his son in order to keep him passive at home and thus prevents him from depleting the family wealth on gambling and prostitutes. The plan backfires, however. As found in pictorial, fictional, and even cinematic representations in late Qing and early Republican China, the son brings complete ruin on himself and his family. In an alternate version of this story, instead of deliberately addicting his son, the father merely indulges and tolerates his son's addiction. He thinks at least to save face by having a son who supposedly stays obediently at home. Whatever version it may be, the life of the opium wastrel also becomes an allegory for the ruin of China, while the chief culprit for this ruin is the greedy merchant from the "Western seas." Thus we have the accusation found in countless documents throughout the nineteenth century and heard by Westerners in their exchanges with Chinese of all levels.

The totalizing allegory is one of opium addiction as a figure of the essential catastrophe of China in this period. Mingled in this story is the sense of helpless loss and devastation and of inferiority before the dominant outsider. In some late Qing satires, moreover, the Chinese are opium addicts because the Chinese "would do that"; others, like the Westerners, know better. Such a totalization of opium is apparent in not only fiction or common assumptions but also the late Qing politics of prohibitionism, especially the movements of the early 1900s (Su Zhiliang 1997, 197ff.; Zhou 1999). The eventual solution to opium addiction and the broader problems that opium represented came to a head in the early 1950s Communist purge of opium, prostitution, gambling, polygamy, and all other signs of "feudal" backwardness and decadence. Any reliance on a foreigner takes on the appearance of addiction, which is categorically rejected in a move to create a new and pristine space of "modern," self-energized independence. Although these post-Qing developments get ahead of my story in this book, it is important in understanding twentieth-century Chinese history to view opium addiction in this allegorizing way as a figure of Chinese dependence on and abjection before modernizing Western nations.

There is also a Western opium story comparable in significance to the Chinese sketch above, which undoes any concept of the complete victimization of China before an all-confident Euro-West. The key to the Western allegory is the conflation of China and the opium smoker that I have spoken of above. This allegory is a précis of what chapters 3–4 relate in more detail.

The Westerners were a "master race" who landed on the shores of another race of people who seemed convinced of their superiority but lived in a very contrary way. For the British, superior reason justified using superior weapons to force the free-marketization of opium on China; thus the Opium War of 1839. It was the Chinese and their "craven" lying and stupefied addiction that kept evading every attempt to listen to reason (i.e., desires based on reasoning about "progress"). China was in fact the drug itself to swallow and inhale, which meant a surrender of reason and clarity. To some, that surrender was at the same time—it seemed dangerously and mysteriously so—also a voluptuous enhancement of reason and clarity such that it was unnecessary to do anything but stay on opium. Opium made perfect sense as the Chinese intoxicant. It represented the essence of a negatingly alternate and equally if not more masterful way of life. The question at the back of the superior mind, then, was whether the "antediluvian" Chinese actually had some knowledge that was more important and closer to the so-called true source of being. The Chinese appeared self-sufficient and impervious to foreign science and products. In other words, they had all the earmarks of another master race.

This story of competing master races resembles the story of the wastrel ruining China in that they both construe opium in a totalizing way. But there are major differences in the way these two arrive at prohibitionism. The British prohibition movement viewed opium as something that threatened to sweep through populations on a massive scale. Opium addiction became a giant symbol of disorder. Opium was marked as something qualitatively different from the traditionally accepted intoxicant, alcohol. It was the mark of a qualitative and alienating difference between Chinese and Westerners. Despite the cross-cultural similarities in the condemnation of opium addiction, prohibition in Britain was significantly defined by the fear of British smokers becoming like the demonic masses of Chinese. As for prohibition in China, it eventually leagued itself with and looked like the movement in Europe and the United States. Nevertheless, it was centrally defined by the Chinese accusation that Britain and other nations deliberately poisoned China in their greedy desire for profit. Chinese prohibitionism was therefore central to nationalistic self-assertion in the face of foreign dominance. In Britain and the United States, on the other hand, the prohibitionist concern was about cultural and racial deterioration. It was fear of potential loss rather than shame about inferiority to another dominant culture. Another way to say this is that Western nationalism "got there first." It thus occupied a central position that had to be constantly defended against infiltration and degradation.

OPIUM ADDICTION IN A CROSS-CULTURAL CONTEXT

Situating and Defining This Study

In one of the most informative pieces on opium in China to date, Jonathan Spence writes about "opium smoking as a phenomenon that radically affected all levels of Chinese society."[13] Following the spirit of his use of the word "radically," I see opium addiction as an outstanding example of so-called nonproductive, irresponsible, and parasitical activity. I want to define what meanings "parasitical" or other like terms take on in the context of the relations between China and Western nations. In particular, what are the varying perspectives on how opium smoking is "unproductive" depending on whether one is Chinese, Western, smoker, nonsmoker, male or female, rich or poor, to name some of the main categories by which I will conduct my discussion.

To a Chinese prohibitionist, for instance, the parasitism of opium addiction took the form of land used for opium cultivation usurping land needed for grain production, a process that led to increasingly frequent famine in the later nineteenth century and after.[14] Chinese leaders and ideologues thus hoped to reinstill people with traditional values of economic activity and well-being. Opium irresponsibility also symbolized China's inability to compete with stronger foreign nations. China was coming under pressure from newly formulating values of modernization in military capability, political and economic institutions, expertise in Western learning, especially science, and general social mores. For Christian missionaries, opium consumption was something that turned people away from salvational religion. Opium euphoria or dependence outdid any call for devotion to God. And for capitalists with industrializing inclinations, the question was whether opium smoking was conducive to the disciplines of mass production and consumption. As unconcerned with the ethical aspects of the opium problem as the capitalists may have been, they were nevertheless driven by speed and efficiency. Opium was something that consumed debilitating amounts of time. The question was, In spite of what capitalists gained from their century-long experience with the opium trade, would opium smoking accommodate their visions of capitalist expansion and accumulation?

I also see opium as vitally productive and functional in the everyday life of Chinese society as it impinged on, and was impinged on by, Western society. Chinese, Indians, Japanese, Europeans, North Americans, and others made tremendous fortunes in the opium trade. Income from opium played an integral role in the economic functioning of China in the nineteenth century, especially in helping the Chinese collect taxes and repay foreign debts. Coolies who carried the baggage of Western travelers who wrote about China and opium used opium themselves as an aid to (or relief from) their grueling work (as did the Chinese laborers who worked in mines and on railroads in the western United States). Prostitutes used opium to lure customers and earn money from them. Some also spent hours around the opium lamp with special lovers who, they hoped, would buy them out of prostitution. Businessmen and other well-off men and women smoked throughout life but nevertheless kept their business and household affairs intact.[15]

Some Chinese, British, and other foreign observers recognized these everyday uses of opium and admitted the serious harms that could result, yet refused to vilify opium to the exclusion of other problems. But these views were the minority. In the prevailing eye opium addiction was loathed as a sign of degeneracy, sloth, and lack of humanity. The seemingly profound detachment of the addict, his apparent "libidinal autonomy," in Avital Ronell's words, introduces a "scandalous figure" into human society. He or she constituted a threat to the sense of "human connectivity." "Perhaps the hint of libidinal autonomy," as Ronell continues, "furnishes the most menacing among social attitudes" (Ronell 1992, 53–54). In Euro-American eyes in particular, the inscrutable Chinese, who were utterly convinced of the superiority of their culture, epitomized self-complacency. In short, the Chinese were libidinal autonomists and opium addicts, all of them!

The "scandalous figure" of the opium addict is a relatively new locution in the study of opium in China. Others have discussed the rise of the opium trade and the origins of the Opium War (e.g., Chang 1970), the consumption and distribution of opium, its prohibition, and its functioning in the Chinese economy (e.g., Spence 1992), its role in foreign policy (Walker 1991), its role in internal Chinese politics of the pre–mid nineteenth century (Polachek 1992), or the efforts of Protestant missionaries in the suppression of opium in China (Lodwick 1996). Of four recent and valuable studies, one focuses on social, political, and economic aspects in the history of proscribed drugs, mainly opium, from the eighteenth century to the present (Su Zhiliang 1997); another on nineteenth-century Chinese and Western efforts toward opium suppression and attitudes about opium smoking as a social problem (Howard 1998); a third on opium, imperialism, and the Arrow War (Wong 1998); and a fourth on drug suppression campaigns and nationalism in twentieth-century China (Zhou 1999). Two other recent studies focus on opium in Asia as a whole (East, South, and Southeast), one on opium and the formation of the global political economy (Trocki 1999), the other on the illegal trade in opium after the international prohibitions of the early twentieth century (Meyer and Parssinen 1998). Finally, a collection of articles on opium in 1839–1952 provides a broad perspective on the political and economic aspects of the opium trade and on the systems of authority that have attempted to control the use, production, and distribution of opium (Brook and Wakabayashi 2000).[16]

In general, these works have tended to limit the perspectives of the opium smokers themselves, including how these smokers might defend or account for themselves. Moreover, they tend not to ask why addiction is viewed as a problem to begin with, that is, why in the social-symbolic order has the addict come to be assigned the role of a pariah? In attempting to answer such questions, I address two topics: (1) opium as a way of life–the culture and experience, both individual and collective, of opium smoking and addiction in China and (2) opium addiction as social disruption–the ways in which this way of life is interpreted as scandalous and antisocial, both in cross-cultural and native contexts.

The Fictional Structure of Addiction

The second of these topics–opium addiction as something scandalous–already appears in studies that have influenced my understanding of opium smoking in China, including Avital Ronell's *Crack Wars* (1992), quoted above. What I add to her work and the others is the consideration of opium smoking and the definition of addiction in the cross-cultural context of China and Western nations. Of special interest is the question of whether the word "addiction" itself and even the experience of addiction can be assumed to have uniform meaning in such different historical and cultural situations.

Ronell's work, although "Western" in focus, is most useful in describing addiction from the perspective of the nineteenth-century Anglo-American outsider looking into China, for example, the missionary, capitalist, diplomat, plant collector, sinologist, or writer and reader of late Victorian fiction about villainous, opium-smoking Chinese. Ronell collects various ways of saying what "we . . . hold against the drug addict," which in effect designates the fictional structure we inhabit whenever we divide ourselves off from the drug addict as alien other (Ronell 1992, 102–4). Besides the addict's supposed "libidinal autonomy," or "narcissistic withdrawal" (pp. 52–53, from Freud), there is also escape into a "world of simulacrum and fiction" (p. 102, citing Derrida), the idea of "mysticism in the absence of God" or "mysticism without mysticism or experience without truth" (p. 103, citing Bataille). These expressions are important to keep in mind when reading De Quincey and others who write of the uncanny feeling they have before the heathen Asiatic masses or the inscrutable and self-satisfied Oriental. Closed off from outsiders, the opium-smoking Chinese are in possession of secret joys. But they appear to be in love with themselves, not the foreigners, who shake their heads at what they see are excessive, inhuman pleasures.

Ronell also speaks of the "structure of addiction," which is "anterior" to the "empirical availability" of drugs like opium or crack (p. 103). This so-called anterior structure is part of a cultural metaphysic that set in soon after the British began trading opium for Chinese tea and silver in the late eighteenth and early nineteenth centuries. Although eighteenth-century British generally held the Chinese in high esteem, the situation changed radically in the next hundred years. The assumption firmly in place by the nineteenth century was that Chinese and other heathens smoked opium but the Judeo-Christian English would not. The same metaphysic applied whether or not it was a question of opium. The Asiatic had become a priori inferior if not subhuman in everything from bodily function to moral values. The addiction of millions of Chinese became the sign of their defiance or "refusal of the organic body," that is, of the conventionally healthy way of caring for the body (p. 114). The addict was a figure par excellence of the unnaturalness of opium smoking. "What do we hold against the addict?" Ronell asks, answering with Derrida's words: "In the name of this organic and originary naturalness of the body we declare and wage war on drugs."[17]

Opium and Victorian England

Conflating China (or "Asiatic") as a whole and the opium smoker in particular figures repeatedly in British literature, especially Victorian fiction (whose authors never went to China).[18] Numerous authors created "narratives about mysterious and evil opium dens in the East End of London," repeatedly figuring this Oriental presence as an "insidious invasion" from within the British empire itself (Milligan 1995, 85). As Barry Milligan observes, oriental associations surrounding opium "have become so entrenched in American, English, and European cultures that they have attached themselves to other controlled substances with no discernible Oriental origins" (p. 8). Coleridge, De Quincey, and later nineteenth-century writers and prohibitionists repeatedly return to the theme of the Asiatic threat to British identity. The same mingling of "fear, desire, guilt, [and] titillation" in the perception of this threat appears (although in somewhat more reserved form) in the writings of the authors I examine in chapters 3–4, who actually traveled through and lived in China in the same period (p. 7).

This late Victorian sensationalization of the Orient takes on further historical significance in light of the role of monstrosity in the nineteenth-century imperial imagination.[19] In natural science from Linnaeus to Darwin, the natural world ideally constituted an ultimately knowable whole, an order in which no species or variation of a species was alien or monstrous. This assumption of "consonant wholeness" was also a figuration for an imperial whole–the British Empire in its exercise of control through a comprehensive and archival knowledge of all aspects of life in the empire.[20] Late Victorian writers, however, as exemplified by Bram Stoker, author of *Dracula* (1897), began to imagine beings that defied the natural order of the Darwinian paradigm (Richards 1993, 49). The newly constructed notion of the "mutant" crystallized a type of monstrosity that escaped existing modes of categorization (p. 58). The opium addict, like the mutant, threatens the imperial center as a peripheral being unhinged from historical lineage and natural form. As Thomas Richards observes, "overwhelmingly the mutation tends to be represented as the revenge of the colonial world on the colonizer" (p. 61). Although not from a British colony, Dracula and his cohorts infiltrate Britain from a peripheral region on the margin between East and West. The vampire is like the Chinese addicts who began in the late 1800s to inhabit London's East End opium dens. Both are like new diseases arriving from peripheries that attempt to "colonize the center" (p. 61). Against such threats, the imperial center summons all its powers of knowledge and mastery of science and technology to defeat the vampire and, in parallel fashion, ultimately to justify legally outlawing the addict.[21]

The organization and production of knowledge as it evolved in late Victorian England play a comparable role in the emergence of state control over narcotics in nineteenth-century England.[22] Scholars have linked this control with the emergence of new explanatory frameworks for theories of addiction, insanity, homosexuality, and poverty (Berridge and Edwards 1981, xxix, 157). Originally, whether in China or Britain, opium was subject to little control and was taken as an effective treatment for a great many ailments. By the end of the nineteenth century, however, British and other Western governments had begun to restrict the sale of opium in their own countries. At issue was the "luxurious" or "stimulant" use of opium and its derivatives, that is, what came to be called addiction or drug dependence. What used to be seen as at worst a "bad habit" engaged in by weak-willed or sinful people, after about 1870, began to be seen in light of theories of addiction as a disease.[23] Addiction had become a "new medical specialism," with science now taking it under control (p. 152). The gradual establishment of professional medicine and pharmacy from the mid-nineteenth century on played a major role in this transformation (p. 113). Specialists who were relied on to formulate antinarcotics legislation, however, tended to ignore social and historical factors in favor of explanations based on the science of the body and individual personality (pp. 153, 170). A person who became an addict or failed to recover from addiction, for example, was deemed to have some inherent psychological or biological defect. Whole populations might suffer such defects, and thus antidrug laws were enacted in reaction to upper-class fears of the spread of opium use among working classes in

England.[24] At that time biological determinism held sway in the classification of degenerate individuals and populations, as numerous authors (quoted below) reflect in their observations of the Chinese.

Anthropological Approaches

Anthropological literature on alcohol and drugs helps situate this study by changing the focus from one that typically concentrated on "excess and abuse" to one that looks at drinking or drug taking as culturally informed acts that "var[y] from one culture to another."[25] Such a focus notes the "culturally and politically specific" nature of the encouragement, toleration, or prohibition of certain states of consciousness.[26] In the case of opium, it is precisely the state of being induced by opium smoking that current laws distinguish from the states of drunkenness or medically induced anesthesia, for example. The evolution of such laws in the last century resulted from historically new modes of drug use which utterly confuse "traditional social practices and contexts of consumption" (Sherratt 1995, 2). These new modes of consumption in turn arose in the context of major changes in world patterns of trade and communication in the last several centuries (p. xii). The trade in opium is one of the outstanding instances of these new forms of contact.[27] The late-twentieth-century system of narcotics trafficking, which is now global in scope, received its earliest contributions from nation-states like Britain and Japan, whose opium operations in China were never fully legitimate even when distantly sanctioned by legitimate governments.[28] The overwhelming focus on drug abuse has repeatedly turned attention away from these and other historical factors that have affected the way drugs have been, and still are, produced, sold, and consumed.

Anthropologists have also treated numerous subtopics that demonstrate ways of conceptualizing the study of drugs in general: ritualization of drug consumption, expectations of how one will or should act under a drug's influence, conventions of time and place, social hierarchy as reproduced in relationships between drug users, power relations in cases, for example, of drug scarcity in which "balanced reciprocity may transform into imbalanced hoarding," or the drug economy, which includes ways in which drugs supplant or exchange with other productive resources.[29] In the case of gender and age restrictions, for instance, women can consume a certain drug but not another, or only men may consume in excess. Also important are the origin and history of a drug, its methods of production and consumption, its physiological effects, and disease problems associated with it (Mansfield 1987). All of these topics are relevant in the Chinese case, although I will only lightly touch on some, including the economic aspects, the physiological and disease effects, and the origin and history of opium, which others have already discussed. In general, opium as a social problem or cause of personal ruin are crucial topics. But since they have dominated most earlier studies and personal accounts, they will take second place to what I am calling the phenomenology of the opium way of life in the context of the global symbolic order.

Autobiographical Accounts

Finally, numerous American and European individuals of the nineteenth and twentieth centuries who themselves became addicted to opium or heroin have left writings about their experiences. A number of them smoked their opium in China, for example, James S. Lee, Claude Farrère, and Emily Hahn. Others were located in the United States, England, or France: Coleridge, De Quincey (both "eaters"), Jean Cocteau, Roger Gilbert-Lecomte, Philip Lamantia, and William Burroughs. Some were only short-term experimenters–Duncan MacPherson, Harry Hubbell Kane (both nineteenth-century doctors), and Emily Hahn, all of whom learned opium smoking from Chinese smokers. I cite some of them because of the information they provide on the process of opium smoking and their observations of the appearance and living conditions of opium smokers in China. They provide cross-referencing evidence of concrete practices and typical situations and occurrences. Some of their observations, like those of nineteenth-century travelers, missionaries, diplomats, or sinologists who apparently did not smoke opium, may be relevant as illustrations of aspects of Orientalist attitudes. Others I cite because, however different their perspective is culturally or temporally from the Chinese, they make brilliant or enlightening statements about their opium or heroin experiences. William Burroughs is not Zhang Changjia, but when they sound alike we have an opportunity to fine-tune what is different between them and corroborate what may have at first seemed isolated, lunatic, or obscure.

As for Zhang Changjia, he is (as far as I know) unique in China in the length to which he went to write an apology for opium smoking. The poets I cite offer shorter, more distilled renditions of their opium bliss and anguish. A substantial literature of poetry and essays on opium deals for the most part with the anguishing and abusive side of opium smoking, for example, in Zhang's "Opium Talk"; in a poetry collection called *The Bell of Qing Poetry* (*Qingshiduo*) compiled between 1858 and 1869,[30] scattered among the works of various Qing poets of reknown such as Gong Zizhen (1792–1841),[31] in Shanghai guidebooks of the late nineteenth century, the great *Collection of Opium War Literature* compiled by A Ying (1957), or Arthur Waley's *The Opium War through Chinese Eyes* (1958), which translates and paraphrases numerous essays, poems, and personal accounts, and also includes official documents. Otherwise novels are my main sources for both the individual and collective representations of the opium way of life in China. I frequently cross between these voices, whether Chinese or European, individual or collective, real or fictional, in order as much as possible to avoid overgeneralizing from any one of them. Each text has its peculiar limits of perspective and assumption; none can be taken to be transparently authoritative. The same caution applies for certain key terms, to which I now turn.

Terms: Addiction, Drug, China, West

"Addiction" is a word that I often let straddle and confuse the divide between its conventional drug-related sense and its use as a metaphor for an intense type of loyalty to any activity, goal, or god. In one typical sense, an addictive drug is a psychoactive substance that induces (1) tolerance (i.e., the necessity for greater doses in order to produce the desired effect) and (2) a withdrawal syndrome. Since some drugs do not produce withdrawal symptoms, another common sense of addiction is simply an intense and compulsive drive to consume the drug. These senses apply in both contemporary global contexts and the Chinese one of Zhang Changjia, where the comparable term for "addiction," *yin*, had already been in use in regard to opium for more than a century. In the metaphorical sense, addiction can occur in regard to a religion or even to oil and guns. Or as the preface to "Opium Talk" implies, addiction can be to delusionary notions of saving China from destruction. In posing this metaphorical sense, I intend to view the usual definition of addiction as marking an attempt (1) to delimit straight consciousness and (2) to protect that consciousness from altered consciousness, which is deemed dangerous and is therefore outlawed. Under the protectionism enforced by straight consciousness, therefore, drug addiction is a kind of adultery that cuckolds the straight consciousness. Addiction can just as easily be defined as comprising the obsessions of that straight consciousness as it seizes on objects or activities for the sake of its ever engorging enrichment and self-glorification. In the terms of "Opium Talk," the true opium demons are officials and ideologues whose blather about saving China comes on like the high of the opium rush, as the preface writer says, always right afterward to subside into sleepless nights of inefficacy.

The use of the word "drug" in the sense of an illegal and addictive substance with psychoactive properties is, like the word "addiction," of very recent historical origin. Both terms beg many questions, not the least of which concerns the very meaning of consuming anything in general. As I have already been asking, what effects on body or mind are considered allowable and in what circumstances? Nourishment and health are the current commonsense reasons for consuming food and medicine or drugs (as long as these "drugs" are not the so-called abused or illegal ones). But everyday consumption also includes numerous items with druglike properties such as soda, coffee, tea, chocolate, and tobacco.[32] These and other much stronger substances have long histories of use in a wide range of situations. Hallucinogens have been taken in some societies in the performance of sacred rituals; elsewhere opium and coca have served as aids to everyday physical labor. As David Lenson shows in *On Drugs* (1995), the truly clinching definition of this newly coined term "drug" arrives only when the word is used pejoratively and then "when and only when a law interdicts it" (Lenson 1995, 3–4). Drugs are such when declared antithetical to what I have called straight consciousness, to sobriety, or to some other hallowed standard, even health. This is the type of definition that I generally apply.

In the second half of the nineteenth century and into the twentieth, the Chinese had several euphemisms for opium intended for smoking, a chief one of them being "Western-seas medicine," *yangyao*. Here the conventional word for medicine or drug, *yao*, carries the sense of something that cures an illness, one of the main uses of opium in those times. The addition of *yang*, however, figures the foreigner as the one responsible for introducing this drug into China. The subtlety of this term came in handy in the 1858 treaty China was forced to conclude with England, the United States, and France officially legalizing the opium trade. Instead of *yapian*, a loanword for "opium" already in use at least since the Ming dynasty, the Chinese text of the treaty writes the euphemistic *yangyao*. The Western-language versions use "opium."[33] The Chinese rulers were in principle opposed to foreigners trading in opium on or near Chinese soil, but were forced by these powers to accept this and other similar concessions. The use of euphemism perhaps couched the note of accusation the Chinese government often leveled at foreigners for pushing opium onto the Chinese people.[34] Such an interpretation would be consistent with the fact that, although forced to surrender to acceptance of opium trade on the international front, China nevertheless maintained its position of official disapproval on the domestic one. It was not until sometime in the twentieth century that a term was coined carrying the clearly pejorative and interdicted sense of "drug," as in "illegal drug." In the Chinese case it was *dupin*, literally, "poisonous substance," which now includes all narcotics as defined conventionally in current international parlance.

David Lenson states that "what characterizes the condition of addiction is above all else . . . the replacement of conventionally measured seconds, minutes, hours, and days with a different chronometry based on the tempo of administration" of the drug (Lenson 1995, 35). Addiction involves "an altered sense of time" that to varying degrees departs from the rhythms of social convention (p. 43).[35] At the same time, it is never appropriate to assume drugs have fixed and predictable effects regardless of factors such as individual constitution and personal, social, and historical environment. The dominant tendency is to define addiction in the heavy sense and thus create the assumption that the drug taker cannot avoid becoming heavily addicted and therefore deeply alienated from the social order. The same tendency results in an intensification of the rule of conventional order to the exclusion of these other internal and external factors.

According to the etymology of the word "addiction," as Lenson continues, the drug user is "*addictus*–the past participle of the Latin verb *addicere* (to say or pronounce, to decree or bind)" (p. 35). This interpretation suggests that the user has lost self-control, "that she or he is already 'spoken for,' bound and decreed" (p. 38). The drug addict's reply might be that he or she finds social convention and contingency–or any belief, custom, or law–equally if not more enslaving (pp. 47–48). Taken up with the drug, the addict is at the same time liberated from the arbitrariness of social imperative by what in contrast appear to be the clean and "absolutely objective" imperatives of the drug (p. 36). If drugs make us ask what it means to consume, they also ask what it means to choose: social convention or the imperatives of addiction, not necessarily equally enslaving depending on an individual's perspective.

The etymology of the Chinese character for addiction, which existed long before it took on this new meaning, yields two semiotic components: the radical for sickness and the word for withdrawing like a hermit. In its earliest usage, *yin* means "internal illness," which echoes the withdrawn and hidden elements of the sense of hermit. Zhang Changjia and other observers affirm that the opium addict is in a state of chronic illness. Opium is both *yao*, "cure" or "tonic," and *du*, "poison," Zhang implies (no. 22). Smokers often begin using opium in order to cure an ailment but then become "sick" with addiction, as if poisoned. As for the idea of withdrawing like a hermit, no one can say that the character *yin* was deliberately chosen with "sickness" and "hermit" in mind. Chinese character etymologies are commonly too unreliable to be used as precise keys to later meaning. Nevertheless, admitting the still very telling resonance between opium smoking and becoming a hermit, we can say that the opium smoker replaces all former pleasures and pursuits with opium, which he or she consumes in a special chamber away from all other social transactions. To be sure, the choice to withdraw like a hermit is traditionally more available to men than women,[36] and to the wealthy rather than the poor, points that lead to the discussion of opium smoking in light of gender and social status in chapters 5–6. With opium the hermit, like the wastrel, enters an unprecedented realm in which whatever he could do before, he can now do to a newly extreme degree.

Although I use "addiction" to translate *yin*, "craving" is often more accurate. In the first appearance I have found of *yin* used in relation to opium, it is referred to as a word deriving from "common" or "slang parlance" *(su hu wei yin)* to indicate the "arrival" of craving, when the individual feels utterly weak and unable to move. The reference occurs in the miscellany of a painter and poet named Yu Jiao, whose *Dream Hut Notebook (Meng'an zazhu)* has a preface of 1801 but was compiled from stories, events, and memories of about the second half of the eighteenth century (Yu Jiao 1988, 154). An

1833 medical work, *Remedies for Rescue from Oblivion (Jiumi liangfang)*, by He Shutian, explains the causes and effects of *yin* and provides a number of cures (He Shutian 1984, 58).[37] He Shutian distinguishes between those whose addiction is light and who have strong constitutions, for whom the cure is easy, and those whose addiction is heavy but who are weak, for whom the cure is difficult. Here *yin* is defined as a general condition that affects the whole body from innermost to outermost. In this case, "addiction" is more suitable than "craving." Another character was sometimes used for *yin* meaning to "draw" or "lure." In this case, the Chinese is more like the Latin *addictus* in the sense that the consumer of opium has surrendered volition and succumbed to entrapment (this usage is far rarer than the other).

The words "China" and "West" present problems as well. The expression "Western attitudes toward Chinese," for example, evokes a realm in which each pole by default competes with the other in both subtle and reductive dialogues of have and have-not, right and wrong, or like and not like. The emblematic ways Western observers classified themselves and then Chinese opium smokers illustrate similarly essentialist uses of these terms. The "West" itself, of course, breaks down into more minute perspectives of its own, such as a certain British view of the French or Italians as "depraved" or "decadent" (a perspective that took hold in Shanghai between the Anglo American International Settlement and the French Concession, which contained many of the low-class opium dens, the so-called flower-smoke rooms, *huayanjian*). I allow such essentialist uses as long as China and the West (or equivalents like Euro-West or Euro-America) are viewed as character types like those that appear in Chinese fiction. In this case, however, it is a global theater of international actors rather than a family drama with the polygamist at the head. In the global theater, China is assigned the role of the opium sot, which it sometimes plays extremely well but also resents and rejects. Playing that role well includes playing it in the mode of eyesore to the colonialist. The Westerner, on the other hand, is assigned the role of most evolved human and rational thinker. Perhaps most of the Western actors liked this role, but there were always some who wanted to join the other side; still others lived in paranoia of being invaded by the other side.

Many questions concerning "China" and "the "West" are taken up in chapter 3 on Orientalism and the production of knowledge about Oriental places like China. In general, the terms have two uses: one referring to someone who is "from" China or the West (which roughly stands for the nations of Europe or of immigrants from Europe), the other referring to emblematic reductions, stereotypes, or caricatures of Chinese or Western people. Whether real or caricature, neither is a secure or permanent totality. Even when used emblematically, they indicate modes or moments of behavior that may sometimes contradict themselves and contain or appropriate features of their supposed opposite. The danger (but also sometimes the necessity) of using these words to stand for mass numbers or integral mentalities arises throughout this book as I address and attempt to "detoxify" the inevitable question in the history of opium consumption: Why did so many Chinese smoke opium?

AN INEVITABLE QUESTION:
WHY DID SO MANY CHINESE SMOKE OPIUM?

Opium as Bridge

Opium is the bridge par excellence between Westerners and Chinese from the end of the eighteenth century on. Frustrated at the Chinese lack of interest in foreign goods to exchange for Chinese silk and especially tea, British merchants finally hit upon opium, which the Chinese began buying in greatly increasing quantities from the 1790s on. By the 1830s opium was *"probably the largest commerce of the time in any single commodity."*[38] "Opium is like gold, I can sell it any time," said one British merchant in 1818 (Greenberg 1951, 118). Another merchant, the American William C. Hunter, wrote of his days in Canton of the 1820s and 1830s: "Transactions seemed to partake of the nature of the drug; they imparted a soothing frame of mind with three percent commission on sales, one percent on returns, and no bad debts!" (Hunter 1882, 72–73). However they may have expressed it or avoided expressing it, many Chinese of the time must have found the British opium merchant a very lucrative trading partner. Others, even those who themselves smoked opium, saw its spread as disastrous. As Zhang Changjia later said, "It was like flood, conflagration, and rampaging armies all at once, making no discrimination between rich and poor, high or low."[39]

Characterizing opium as a bridge between Chinese and Westerners means that it was a medium of significant, flowing contact on a scale that exceeded anything before. How can this contact be described in terms of the questions posed above about the meaning of addiction in this cross-cultural situation? How are the actors to be assigned roles in terms of motivation and responsibility? To repeat one of the main themes of this book, how is the addict's experience to be described as something vital and even productive instead of something that is only unnatural and is only about abuse and waste? In other words, how is the addict acting in a way that entirely makes sense given the social and psychic upheaval of this era?

All such questions have to do with how to approach this historically new phenomenon of drug addiction across cultures that are newly and nonuniformly defined because of this interaction. Questions posed in certain ways invite answers that arrest themselves at the level, for example, of free will and individual moral responsibility ("all the addict has to do is quit"), or of the assumption that once cured the addict can return to normal life. The most overly demanding yet inevitable question of all is, Why did so many Chinese take up opium when they did? Similarly constructed questions ask, Was the appearance of opium purely accidental or was China ready for it? Is it the chemical nature of opium and the particular constitutions of individuals that we should mainly be dealing with or are social conditions and symbolic values more important? I cannot fully answer these questions in this book, nor can I conjure these alternatives away. Perhaps, as Avital Ronell says in *Crack Wars*, "we are dealing in a way with the youngest vice, still very immature, still often misjudged and taken for something else, still hardly aware of itself" (Ronell 1992, 49). There is some illness that the collective "we" do not yet have a name or a cure for that these so-called addicts have come down with. Or else "we" suffer from the same illness, which we try to cure in other ways than smoking opium, all the while denying the drug addict's quest to help us out.

Instead of the Normative Definition of Addiction

In the most desirable type of discussion about opium, it is one thing to say that the drug has certain chemical properties that produce certain reactions, for example, constipation, euphoria, dependence, sleeplessness, itchiness, and so forth. It is another thing to say that opium is addictive or destructive or that someone or some race is "weak" because of having taken up opium smoking. I argue that the appearance of opium smoking and the phenomenon of addiction in the eighteenth and nineteenth centuries immediately expanded the meaning of addiction. In this expansion cultural loyalty and identity of any sort are thrown into abeyance, making the transfer of loyalties between cultures, gods, and substances therefore seem (though not necessarily actually become) infinitely fluid or chaotic. If an opium smoker feels like the "absolute equal of God" (Farrère 1931, 201), then he defies and even terrifies the nonsmoking believers in God or Oil in such a way that they can only oppose opium by becoming like addicts themselves. One may be as addicted to God as to opium or any other substance, idea, or activity. Such a seemingly loose application of the word "addiction" revolves around the idea of transfer of loyalties, not the literalist interpretation of addiction as physical dependence on a drug. The scandal of the addict lies in his or her uncanny fascination with the drug. This fascination has come to stand for a disloyalty comparable to that of a traitor in war, a believer in a deviant religion, a sexual pervert, or an opponent of the established political-economic system. Thus it has come to pass that all-out war has been made on opium and other such drugs.

Addiction in its normative clinical sense, then, is a reduction of qualitative social effects onto a discrete quantifiable substance called a narcotic. In this normative sense, only drug addicts are addicted, one can only be addicted to drugs, and it is a combination of the chemical properties of the drugs and the personal and inherent tendencies of the addict that produce the addiction. Last but not least, in this normative definition it is assumed that life for addicts will be better once they are off drugs. It is then assumed that they can transfer their loyalties to more socially approved activities. These are the assumptions toward which nineteenth-century Euro-Americans were heading ever since they first wrote about China and opium smoking beginning in the 1830s, as I show in greater detail in chapters 3–4.

As for the idea that opium addiction is destructive, the normative sense of this destructiveness likewise reductively centers on the drug itself and the individual who smokes it. Addicts alone are said to be ultimately responsible for both self-destruction and harm to others, such as spouses or children. Other explanations of opium's so-called destructiveness, however, must take into consideration such things as the corruption and relative weakness of the Manchu imperial system and the social order as a whole already present when the British began to succeed in the opium trade and which contributed to that very success.[40] Destruction also includes that of the British military, which with a few ships thousands of miles from home ports managed to subjugate Chinese coastal cities that had populations in the millions. Other factors in China of the latter half of the nineteenth century include the breakdown of traditional and reliable forms of employment due to, for example, the introduction of labor saving devices (most prominently, steamships and trains) and the concentration of capital in newly grown treaty ports that flourished in great part because of a massive supply of cheap and expendable labor.[41]

What is important here is not the mere availability of opium and the allegedly overwhelming temptation it constitutes for the weak human being. We should rather attend to how the words "addictive" or "destructive" have come to be attached to or defined in relation to opium. The clinical and legal definitions of addiction that need revision use quantitative scales for measurements, but suddenly off the cuff, using so-called common sense, arrive at their own pseudo-objective standards of what constitutes pleasure and pain, health and unhealth, or citizens fit or not fit.[42] As Richard Klein writes in *Cigarettes Are Sublime*, health and fitness in this common sense confer "moral distinction" to the "survivor." "But another view," Klein continues, "the dandy's perhaps, would say that living, as distinct from surviving, acquires its value from risks and sacrifices that tend to shorten life and hasten dying" (Klein 1993, 191).[43] I would modify Klein's statement by changing "dandy" to "coolie laborer," for example, who engages in or grabs any mode of escape, insulation, or belonging that is possible. The smoker does this, moreover, even if life is shortened and even if dying comes to mean abandonment by the side of the road where his corpse is then eaten by wild dogs.[44]

Another illustration of my approach is the following statement: long-term opium addiction produces nightmares that do not occur in a normal nonaddict. Saying this trivializes the nightmare and refuses to listen to the opium smokers who tell us repeatedly that those nightmares are worse than anyone could imagine or than nonsmokers could possibly fathom (Farrère 1931, 263). In her study *Opium and the Romantic Imagination,* Alethea Hayter speaks of the opium eater's "serene self-assurance, for which," she adds, "there is no objective justification" (Hayter 1988, 42). In an otherwise important work on opium and the literary imagination, Hayter concludes that whatever the opium addict does, thinks, or sees, including euphoric visions and horrific nightmares, is not qualitatively different or better from what that person could accomplish without opium. The addict's self-assurance has no real, objective value, in other words. The addict's words and visions are false and hollow because they result from chemical processes. These processes in turn are seen as artificial influences upon what by implication is or could be a natural and therefore innately good mind-body system.

The approach I prefer is like that of Thomas Szasz, for example. In *Ceremonial Chemistry* he compares the lure of opium craving with the call of God or other deep convictions that represent "profound inner desire or urge" (Szasz 1974, 44). Roger Gilbert-Lecomte, a French opium smoker of the 1930s and 1940s, wrote, "There are no two ways of being a seer. The only way to see is via asphyxia or congestion, whether by yoga, drowning, or narcosis."[45] At the same time, I include statements of flat need such as Cocteau's: "Without opium, plans, marriages and journeys appear to me just as foolish as if someone falling out of a window were to hope to make friends with the occupants of the room before which he passes" (Cocteau 1930, 31).[46] William Burroughs's words are even flatter: "I need junk to get out of bed in the morning, to shave and eat breakfast. I need it to stay alive" (Burroughs 1953, 23). Richard Klein states broadly, "Drugs may be necessary for the survival of civilization, perhaps even of the species, but most particularly at moments of social crisis or at trying times of life" (Klein 1993, 191–93). Neither do I eliminate bleak statements like Avital Ronell's, "You can only be addicted to what is available, which is what traps you in a circle without futurity" (Ronell 1992, 42), although "without futurity" is a little too close to Hayter's "no objective justification." Or as Thomas Szasz says with studied sanity, "Addictions are habits [which] enable us to do some things, and disenable us from doing others" (Szasz 1974, 85). Euphoria-inducing drugs are "neither panaceas nor panapathogens" but have "certain chemical properties and ceremonial possibilities" (p. 81). There are of course additional layers between "chemical properties" and "ceremonial possibilities." It is an exaggeration to say that everyone smoking opium becomes a seer. But the dominant stance ever since the nineteenth century has been that the addict is anything but a seer. This stance was basic to the British rationale in carrying out such acts as fighting the Opium Wars.

Opium and Cultural Self-definition

Opium was a medium through which one side viewed the other and defined itself. Americans observed the talkative friendship and the code of honor that obtained between smokers in Chinese opium dens in the United States,[47] but they also imputed debauchery, passivity, and low morals. Alcohol was the intoxicant of active and impetuous peoples. Opium led to sottish and immobile indifference. The smokers and eaters of opium all "knew better," as the American Emily Hahn said, herself a one-time addict in Shanghai of the 1930s (Hahn 1970, 229), for each had turned himself or herself into a "masterpiece" whom no one could touch, as Cocteau wrote (1996, 70). Arrested or even sentenced to death, all the addict wanted was one more smoke, wrote an eighteenth-century Chinese observer (Zhao 1983, 31). "Opium leads the organism towards death in euphoric mood," Cocteau declared (Cocteau 1996, 22).

The image of a euphoric Chinese addict about to have his head cut off rouses the indignation of a hypothetical Western observer, who accuses the Chinese government of barbarism for dealing with its addicts in such a "brutal" way. The same Westerner may have been an opium trader in Canton or Shanghai who never touched opium, or only in the form of an occasional drop of laudanum to relieve pain or cure diarrhea. In these patterns by which each individual or collective views others or defines themselves, there is a hazy middle ground where the so-called brother- and sisterhood of opium occurs. How much do the Chinese and the Western addict or the male and the female addict share? In some anti-opium eyes of the late nineteenth century, such so-called sharing threatened a loss of identity. To some opium smokers, it was precisely the fantasy of identity produced by this sharing that made opium so attractive.

Whether or not opium can neutralize such differences, whether or not anyone wants it to, the consideration of opium as "bridge" must include, even if hypothetically, persons of different cultures or gender who smoke opium, whether together or separately. I have found few pre–twentieth century references to Chinese and Westerners smoking opium together, and none by Chinese.[48] A few cases exist from the turn of the century and after and are likewise written by Westerners only, for example, Claude Farrère (1931, fiction taking place at the turn of the century), James S. Lee (1935, 239–41, autobiographical writing about 1906–1907), and Emily Hahn (1970, autobiographical writing about the 1930s). The imbalance of these few sources tends to suggest that cross-cultural brother- and sisterhood is a particularly Western fantasy. Nevertheless, aside from idealizations or vilifications of cross-cultural or cross-gender commonality, addicts in general are united in consuming opium or its derivatives in historically unprecedented ways. It may not be easy to sort out what "unprecedented" exactly means, since the many aspects of that history, I think, defy what any of us are ever able to explain. But suffice it for now to say that in the historical framework of this book, Cocteau and Zhang Changjia have more in common with each other as consumers of "mind-altering substances" than either would with a shaman who eats psychotropic mushrooms as part of a religious ritual or with an Andean chewer of coca leaves in the period before the widespread use and production of coca in its refined form of cocaine. It is the context of the globalizing capitalist market of the nineteenth and twentieth centuries that most distinguishes this use of opium from that of any other drug in previous history.

The Crossing of Categories

Humans have used opium in some form as both medicine and agent of euphoria for millennia. As Mark David Merlin has said, no truly wild kinds of opium can be traced (like coca and tobacco). It was cultivated and artificially selected from a long time back (Merlin 1984, 53–54). Before the restrictions of the late nineteenth and twentieth centuries, it was used to relieve pain, fever, diarrhea, cholera, malaria, ague, and discomfort after childbirth, or to quiet infants. Its use as intoxicant also goes back to very early times (e.g., Neolithic Europe and ancient Egypt).[49] But by the nineteenth century, opium consumed for euphoric effects became something for which smokers or eaters, whether Chinese or English, often felt it particularly necessary to make medical excuses: they made as if they were using it as medicine, not for pleasure. This defensiveness in retrospect looks like a vain effort to hide the incredible secret of the need for opium and of opium's marvelous properties: "the euphoria it induces [is] superior to that of health" (Cocteau 1996, 24); "the pain erased by Opium can be equaled by no other pain killer!" (Lamantia and Artaud 1959, n.p.); with it De Quincey enters the "abyss of divine enjoyment" (De Quincey 1994, 180).[50] "Truly, opium is something that the world cannot do without," says Zhang Changjia (no. 21). Nothing but the most extreme vilification and draconic measures come close to controlling or seeming to control the flow and use of this and other such substances. Again, it is tempting to ask, What new and unprecedented illnesses were opium smokers trying to cure?

Opium forces a confusion and crossing of categories and subjects and objects. It forces the question of what constitutes the consumption of everything from food to vitamins, aspirin, or opium. Is addiction pleasure or pain? "Junk is not a kick. It is a way of life," William Burroughs says (1983, xvi). We who do not smoke or inject are definitively outside what the true addict comprehends when seeing "life measured out in eyedroppers of morphine solution," or conceiving the "idea of that other speed of plants," their "vegetable calm," as Cocteau wrote (1996, 92, 77). Are addicts "humans or things?" Zhang asks. "There is no way to answer this" (no. 23). Who menaces whom? "In the end," as already noted, "what is the greatest addiction in today's world? How can it only be opium?" (from Zhang's preface). What is solved by attempts to stamp out addiction? "What is this black smoke that so vexes you, sir?" asks Zhang Changjia (no. 16). His poet friends answer, "In famine I would willingly put it before food" (no. 58); "morning and night the taste of love-sickness. Rain and wind to sleep the day through" (no. 58); and "life is either smoking or waking from dream; it is like thirst, then like starvation," which, Zhang concludes, "is quite like it is" (no. 61).

NOTES

1. An English writer who in 1821 published *Confessions of an English Opium-Eater*.

2. I have numbered each paragraph in the translation of "Opium Talk" appended at the end of this book; the above quotes are no. 15 and no. 13, respectively. All quotes are cited by the numbered paragraph. See chapter 5 for bibliographical information.

3. *Yang* does not specifically mean European until sometime in the early to middle nineteenth century. Originally it referred to foreign things in general.

4. He began taking laudanum for medical purposes but became interested in the luxuriant effects as well.

5. As William Burroughs wrote much later: "Junk is the ideal product . . . the ultimate merchandise. No sales talk necessary. The client will crawl through a sewer and beg to buy" (Burroughs 1960, 16).

6. As Gregory Blue states, "From British manufacturers . . . concern was repeatedly expressed that opium was soaking up Chinese demand" (Blue 2000, 38). See J. Y. Wong, who also notes the British assertion that Chinese purchases of opium hurt China's capacity to buy British products (Wong 1998, 378).

7. See Trocki, who states: "Though difficult to prove beyond question, it seems likely that without opium, there would have been no empire. Opium, both in the case of capitalist development as well as in the case of colonial finance, served to tighten up those key areas of 'slack' in European systems and facilitated the global connections that in effect, were the empire" (Trocki 1999, 59).

8. At the turn of the century, the early manufacturers of Coca-Cola removed one of the original ingredients, cocaine. See Musto 1973, 3, 46.

9. The domestic growth of opium was illegal until 1890 but nevertheless grew tremendously. Wong demonstrates convincingly that the British government's opium monopoly had a great deal to do with British dependence on revenues generated by the monopoly to support British imperial expansion in India (Wong 1998, 390ff., 416–17, 483). Hence the justification for the Arrow War by way of forcing legalization of opium trade on the Chinese.

10. Many believed that the Chinese had too small a native market and too inflexible a capital base, compared with the British and other Western nations. See Greenberg

1951; Chang 1970, 13–15; and Wakeman 1966, 97. Also see Kenneth Pomeranz (1997), who lists the usual negatives about traditional Chinese business practices that supposedly prevented the Chinese from competing with Western counterparts. But he also notes some important nineteenth-century exceptions which suggest that Chinese business practices and organization were more flexible than was believed at the time and has been since asserted. In the period prior to Lin Zexu's posting to Canton, Chinese statesmen proposed the legalization of the opium trade, one of their ideas being that domestic growth would counter the loss of silver to the import trade. See Polachek 1992, 113ff. These statesmen, of course, lost out in the power struggle that resulted in the anti-opium campaign of Lin Zexu.

11. For an example of similar views in the context of the contemporary "war on drugs," see Dally 1996.

12. I have discussed these character types in a previous work on eighteenth-century erotic fiction (McMahon 1995).

13. See Spence 1992, 229; originally written in 1975.

14. On the great famine of 1876–1879 and its alleged relation to poppy cultivation, for example, see Howard 1998, 202–6.

15. See Alexander Des Forges (2000) for a discussion of opium and leisure in Shanghai of the late nineteenth century.

16. See also the book by Martin Booth (1998), which looks at the history of opium in China. Trocki provides the best overview so far on the opium issue in Asia (Trocki 1999, 174–78). Des Forges in Brook and Wakabayashi (2000) comes the closest to the current study in his focus on the culture of opium consumption.

17. Ronell 1992, 114, from Herviev 1989, 205.

18. See Barry Milligan's *Pleasures and Pains: Opium and the Orient in Nineteenth-Century British Culture.* Of particular relevance is his examination of "the ways in which perceptions of and responses to the Orient–including fear, desire, guilt, titillation–are paralleled, mediated, and represented metaphorically by attitudes toward opium, and the ways in which these intertwined phenomena complicate notions of identity, both national and individual" (Milligan 1995, 7).

19. See Thomas Richards, *The Imperial Archive: Knowledge and Fantasy of Empire* (1993).

20. Richards 1993, 50, 57; chaps. 1–2.

21. "At every point Stoker makes it crushingly clear that Dracula must be defeated through a mastery of the means of information" (Richards 1993, 62–63).

22. As discussed in another book that is vital to any consideration of opium in the last two centuries, *Opium and the People: Opiate Use in Nineteenth-Century England,* by Virginia Berridge and Griffith Edwards.

23. See Berridge and Edwards 1981, xxix, 49, 150ff.; Courtwright 1982, 126–27; and Parssinen 1983, 86ff. See also Musto 1973, 1–6.

24. Berridge and Edwards 1981, chap. 9.

25. See books like *Essential Substances: A Cultural History of Intoxicants in Society,* by Richard Rudgley (1993), or *Constructive Drinking: Perspectives on Drink from Anthropology,* edited by Mary Douglas (1987). Quote is from Douglas 1987b, 3–4.

26. See Jordan Goodman, Paul E. Lovejoy, and Andrew Sherratt, eds., *Consuming Habits: Drugs in History and Anthropology* (1995), x.

27. See also Trocki 1999.

28. On Japan's involvement in Taiwan, Manchuria, and elsewhere in China, see Meyer 1995; Meyer and Parssinen 1998; Wakabayashi 2000; and Kobayashi 2000.

29. See Lindstrom 1987b, 5.

30. See Zhang Changling 1983, 1004–13. Thanks to Paul Ropp for supplying me with copies of those poems.

31. For a translation of such a poem, one of his most well-known, see Owen 1996, 1147.

32. See Sherratt 1995, 2; Lenson 1995, 3–4.

33. See Su Zhiliang 1997, 127–28.

34. In the 1890s, when British missionaries complained that the Chinese often blamed Britain for China's opium problem, one of these missionaries remarked on the term *yangyan*, "foreign smoke," which was used even when referring to domestically grown opium: "That is the stigma put upon us." See United Kingdom 1894, 1:128–29.

35. Moreover, "different drugs create different rhythms of desire," which in the simplest sense means urge for readministration. Opium and heroin are on the slow end of the scale, while cocaine is the relative opposite (Lenson 1995, 38).

36. See McMahon 1995, 93–98 and passim on the "ascetic" and "self-containment."

37. Thanks to Paul Howard for supplying me with a copy of the relevant section. See his dissertation for a discussion of Chinese medical views of opium addiction (Howard 1998, 60–62).

38. As the scholar Michael Greenberg has written (his emphasis); see Greenberg 1951, 104–5, citing Phipps 1836; see also Chang 1970, 30.

39. From Zhang's preface writer; also see the poems on opium in the poetry collection *Qingshiduo*, for example, Zhang Changling 1983, 1004–1013.

40. See Polachek 1992, 52–53, 79.

41. See, for example, Wakeman 1966, 98–101, 131.

42. See Barry Milligan, who speaks of the standard addiction model's overly "stable definitions of pleasure and pain" (Milligan 1995, 67).

43. See also 99–100 on sickness and health, especially the idea of "health [as] a conviction."

44. See the beginning of chapter 6.

45. Cited in Rattray 1992, 195. Thanks to Ken Irby for introducing me to this piece.

46. Cocteau's book was originally published in 1930. The Margaret Crosland translation I use is originally from 1957; the edition I refer to was published in 1996, which is cited in all future references.

47. Courtwright 1982, 73.

48. See David Courtwright's *Dark Paradise: Opiate Addiction in America before 1940* (1982). The presence of Chinese in the western part of the United States was the first condition for white people (unless they had already been in China) to learn opium smoking and to have access to opium (pp. 65, 71, 78). In Courtwright's account, it was white gamblers, prostitutes, and other underworld individuals who made this first contact. Smoking in company was supposedly one of opium's special attractions (p. 72).

49. See Rudgley 1993, 24–25, 27–28.

50. Lamantia's quote is from his poem, "Opium Cocaine Hemp," in Lamantia and Artaud 1959 (thanks to Ken Irby for supplying me with this text).

Chapter Two

A Short History of
Opium Smoking in China

OPIUM IN CHINA

Material on the history of opium smoking can be found in numerous sources produced over the last 150 years. The following short history focuses on what is most important as background for this study: the origin of opium smoking, the techniques of smoking (especially the "classic" Chinese style), its early spread and economic impact, and some critical differences between opium use in China and Britain or the United States.

In China opium served as a cure for numerous ailments long before the nineteenth century. It was also known as an aphrodisiac and an agent of euphoria.[1] The practice of smoking it, however, was not the original method of ingestion. It first came about with the introduction of tobacco, which reached China sometime in the sixteenth century from the interaction between peoples along coasts and in port cities that were outside or on the fringes of China. These early points of contact were mainly in Southeast Asia, including parts of what are now Malaysia and Indonesia. Some version of opium smoking probably existed as early as the sixteenth century but did not necessarily begin among the Chinese. When the Chinese took up the custom, it was practiced by people—merchants, sailors, and laborers—who were in frequent contact with foreign populations and were exceptional because of that contact.

The imperial governments of the Ming and Qing dynasties were averse to opening China's coasts to unimpeded and unpredictable exchange with foreign countries. Until China was defeated in the Opium War of 1839–1842, imperial policy shifted from time to time, sometimes became lax, but generally restricted contact with foreigners to the southern city of Canton and strongly discouraged people from entering any but officially sanctioned channels of exchange. Nevertheless, great numbers of coastal people either left China to settle in Taiwan and many parts of Southeast Asia or engaged in trade, smuggling, and piracy that took them out to sea along the southern coasts of China and beyond to the south. Opium smoking arose in this highly fluctuating milieu, where official sources from the start portrayed it as a dissipative and corrupting activity. The same sources placed ultimate blame for the spread of opium on Western foreigners who were said to use opium to weaken the Chinese in order to cheat them of profit.[2]

The Early Period of Opium Smoking

Early on referred to as *yingsu* or *minang*, the opium poppy was also valued for the beauty of its flower.[3] As far as we know, the currently most common word for opium, *yapian*, did not appear in records until the Chenghua reign period of the Ming dynasty (1465–1487). At that time an official named Wang Xi (died 1488) used this and an alternate term, *afurong*, both loan-words, to describe the method of making opium extract, a gummy substance that in his description was infused in warm water and administered as a cure for chronic dysentery (the head of the poppy was incised, and the sap was collected and dried in a dark place). Having spent twenty years as an official in Gansu, Wang may have learned about *yapian* from Muslim Chinese inhabitants, as the scholars Joseph Edkins and Yu Ende suggest.[4]

Yapian yan—opium to be smoked—did not appear in Chinese records until the late Ming in the early seventeenth century. Smoking pure opium was preceded by smoking opium mixed with tobacco, which started sometime in the sixteenth century, as already noted. The habit-forming nature of tobacco, as well as the opium and tobacco mixture, was probably soon apparent, but written reports of the habit and its physical effects did not appear until the seventeenth century. (The addictive effects of opium presumably had long been known.) What are now parts of Indonesia and Malaysia and southern coastal China including Taiwan were some of the earliest places in which the opium smoking custom was said to exist. In the earliest Chinese source that Spence cites, a gazetteer writer from Macao who died in 1626 reported simply that opium could be smoked and that there was a prohibition against selling it. Another seventeenth-century author said he had heard of *yapian yan* but had never seen people smoking it.[5] Non-Chinese sources indicate that trade in opium from Patna in northeast India to Burma, the Malay peninsula, and other parts of Southeast Asia existed as early as the sixteenth century.[6] The custom of chewing opium or drinking it in solution was already common in India and other places that Portuguese, Dutch, English, Chinese, and other sailors visited or traveled through. As a Dutch physician reported in 1629, opium was particularly useful in "hot countries" like Java because of diseases such as dysentery and cholera (Edkins 1898, 29). In 1689 the German pharmacist Englebert Kaempfer observed shops selling pipefuls of the opium-tobacco mixture in Batavia.[7] He also described "porters" at Kasan who would fill a "cow's horn with tobacco leaves, place . . . it over burning coals, and smoke . . . through a hole in the horn; after a few whiffs they fell down in a state of something like foaming epilepsy."[8]

From these fragments of information it is not difficult to imagine that both sufferers of disease and discomfort, on the one hand, and inventive seekers of excitement or relief from fatigue (e.g., sailors and laborers), on the other, were fast finding ways to make the combination of opium and tobacco work to their satisfaction. Studied refinements of the smoking methods and utensils were a part of this development. The water pipe was introduced to help remove impurities and moderate the smoke, Kaempfer reported (Edkins 1898, 35). Then came the unique and significantly more specialized opium pipe, described for perhaps the first time in a Chinese source published around 1765, the *Affairs of the Eastern Seas (Haidong zhaji),* which quotes earlier material.[9] A lamp is set in the middle of the floor, around which smokers recline, using a pipe with a clay bowl molded into the shape of a gourd, hollow inside, and fitted with a tiny hole. The bowl comes so close to the classic Chinese pipe for smoking pure opium that it sounds as if the smokers were no longer combining tobacco with their opium. The leafy tobacco-opium mixture smokes relatively easily, but by itself the sappy opium cannot come into direct contact with the flame or it will burn too fast and ooze away, clogging up the bowl. To prevent this, a pea-size pill of opium is placed around the smoke hole and brought near the heat focused above the lamp;[10] in addition, the smoke hole must be very small (1–2 mm). When sufficiently heated, the opium sizzles away from the hole, some going to the lungs but most going as dross that collects on the inside of the hollowed-out bowl and the pipe. Pure opium is much more potent than opium mixed with tobacco or other leaves. At the same time, opium is less toxic smoked than ingested in solid form. In China the smoking of pure opium seems to have taken off in the mid to late Qianlong period, perhaps from the 1760s or 1770s on (Spence 1992, 232–34).[11]

A prominent feature of the early descriptions is the group of dissolute and villainous *(wulai)* men smoking and carousing all night long. An official in Taiwan in 1721 submitted a report about the no-goods who customarily gathered and smoked opium all night. He added that opium ruined people physically and financially, and that the custom was common in Amoy and Taiwan—areas of highly mobile inhabitants such as sailors and emigrants.[12] Huang Yufu, an inspecting censor in Taiwan in 1723, reported that smokers of the opium-tobacco mixture could not break their habit, and that their bodies became emaciated (the German Kaempfer made similar observations of opium eaters in 1689; Trocki 1999, 25). Even those about to be arrested for smoking would ask for another smoke. "They won't stop even if you threaten to kill them."[13] The author of the *Affairs of the Eastern Seas* (c. 1765) also stated that opium smoking led to "ruin and death." According to his description, smokers at first experienced a sudden increase in appetite for "fatty and sweet" things.[14] They had darkened complexions and "sunken" shoulders, suffered watering of the eyes, and died from "prolapse of the anus." After a few months of smoking they could still quit, but after a longer time suffered extreme pain if they tried to break their habit (Zhao 1983, 31). Writing sometime in the last quarter or so of the eighteenth century, the painter, poet, and sometime official Yu Jiao described the addicted smoker: "When craving hits, his eyes water and his nose runs; he can barely lift his hands and feet. Even if a bare blade were applied to his neck or if a ferocious tiger jumped out in front of him, he would simply surrender and submit to his death."[15] Yu Jiao's is the earliest account that I have seen using the word *yin* for addiction.

The first major official prohibition came in 1729 and punished sellers of opium, especially those who ran opium shops (or dens, called *yanguan*), but did not punish the smokers themselves, who were thought to suffer badly enough from the effects of addiction (Edkins 1898, 44; Yu Ende 1934, 15–16; Howard 1998, 76–77). In the official eye, opium was associated with gambling and crime, and was considered an aid to sensual indulgence. The *Taiwan Gazetteer* of 1737 (*Taiwan fuzhi*) asserted that opium smoking began in Java during Dutch occupation when Westerners prohibited opium to themselves and the Chinese, but allowed it to the natives in order to soften and control them (the *Affairs of the Eastern Seas* likewise says that opium smoking came from Java and the Philippines). Chinese smoked it anyway, however, and brought it back with them to Fujian and Taiwan (Yu Wenyi 1984, 685). The *Amoy Gazetteer* of 1832 (*Xiamen zhi*) with Tongzhi period (1862–1874) supplements described addiction using the word *yin*, to draw or attract, instead of the usual character, *yin*, meaning addiction (Zhou Kai 1984, 655). Reflecting a common Chinese official view, the author of the Tongzhi supplements claimed that opium smoking was introduced into China in the Wanli period (1573–1620) in order to weaken the Chinese and siphon off their wealth.[16]

Prohibitions never halted the growth of opium smoking,[17] which at first was mainly concentrated in the southern coastal regions but reached Beijing at least by the 1790s (Edkins 1898, 52). The spread beyond Guangdong and Fujian came to the emperor's attention in 1807, and its use by imperial guards and eunuchs was a source of alarm to him in 1813 (Chang 1970, 19). By then foreign opium traders and the network of Chinese buyers and distributors were well established in the area between Macao and Canton. Portuguese traders of opium appeared as early as the late Ming (Chang 1970, 17–18), but the British and their East India Company were the first to find a solid market starting in the 1770s. This trade grew and prospered for the next century until the 1880s, when domestic opium production finally exceeded imported opium.[18]

The growth and spread of opium smoking has often been derived from the number of "chests" of Indian opium that were recorded as having been sold to the Chinese, for example, starting at 200 in 1729, reaching 1,000 by 1767, and jumping from 5,000 to 18,760 between 1821 and 1830–1831. The number peaked in the 1830s, at between 13,000 and 26,000 each year (Chang 1970, 19, 21).[19] The final peak was over 80,000 chests by 1879–1880 (Hao 1986, 336).[20] In 1813 the government seriously tried to tighten its laws prohibiting opium (Spence 1992, 241) and then again in 1830–1831 after the great increase had become apparent. Official investigations at that time reported that opium smoking was widespread, including among government officials and the army, but still had not reached the people of the countryside (Spence 1992, 230, 234–35; and Yu Jiao 1988, 372).

Economic Impact

During the 1830s numerous Chinese officials asserted that the importation of opium had caused a reverse in the balance of trade with Western countries, resulting in what they saw as a drastic outflow of silver (Chang 1970, 40–41). Yen-p'ing Hao states that this trade imbalance was virtually unprecedented in Chinese history (Hao 1986, 121). In fact the Chinese economy suffered a severe contraction of its money supply in the second quarter of the nineteenth century, accompanied by economic dislocation that many scholars cite as a major cause of the Taiping uprising of the next few decades (Wakeman 1966; Hao 1986, 121–23; von Glahn 1996, 256). James Polachek, however, reports that the silver crisis was mainly a matter of "domestic currency management," as numerous officials then thought (Polachek 1992, 103–4). Richard von Glahn notes that the "scale of opium imports could not account for more than half of the outflow of silver."[21] He calls for a reexamination of the thesis that massive opium imports caused this drain of silver, which he says should be viewed in a global context (e.g., against the worldwide reduction of silver output and the economic depression of the 1830s and 1840s). What is obvious from the Chinese point of view, however, is what I have referred to as the totalization or emblemization of opium as the cause of China's problems. In fact, many other crises already plagued China during this period: extensive government corruption at the highest levels in the form of cronyism and patronage, weakening of the central government in general and of the military in particular, piracy, banditry, growth in operations of secret societies, and salt smuggling (these last four were often tied together and to the opium trade as well), plus organized rebellion (e.g., the White Lotus Rebellion of the end of the eighteenth century and again in the early nineteenth). Government officials had been observing for a century or so a population growth that appeared to outstrip the economic capacity to sustain it. These are all examples of what in retrospect already signaled problems in urgent need of solution by the early nineteenth century.

The Opium War and Its Aftermath

Nevertheless, opium became the center of heated debate among government officials. One Chinese statesman submitted a memorial to the emperor in 1836 advocating the legalization of opium as a solution to the growing crisis, but the majority of men the emperor consulted were on the side of strict prohibition.[22] The opium trade, they said, was harmful to China economically, while opium smoking produced extremely undesirable social elements whose menace to society seemed to increase precisely because of their involvement with opium. The Daoguang ruler (reigned 1821–1850) then sent the highly respected official Lin Zexu to Canton to carry out the new prohibition, which resulted in the famous seizure, dumping, and destruction of a large amount of British opium by means of water mixed with salt and lime in 1839 (Chang 1970, 173–75). Foreigners witnessing the event recorded a horrible smell. In his late Qing novel *Souls from the Land of Darkness,* Peng Yang'ou facetiously recreates the scene, portraying pitiful, opium-deprived addicts ("smoke ghosts," *yangui*) standing around taking whiffs of the odor and then going three days before experiencing craving again.[23]

This dramatic event was followed by numerous isolated small-scale conflicts and battles, the sum of which finally led to the British expeditionary force that arrived in June 1840 to launch what would be called the First Opium War. The Chinese forces crumpled in the face of superior firepower, while opium-selling ships followed the British forces as they secured their hold and made themselves invincible. Captain Arthur Cunynghame, one of numerous British participants to publish an account of this event, reported that an American merchant ship, the *Anne,* followed the British fleet up the Yangtze River and sold opium to the Chinese in exchange for poultry, which was sold to the British in exchange for plunder, which was in turn sold to the Chinese for a supposed 1,000 percent profit (Cunynghame 1845, 152–53).[24]

Although the Nanking Treaty of 1842 did not specifically mention opium, it had the effect of informally sanctioning the British sale of opium and thereafter discouraging the Chinese from much more than "sporadic punishment of opium offenders" (Spence 1992, 244). Still, the foreign opium merchants anchored their ships away from the full view of both the Chinese "mandarins" and the foreign consuls (Fairbank 1978, 222–23; Hao 1986, 128). It was not until 1858 that the opium trade was fully legalized and that opium merchants moved from the "outer waters" to the treaty ports, especially Shanghai, which was already handling about one-half the total import to China by this time (Hao 1986, 132–34). At this point, the opium trade also came under taxation. Besides benefiting foreign and Chinese merchants, the commerce in opium became a source of government income. Then, to the advantage of many Chinese people, the domestic production of opium began to compete successfully in price and quality with the import market, finally surpassing it by the end of the century.

By the 1870s the impression was that Chinese peasants and workers were smoking opium on a massive scale, in part at least because more smokers could afford the domestic product. By the last quarter of the nineteenth century opium was a fixed part of the Chinese economy, serving among other things as a substitute for money, helping officials achieve taxation quotas, and helping pay off foreign loans. According to one scholar, China consumed 95 percent of the world supply of opium at the beginning of the twentieth century (Trocki 1999, 126).

OPIUM IN BRITAIN AND AMERICA

During all of the time covered so far, opium in various forms such as laudanum (originating in the 1660s) and other solutions or pills taken by mouth was widely available and legal in both England and the United States. By the seventeenth century the habitual "eating" of opium was a known practice in England; and by the eighteenth century it is said that the habit "could be met in most walks of life" (Hayter 1988, 23, 25; Berridge and Edwards 1981, xxiv). Up to the mid-nineteenth century and somewhat after, opium was considered something that "every household should have" and was valued as an analgesic and a tranquilizer (Hayter 1988, 29; Berridge and Edwards 1981, 21ff.).

Although what later would be qualified as its addictive properties were known and discussed as early as the seventeenth century (Berridge and Edwards 1981, xxiv–xxv), opium was not widely reputed to be dangerous or addictive until about the 1870s. During these years Chinese opium dens in England and the United States began to draw white condemnation. Before this time opium was at worst a "bad habit." Taken in the form of poppy head tea, "black drop," or numerous patent medicines, it was used as needed for the relief of many kinds of discomfort. Working people commonly used it as a remedy for "fatigue and depression" and many other complaints (Berridge and Edwards 1981, 31), especially in the Fen district where, as in other damp lowlands around the world, it was taken as a cure for ague or malaria. Although opium consumption was in general decline by the last two decades or so of the nineteenth century, its use in the Fens stayed "notably higher" as late as the early twentieth century (Berridge and Edwards 1981, 48; Parssinen 1983, 48ff.). One scholar reports that most people in England used the drug moderately, but if an occasional user became an addict, opium became "ruinously expensive, especially for working class families" (Parssinen 1983, 30–31).

Concerted opposition to opium and other narcotics arose as the result of several factors: fear of the habit spreading among working classes; the discovery of morphine, the hypodermic needle, and the realization of morphine's addictive properties; the professionalization and specialization of medicine and pharmacy; and the increasing hostility against opium smoking as engaged in and supposedly spread by Chinese in England and the United States.[25] The debate over opium use in England and English involvement in the opium trade in China grew especially intense in the 1870s and 1880s and centered around two opposing positions: one that opium, especially if smoked, could never be used in moderation, and the other that opium was for the most part harmless and was in fact beneficial as an aid to both work and relaxation. In the United States morphine addiction had become fairly common by the later nineteenth century, and its dangers were widely broadcast. Many states enacted antimorphine laws in the 1890s, while opium smoking, though often condemned, was not outlawed until 1909 (see Musto 1973, 3–4).

Early descriptions of Chinese opium dens in East End London were calm and nonvilifying. One report spoke of the Chinese in a den as a "pleasant looking, good-tempered lot" (from the 1860s; Berridge 1978, 4–5). Depictions like the one in Charles Dickens's unfinished novel *Mystery of Edwin Drood* (1870), however, signaled the beginning of the "more melodramatic" and vilifying view of the den as "haunt of evil," which became a staple of popular literature for the rest of the century (Berridge 1978; Milligan 1995). In the United States as well, by the mid-1870s white men and women mingling in Chinese opium dens had become a source of alarm (Kane 1976, 2–3, 14; Courtwright 1982, 78–79). The mixing of sexes and races and the menacing effects of opium smoking in general were the focus of an evolving racial stereotype that by the late nineteenth century was solidly in place. Passivity, loose morals, and evil cunning were some of the traits attributed to the Chinese sailors and workers who frequented these dens in their otherwise laborious lives. At the same time, import statistics in the second half of the 1800s pointed to steadily rising consumption in the United States (Musto 1973, 3).

THE LATER PERIOD IN CHINA

Opium smoking continued on a massive scale in China, augmented in the late 1800s by other drugs such as morphine and on a smaller scale cocaine. As the result of an intense prohibition movement, opiates were effectively restricted between 1906 and 1915. The restrictions were linked to mutual accords drawn up with Britain in 1906 and further formulated at an international meeting on opium in Shanghai in 1909 and another in the Hague in 1912. The energy of this prohibitionism coincided with the surge of nationalism that came about at the end of the Qing and beginning of the Republic in 1911–1912.[26] A relapse followed, however, when warlords began dominating the various regions of China, in some cases encouraging or even forcing farmers to increase opium cultivation, a lucrative source of tax income for warlord governments. Su Zhiliang states that opium consumption reached its highest levels ever in the 1920s and 1930s.[27]

The Nationalist *(Guomindang)* government under Chiang Kai-shek did not strictly enforce prohibition until 1935 under its New Life Movement. The Anti-Japanese War and the civil war between the Nationalists and the Communists made this enforcement more difficult to carry out, although the Communists made prohibition a firm part of their political line.[28]

After the Communist victory in 1949, the government estimated that China had 20 million drug users. Opium prohibition became law in a 1950 proclamation. Addicts were required to register with the government and terminate their drug use by a stipulated time (these measures had been used in pre-Communist times as well). All branches of the opium industry devoted to opium supply were outlawed. Addicts who complied were to receive sympathetic treatment; others were subject to arrest and, in the severest cases, a death sentence. By 1953 China announced that it was a "drug-free nation" *(wudu guo)*.[29]

CLASSIC OPIUM SMOKING

The American Emily Hahn went to Shanghai in the 1930s and "loved" it. Part of this love derived from an "old ambition" she had since childhood to become an opium addict–like becoming "the world's best ice skater, the champion lion tamer, you know the kind of thing" (Hahn 1970, 220). She soon learned that an odor she smelled "here, there, and everywhere in town" was that of opium, which she had a Chinese friend of hers teach her to smoke (p. 221). She enjoyed long hours with him, his wife, and other Chinese friends, talking and reading aloud to each other, living what she called a "fin-de-siècle life." In fact, she adds, "the modern Westernized Chinese of Shanghai frowned on smoking," considering it "lamentably old-fashioned" (p. 227). In Paris in the 1920s Jean Cocteau had already written his impression that "young Asia no longer smokes because grandfather smoked" (Cocteau 1996, 28). Hahn's Chinese opium friends wore long gowns, were "deliberately, self-consciously reactionary," and enjoyed reading Cocteau's *Opium: Journal of a Cure* (Hahn 1970, 227–28). Cocteau in the 1920s, Hahn in the 1930s, and Gilbert-Lecomte in the 1930s and 1940s, among others, smoked because "grandfather did not smoke" (Cocteau 1996, 28).

As a method of usage, opium smoking in the "classic Chinese style"—which "is at once the hardest and the best," asserts David Rattray (1992, 206)—has for many decades been largely superseded by faster forms of delivery (e.g., heroin and morphine via injection). Drug addicts of the 1920s, 1930s, and 1940s in New York, for example, reported that compared with heroin users, opium smokers were a classier lot. But stricter drug enforcement and rising prices made opium smoking too expensive.[30] Writing in the 1920s, one of the early scholars of the anthropology of drugs, Louis Lewin, compared "morphia" and "its ancient and clumsy rival," opium:

> There will always be some who seek a life of dreams and visions, such as the smoking of opium produces, who will prefer the latter drug because its effects are more attractive and alluring than the cold action of morphia. That is why even in our days isolated devotees of opium are to be found all over Europe. (Lewin 1931, 46–47)

Opium smoking was a "way of life," to borrow William Burroughs's words in regard to heroin, in terms of its "cellular" (another Burroughs word) effects on the addict as well as the network of relations starting from the labor-intensive cultivation and harvest of opium in India and later in China to its lengthy processing and then delivery and sale to merchants and users. In China this network was ridden with connivance and illegality, even though suppression was only sporadic. The processing of opium before its sale was a multistage, time-consuming method of boiling, purifying, repurifying, and packing (see Allen 1853, 25–27). The wealthy connoisseur often demanded another layer of preparation with ginseng and fragrances added to create an especially mellow and highly prized smoke. Utensils were another site of specialization, with different craftspeople creating and refining each separate component, including opium containers, trays, pipe shafts, and pipe bowls.[31]

In the final stage of this elaborate operation, the attendant in the opium den or the smoker scooped up the opium with a special long needlelike tool, rolled it over the flame, and traded the expanding globule from one needle to another until the opium reached the proper consistency. After shaping the small mass around the point of one of the needles, the smoker deftly set it around the vent hole and poked a hole in the middle of the opium; then it was ready for smoking. Doing all this well took considerable practice. One such preparation disappeared in a single long draw and could be followed by numerous others depending on the capacity of the smoker. Rich addicts could spend nearly all their time in the opium world, but even poor coolie laborers would, if they could, stop everything at set periods and go off and have a smoke, using less elaborate paraphernalia and smoking grosser, recycled forms of the drug. The same set periods punctuated the life of the brothel, where connivance, dependence, and blackmail infiltrated the opium way of life to an extreme degree.

The "classic" style of opium smoking is almost extinct, too inefficient and detectable in the age of strict prohibition. It received its final blow in China when the Communist government eradicated it in pursuing policies of social cleansing in the 1950s. Not that opium smoking was purely "good" or should necessarily be revived, but who decided that things should be this way? Although this way of life was condemned, what was the world like from the position of those condemned? What have they, and all those involved in the opium economy, bestowed, so to speak, on later periods and manners of drug use around the world?

NOTES

1. See Edkins 1898, 21–22, citing Li Shizhen; see also Huang Yufu's 1723 passage cited in Zhao 1983, 31; and Li Shizhen 1982, 1495–96.

2. For more detailed accounts of the history of opium in China, see Morse 1910, chap. 8; Edkins 1898; Spence 1992; Su Zhiliang 1997; Howard 1998; Brook and Wakabayashi 2000; and Blue 2000.

3. It blooms for only a day or two in April-May. For detailed accounts of the earliest presmoking references and uses from the Tang dynasty on, see Edkins 1898, 6–30; Yu Ende 1934, 3–4; and Howard 1998, chap. 2.

4. Edkins posits that *yapian* and *afurong* are from Arabic or Persian, which in turn received the word from the Greek. Wang Xi's is the first known Chinese description of the incision method of extracting sap and drying it. At this point it would have been opium extract infusion or pill, not opium prepared for smoking. See Edkins 1898, 5, 18–20; Yu Ende 1934, 4–7; and Su Zhiliang 1997, 37. On opium and Chinese Inner Asia, see Bello 2000, who refers to a report of indigenous growth of the poppy in Gansu as early as 1657 (p. 145 n. 8).

5. See Spence 1992, 231; Su Zhiliang 1997, 43, for the second reference, possibly late Ming, by a man from Fujian Province.

6. See Trocki 1999, 24–25, citing a British merchant in the 1580s.

7. The former name for Jakarta; Edkins 1898, 33ff.; Trocki 1999, 181–82.

8. See Edkins 1898, 35. Europeans in the New World reported similar practices among Indians. See Lewin 1931, 287–88; Emboden 1979, 39.

9. Earlier by how much is unclear. See the *Haidong zhaji* in Zhao Xuemin's *Bencao gangmu shiyi* 1983, 31; and Spence 1992, 233–34, which gives a translation of the passage.

10. See, for example, the description in Rattray 1992, 199.

11. See also the description of smoking pure opium in this classic style in Yu Jiao's *Dream Hut Notebook*, that is, *Meng'an zazhu* 1988, 154, which dates from the same period or one or two decades later.

12. See Liu Mingxiu 1983, 7, citing Ying Lida's "Concerning Matters of Government in Taiwan."

13. From *Taihai shicha lu* (Record of a Mission to Taiwan) in Zhao 1983, 31.

14. See also a poem by Yue Jun in *Qingshiduo* (compiled between 1858 and 1869), Zhang 1983, 1005. In *City of Lingering Splendour*, John Blofeld is given sweet gruel the

morning after he smokes opium. His hosts act according to the common assumption that this is what the smoker wants and needs to eat. Blofeld does not give evidence of smoking other than on this rare occasion, perhaps his first (from the mid–1930s; 1989, 155–57).

15. From his *Meng'an zazhu* 1988, 154, prefaced 1801. For further observations on opium, see 371–72.

16. Zhou 1984, 656; this view also appears in Yu Jiao's *Meng'an zazhu* of 1801.

17. As affirmed in the 1737 *Taiwan Gazetteer*, Yu Wenyi 1984, 685.

18. Trocki cites a workshop paper by Lin Man-huong (1993) which states that domestic opium production was nine times greater than opium imported from India by the end of the nineteenth century (Trocki 1999, 126).

19. H. B. Morse believed that a significant turning point occurred in the late 1830s, when "foreign smugglers" began eluding the network by which Chinese officials of all ranks connived at profit from this illegal trade (Morse 1910, 182–84). A significant factor in the mid-1830s has to do with an increase in the foreign supply of opium, which expanded as a result of the abolition of the British East India Company's monopoly on the opium trade.

20. Trocki has a peak of 105,000 in 1880 (1999, 110).

21. Von Glahn 1996, 256, citing Louis Dermigny.

22. See Chang 1970, 85ff. For a study of the intricacies of this debate and the extremely moralizing stance of these opium opponents, see Polachek 1992 (especially chaps. 3–4).

23. Peng Yang'ou 1982, 126.

24. He also noted that the *Anne* wrecked in 1842 on return from Chusan, an island off Ningbo that was temporarily occupied by the British (p. 187). The *Anne* (also referred to as the *Ann*) wrecked on Formosa, as Gully and Denham reported in their diaries of 1842, when both were captured by the Chinese. The two men had been on the warship *Nemesis* when Ningbo was taken and were returning to Macao on the *Anne* when it wrecked. Gully died in captivity but left his diary, which was published along with Denham's in 1844. There are no mentions of the opium dealings of the *Anne* in their accounts.

25. See Berridge and Edwards 1981, 47, 97, 113, and 142ff. See also Musto 1973, 1–6; Courtwright 1982, 78ff.; Parssinen 1983, passim.

26. See Zhou 1999, chap. 2; Wong 2000.

27. Su Zhiliang 1997, 14; see also pp. 262, 287, 290, regarding warlords and opium cultivation.

28. See Slack 2000; Baumler 2000.

29. See Su Zhiliang 1997, 454–71; Zhou 2000.

30. "Your better class of user was a pipe smoker," said one interviewee in Courtwright 1989, 181 (see also 77, 86, 92, 329).

31. For a detailed analysis of opium paraphernalia, see Wylie and Fike 1993.

Chapter Three

Westerners' Intercourse with China

CHARACTERIZING CHINA

"Natural Disposition"

Nineteenth-century Anglo-Americans who wrote about China frequently described opium smoking and, as a glance at journals like the *Chinese Repository* shows, debated the issue at length. A characteristic though not necessarily articulated assumption of many of those visitors can be expressed in the form of a simple statement: a person of the West (more specifically, a Christian) cannot smoke opium. As an American, Reverend R. H. Graves, said in his *Forty Years in China* (1895), "The devil never made a wiser move than when he introduced opium smoking among the Chinese. It just suits the natural disposition of the people, as alcohol suits the active, impetuous disposition of the West" (p. 75). The active, impetuous West encountered the slow, inward-turned China. The self-loving land of opium smokers was profoundly apathetic, long beyond any need to account for its status as a superior culture.

Whether merchant, missionary, diplomat, or explorer, these visitors in nineteenth-century China felt impeded by what they saw as the unnatural lack of openness toward them on the part of the Chinese authorities. They were also frustrated with what they called the lack of "free intercourse" with China. Once the trade in opium and other goods allowed the British and other Europeans to establish strong expatriate communities in Macao and Canton, they began to produce a voluminous literature to serve themselves and those needing to know about China. "Intercourse" is the word they often used in these works—newspapers, journals, travel accounts, and scholarly studies. Although it did not connote sexual intercourse, I want to view the contact Westerners sought as also a bodily observation and a mingling that sometimes involved friendship and even love. But it was also coupled with a will to dominate and be served. In using terms like "natural disposition," American and British observers like Graves defined physical and behavioral traits of the Chinese in comparison to their own. They had their own felt presence against which the Chinese other had to be defined. Mingling in a bodily sense was a subject of study and commentary, especially as concerned the deciphering of Chinese physical and mental characteristics. In all these endeavors, the practical needs of infiltrating and opening up China were at stake. Such infiltration at times took the form of European or American visitors dressing as Chinese in order to travel where they were otherwise prohibited to go. No one could do this without first closely examining how the Chinese dressed, ate, and behaved in general, at the same time trading such information with other foreigners who had relevant insider views.

In this chapter we examine how Westerners made assumptions about the Chinese. My sources are writers of travelogues, narratives of war and daily experience, and studies of subjects like Chinese life or "Chinese characteristics." The question about Western assumptions regarding China is important for two reasons: (1) it will allow us to illuminate the motivations for "opening up" China—how these motivations were arrived at—and (2) it will further clarify the conflation between unfit human being and drug addict. This conflation underlies both the characterizations of China in the nineteenth century and the formulation of rationales against what would eventually be outlawed as dangerous drugs. In other words, the emphasis will be on the range of conscious behavior and physical being that the Chinese were supposed to represent. More specifically, the emphasis is on what the Chinese represented regardless of whether they smoked opium, but as if they were already like opium smokers anyway. This focus is critical because of the overlap between viewing the Chinese in general as "sottish" or "phlegmatic" and seeing the actual opium smoker in his "stupor." For now I will concentrate on the foreign observations of "Chinese characteristics," saving observations of actual opium smokers for the next chapter.

My chief questions are, How did visitors from Western nations inform themselves about and become experts on China? What rights of intercourse did they assume and how did they state and act out these assumptions? The questions they pursued were ones such as, What are the Chinese like and how human are they after all? which led to, What treatment do they deserve from us, given this nature that is alien but also human after all? Finally, the extent of contact (how close or personal) had also to do with how much Chinese counterparts allowed and how much Western visitors could get away with. In other words, how much does an intruder "actually" see? What situations of violence and antagonism ensue when, as usual, the intruder always wants yet more freedom of contact?

A summary statement serves as the theme of this chapter: The mean, masculinist appropriation of Chinese space was also paralleled by the assertion of common humanity. This commonality could mean pulling the Chinese up to a "higher" state of being. Or it could mean joining in a sort of ultimate union with the Chinese. Sentimental travelers (e.g., foreigners "with a conscience") could move in either or both of these directions. In the case of an especially sentimental type, the sinophile, China became a kind of fantasy land or explorer's paradise. Their experience points to an overlap between the presumed fantasy world of the opium smoker and the roaming disengagement of someone like the naturalist whose heart's desire is to travel unmolested through China collecting new species of insects and flowers. Western visitors of all sorts experienced pleasure in their very presence in China. It was sensational to have gained access to a person or place, to arrive at some significant understanding, to enjoy camaraderie with their associates, whether Chinese or Western, or, for example, to learn to appreciate a certain Chinese pleasure. The necessity of pursuing these and the other topics I have just proposed has to do with how these people from Western nations presumed to establish their presence in China and at the same time institute the opium trade. Again, the all too obvious but as yet actually quite unexamined assumption was: the Chinese smoke it, we do not. What then is the way the so-called we acted out this assumption in their writings about China and in their daily activities and interactions there?

China, Modernity, and Orientalism

Answers to these questions must take into account the radical critique of "Orientalism" that has opened up since Edward Said's 1978 book of that name. Whether we focus on Euro-Western images of the Islamic or the East Asian Orient, it is a matter of examining the representational frameworks that have guided Western endeavors in these zones from the late eighteenth century on. The opium smoker was in fact categorized as another essentially oriental character. In other words, the smoker was fulfilling another aspect of the stereotype of the immoral, sensual Asiatic. This chapter is mainly about the representational framework that results in such a stereotype. With this in mind, I want opium smoking to be seen as something that had to be outlawed because it was such a scandalous sign of the defeat of Western rationales for this and other such stereotypes. Of chief significance is the idea that the confidence of the Western colonizing enterprise could only be sustained when not mirrored by an opposite that was so scandalously narcissistic (or even more narcissistic than itself). Rather than countenance this impossible other, it was far better to reduce it to an example of an inferior. To reduce meant to effeminize, orientalize, and subhumanize. This goal would be accomplished by means of a studied examination backed by firsthand accountability. Woven into this endeavor was a rationalism that systematically propped itself up via sets of reductive dichotomies between West and East.

Some general points about this colonialist rationalizing process need to be summarized in order to frame the discussion of Westerners' reports of their firsthand "intercourse" with Chinese. We begin with a brief consideration of the concept of modernity as it had arisen since the end of the eighteenth century after the French Revolution. Not uniform in its arrival at different times or in different places, it nevertheless comes down to a conviction that the Euro-West had entered a radically new age. It was an age that gave rise to a new sense of world space with Europe at the center. Europe was the designer of this space in which various anomalous cultural areas were assumed to be in need of conforming to modernity's forward progress.[1] The fact that certain cultural areas were out of sync tended to justify rather than challenge colonialist domination and expansion.

The ideology of nationalism as it began to take shape in the early nineteenth century was an important component of the process of modernization. Nationalism gave rise to the theory that all cultures had a potential claim to a rightful place among the world of nations. By the end of the Qing, nationalism had taken firm hold among a Chinese elite led by people such as Liang Qichao.[2] He and others were well aware of the concepts of modernity and the progressive merging of all nations into a single global sphere of equal participation. Part of the Chinese elite of the late Qing period was quite willing to condemn Chinese backwardness and lack of collective awareness of the urgency of reformist modernization. The most succinct summation of the theme of modernity as also reflected in nationalist ideology is the subordination of cultural difference to the uniform model of Western progress.[3] In the words of Jean-François Lyotard:

> the grand narratives of legitimation which characterize modernity in the West . . . are cosmopolitical, as Kant would say. They involve precisely an "overcoming" *(dépassement)* of the particular cultural identity in favour of a universal civic identity.[4]

Such universalism dismisses and overrides the uneven landscape of disparate cultures, each of which must abandon cultural particularism (e.g., antiquated traditions) in favor of abstract equality (e.g., modern uniformity).[5]

We must also remember, as James Hevia writes, "that knowledge about the Orient was intimately linked to European domination of the Orient," this being an axiom of postcolonial theory in general. The Western visitor to China was in essence a "knowing observer" who felt superior to the object of his observations. This same superiority of eye supported the imperial expansionist ambitions that harnessed actual power and resources in order to dominate China militarily and then in gradual fashion politically and economically as well.[6] Such a vision also generated violence in countless small-scale and even routine incidents, as I touch upon later in this chapter.

China Specialists of the Nineteenth Century

Many of the characters of this and the next chapter are already well-known to scholars of nineteenth-century China, including the Prussian Charles Gutzlaff (1803–1851), one of the earliest and most famous Protestant missionaries in China; the American William C. Hunter (1812–1891), who from 1824 to 1842 worked for the firm Russell and Co. in Canton and Macao; the English Charles Toogood Downing, a doctor who visited Macao and Canton during the late 1830s; the English Robert Fortune (1813–1880), a botanist and traveler who wrote three books about his experiences in China of the 1840s and 1850s; Walter Medhurst Sr. (1796–1857), a British missionary in Shanghai from the 1840s to 1856; John Scarth, a British merchant who stayed in China for twelve years in the 1840s and 1850s; and Samuel Wells Williams (1812–1884), an American diplomat who served in the first embassy in Beijing. A number of British authors wrote of their experiences during the Opium War, including Lord Robert Jocelyn (1816–1854), Elliot Bingham, Arthur Cunynghame (1812–1884), and Dr. Duncan MacPherson (d. 1867). Missionary writers were especially numerous. Besides Gutzlaff and Medhurst, they include Robert Morrison (British, 1782–1834), Joseph Edkins (American, 1823–1918), R. H. Graves (American, 1833–1912), Arthur Evans Moule (British, 1836–1918), and Arthur Smith (American, 1845–1932). Virtually everyone mentioned here was a self-styled expert on China and "Chinese characteristics," one of them, Arthur Smith, even writing a well-known book by that name (1894). Most have something to say about opium as well. Edkins authored the book *Opium: Historical Note*; Duncan MacPherson wrote at length of his own experiments of smoking opium.

In what follows, I take a sampling of these and other accounts about China from the so-called pre-Treaty days (before the Opium War of 1839–1842) to the early twentieth century. Since a great number of the earliest accounts were produced up to, during, and soon after the Opium War–the first period of especially intense interaction–my selection draws mostly from them. Some of these individuals stayed many consecutive years in China, such as Gutzlaff, Hunter, Medhurst, Scarth, Graves, and Moule. Others made relatively brief trips (from a few months to at most two or so years at a time), such as Bingham, Cunynghame, Downing, Fortune, Jocelyn, and others. The original editions of these have become collectors' items in antiquarian book shops in the United States, and many have been reissued in photo reprint editions.

TRAVEL WRITING IN CHINA

"Free Intercourse"

The words "free intercourse" appeared prominently in many writings of the early nineteenth century, including those of the famed Charles Gutzlaff, Prussian author of *Journal of Three Voyages along the Coast of China in 1831, 1832, and 1833* (published in London in 1834).[7] In the introduction to his book, he stated that nothing was more "unnatural" than the "system of excluding foreigners from all intercourse with China." "Refusal" of intercourse was a "transgression of the divine law of benevolence, which is equally binding upon all the nations of the earth" (pp. 1–2).

Gutzlaff was not unique in making such statements or in going on such a mission. He was representative of many writers of that time—particularly those who wrote travel accounts—who had already begun to appear in the second half of the eighteenth century. In the spirit of modernity similar to that of Linnaeus and his "global classificatory project" of naming and categorizing all plants on earth, explorers set out with a newly established confidence in European superiority over parts of the world as yet unknown and unopened to them and therefore of demanding interest as destinations for the global exploratory mission (Pratt 1992, 15, 24–27). Along with these developments in scientific method and exploration of the natural world came the development of a "new kind of history" based on "notions of qualitative progress," which was defined as a decisive movement away from the past and its burdensome and stagnating traditions (Hevia 1995b, 70–71). China was considered out of step with this rational progress because of its excessive uniformity and rigidity.[8] The Westerner was assumed to be more logical, objective, and realistic than the Chinese, and thus justified in his goal of overruling the Chinese determination to remain unchanged. When Gutzlaff asserted that the "system of excluding foreigners from all intercourse with China" was unnatural, he was echoing an axiom of European thought of his time, the idea that nations and humans in general should benefit from the circulation and exchange of goods, and that rulers had a moral duty to foster the flow of commodities and the increase of wealth.

Among Gutzlaff's predecessors were famous men who had explored the interior of Africa and South America, writing accounts that were widely read and highly profitable as marketed books. One terrain, China, was as yet very underreported. Except for Catholic missionaries, few had written about China, which was waiting for the kind of daring explorers who had written so much about Africa and America.[9] Compared with their sensational predecessors, some of whom wrote about their love affairs with women from the places they visited,[10] travelers to China in general went on less sentimental missions. Until 1860 they could only take far more restricted journeys, however fascinated with China they may have been and assiduous in their efforts to expand knowledge about China. In particular, love affairs with native inhabitants were virtually absent in the reports of these travelers, and equally absent or severely obstructed in the experience of others they witnessed, as one outstanding example below demonstrates.

Access to China, Wearing Chinese Clothing

Charles Gutzlaff was one of the flashier visitors to China. An "old coaster," in the words of William C. Hunter (1882, 70), he made his lengthy stay in East and Southeast Asia from the 1820s to midcentury. He mingled extensively with itinerant Chinese, especially along the coasts from Siam to northern China.[11] He also learned to speak Chinese and in his earlier days there sometimes dressed in Chinese clothing. According to Hunter, Gutzlaff "resembled a Chinese very much, while *they* declared him to be a 'son of Han' in disguise!" (Hunter 1882, 70; original emphasis). Gutzlaff was well acquainted with Chinese sailing vessels, having traveled on them as the lone European. On one voyage he was secluded in his cabin which, as he wrote, was filled with the "vile smell of opium fumigation," and from which he heard the crew indulging in the "most obscene and abominable language."[12] He also claimed great success in distributing free Christian tracts along the coast, and in his 1832–1833 voyage continued to do so while serving as interpreter for a well-armed East India Company ship searching for new opium markets along the northern coast. In his book, however, he does not mention the opium-related aspect of the journey.[13]

One of the most important documents of the expatriate community in Macao and Canton of the pre–Opium War days was the *Chinese Repository*, published in Canton between 1832 and 1851.[14] In the introduction to volume 1, the anonymous author (presumably Bridgeman and/or Williams) referred to the Chinese empire as a "stupendous anomaly," offering the "widest, and the most interesting field of research under heaven" (May 1832, 1). The twofold purpose of the *Repository*, as the author stated, was to conduct this research into all aspects of China, including natural history, social relations, commerce, and religion, and then eventually to make "that which is most valuable to man, and now so richly enjoyed by the nations of the West . . . equally enjoyed . . . among the nations of the East" (p. 5). The *Journal of the North China Branch of the Royal Asiatic Society* (JNCBRAS) was another such journal, published in the Shanghai concessions starting in 1858 and lasting almost a century to 1946 (with a gap between 1940 and 1946). Joseph Edkins, one of the preeminent members of the society and, as already mentioned, the author of a major study of the history of opium in China, stated in his 1902 retrospective address to the society that the purpose of the journal was likewise to research all aspects of China. Speaking of himself and other early organizers of the journal, moreover, he said of their mission: "We were determined to understand both their religion and their want of religion. We wished to know what makes the Chinese hate us and how far they love us" (1903–1904, iv).

After the Nanking Treaty of 1842, Westerners were allowed to settle, trade, and propagate their faith in a number of specially designated zones of cities along the Chinese coast. Travel inland was still prohibited, leading some adventurers to copy others before them (especially the Jesuits from the sixteenth century on) by donning Chinese clothing. They would have their hair cut in Chinese fashion with a braid attached and thus infiltrate beyond the mandated perimeters. Gutzlaff had done this long before the Opium War, as had the Frenchman Abbé Huc shortly after the war, going from Beijing to Lhasa in the mid-1840s in Chinese dress.[15] In *A Glance at the Interior of China*, Walter Medhurst provided other would-be disguisers with a detailed description of how to dress and look like a Chinese (1850, 1–11). His journey took place in spring 1845, starting from Shanghai, which at the time was for Europeans very newly settled, and went through Jiangsu, Anhui, and Zhejiang Provinces. Author of *Twelve Years in China* (1860), John Scarth was another such disguiser, setting off in the spring of 1848 from Shanghai, determined "to penetrate as far as possible into the silk districts" (p. 65). He traveled with his Chinese Singaporean teacher and a barber, who kept Scarth's hair properly shaved and braided and also served as cook.[16]

Another traveler of that early post–Opium War period was the naturalist Robert Fortune, who first arrived in 1843 and eventually wrote three books about his explorations of coastal and interior China from Canton to Shanghai. In spring of 1845, when Medhurst made his journey from Shanghai in disguise, Fortune traveled undisguised along an "interdicted route" on his return from Ningbo to Shanghai. He flouted the "mandarins" who tried to stop or make complaints against him. The matter then simply dropped (Fortune 1847, 351–66). Although he made many lengthy journeys during his three visits, he nevertheless spoke of longing for the day "when China shall have been really opened to foreigners, and when the naturalist can roam unmolested" (Fortune 1852, 247).[17]

Whatever the nature of their claim to roam in China, these visitors are engaged in a kind of love affair with the Chinese. When Edkins casts a retrospective look at the nineteenth century and speaks of the wish to know "what makes the Chinese hate us and how far they love us," he exemplifies the colonizing humanist who stands at a distance yet wishes to get close. The love–hate relationship illustrates the combination of contraries in which Chinese are also involved. The visitor uses force to exercise benevolence while relying on the complicity of Chinese helpers. Gutzlaff rode on and worked for the powerful European ships looking for opium markets, but at other times must have enjoyed the compliment of "son of Han in disguise." He was confident in his popularity among Chinese, but what were the Christian tracts he distributed actually used for (sometimes read but also taken for papering walls or windows, wrapping things, stuffing shoes, or for toilet paper, a luxury to people who customarily used such things as grass or leaves)?[18] Fortune audaciously flouted the mandarin authorities but frequently wrote of his friendly, human contacts with Chinese companions. In 1853 Edkins worked extensively with Wang Tao (the man who later advised Legge on the monumental translation of the nine Chinese classics) during a period when Wang Tao was writing in his poetry and letters of his extreme uneasiness with assisting foreigners (Zhang Hailin 1993, chap. 2). The symbiosis between Chinese and foreigner in such instances evokes the complex relationship of antagonism and attraction between colonizer and colonized that is one of the persistent issues of the colonial and postcolonial experience to the present day (Gandhi 1998, chap. 1).

GRAND SUMMATIONS

Specimen Taking

Westerners who wrote books or articles about China mingled diary-like narratives of their journeys with observations and generalizations presented from the viewpoint of an expert. Writing as if to further scientific knowledge, they treated Chinese people and their material culture, no less than the flora and fauna of China, as specimens to be gathered, described, and classified.[19] In its most standard sense, specimen taking included gathering plants, insects, and other such things that could be put into some sort of catalogue or collection. As a mode of observation, the taking of specimens broadens to include the recording and classifying of a vast array of information in the creation of an enormous and putatively all-embracing archive (Richards 1993). Medhurst reproduced woodblock illustrations of implements used in silk production. Articles in the *Journal of the North China Branch of the Royal Asiatic Society* documented yearly variations in the climate for Shanghai and other areas. In *The Fan-qui in China in 1836–7* (1838), Dr. Charles Toogood Downing wrote of his examination of the "skull of a Chinaman" and proceeded to give a general description of Chinese racial characteristics (Downing 1972, 3:317–21). Physical examinations and descriptions betray a fondness for finding the concrete edge of difference between the standard European and the standard Chinese.

In all such examinations, little surpassed the bound feet of Chinese women as objects of fascination. Authors not only described the process of foot binding but found women whom they could persuade to display their feet. In his 1843 *Narrative of the Expedition to China*, Commander Elliot Bingham had the opportunity of "minutely examining the far-famed little female feet" when he and his group, while on an outing in British-occupied Chusan, succeeded in persuading a "bashful" sixteen-year-old to display hers. The men were "agreeably surprised" to find it "white and clean," but found that "the leg from the knee downwards was much wasted" (Bingham 1843, 358).[20] Authors drew diagrams and later took photographs of such specimens. In *The Opium War*, Captain Arthur Cunynghame reproduced a facsimile of a bound foot, which he helped a doctor obtain from the body of a woman who had been laid out in a coffin of a house occupied by British troops. The doctor had "begged" his assistance in this "laudable desire to forward the ends of science" (Cunynghame 1845, 91).[21]

In these examinations of Chinese women, it is not clear how much these men knew about the historical and cultural significance of bound feet[22]. In lovemaking as portrayed in Chinese fiction and illustration, the otherwise naked woman covered her feet. A man was especially privileged and thrilled if he could touch a woman's bound foot. The size and fineness of the foot was a determining factor in a woman's attractiveness, whether she was to be married, hired as a maid, or sought as a prostitute. But having young women display their naked feet for either curiosity's sake or scientific examination and neither for intimacy nor transaction was something presumably only a complete outsider would think of doing. For the sake of chastity, some women would commit suicide or mutilate themselves rather than let strange men, foreign or Chinese, approach their bodies in any way and for whatever reason. Needless to say, we lack a great deal of information in these instances above–how, for example, did these women come to agree to expose their feet? How were they compensated, if at all? What was their status in their particular communities?

In these accounts, authors rarely hesitated to make grand summations about the attributes of the Chinese character, illustrating the absolute otherness of the Chinese people even without the introduction of opium. The foundation of this belief lies in the assertion, as Commander J. Elliot Bingham states, that the Chinese "may be said to be a mass of contradictions to all European nations,–the very opposite to ourselves in almost everything" (1843, xiv–xv). It was standard for authors to dedicate chapters or sections of their books to the topic of the "character of the Chinese." In his *Twelve Years in China*, John Scarth began his chapter on that subject sounding very much like Commander Bingham: "The Chinese character is the exact opposite to that of Europeans generally" (Scarth 1860, 95).[23] Even Westerners who were fond of China and lived major portions of their lives there accepted this generalization as a given. For example, William Hunter once wrote in passing that "all customs [in China] are the antipodes of those existing in the West" (Hunter 1855, 120). According to the highly respected missionary and expert on China, Reverend Doctor Robert Morrison, for example, "The Chinese are generally selfish, cold-blooded, and inhumane."[24] In *The Opium War*, Captain Arthur Cunynghame referred to "the unceasing industry of this ant-like population" (Cunynghame 1845, 70). The famous opium eater Thomas De Quincey referred to Asia as that "part of the earth most swarming with human life," asserting that "Man is a weed in those regions" (De Quincey 1994, 243). Cunynghame proved Chinese inhumanity when, for instance, he noted their "habit" of nailing rats by their four paws to a board and seeming "amazed at anyone taking compassion upon the wretched beast" (p. 231).

Arthur Smith's influential book, *Chinese Characteristics* (1894), later translated into Japanese and Chinese, was a culminating work in this vein. It was dogmatic and often sounded angry, divided into chapters such as "Disregard of Time," "Disregard of Accuracy," "Intellectual Turbidity," "Absence of Nerves," and, never to be omitted, "Contempt for Foreigners." This book was known to Chinese authors, Lu Xun (1881–1936) in particular, who in their concern with issues of national character read such works with great curiosity, though they also found them full of ridiculous errors (Liu 1995, 51ff.). Two points are crucial in summarizing Smith's book and those of other Western writers of this period: (1) the extent to which these authors were writing about themselves, that is, their own experience in China, even though they pretended to be generalizing and objective.[25] In Smith's case, much of what he wrote was about his frustrating experiences with Chinese servants and other hired workers. Like those who preached about opium smoking, he did not associate (or "smoke") with the upper classes, who were often openly hostile to the missionary cause (Liu 1995, 56–57). The other point has to do with (2) the unpredictable ways Chinese readers and writers understood and appropriated Western generalizations about China. Lu Xun did not swallow Smith's study but used it to satirize or depict both the foreigner and the Chinese, most famously in the form of the fictional character Ah Q.

Phlegmatic but Human After All

To these British and American writers the Chinese were not only "opposite to us in everything." They were also in a state of darkness and intransigence. Such condemnations were already firm features of English discourse by the middle to late eighteenth century. The idealized view of China that held sway in Europe from the sixteenth into the eighteenth centuries had come under attack and given way to a view of China as constituting a "negativity" against which to construct a superior and progressive English identity.[26] This negativity is likewise apparent in the context of opium discourse. In the opium visions of China and the Orient as portrayed by Coleridge and De Quincey, we find a merging of the "demonic and the serene." No longer providing only "escapist settings for titillating fantasies," China in Coleridge and

De Quincey evoked an invading presence that threatened to seduce and contaminate the unwary Westerner (Milligan 1995, 20).

Whether or not travel writers about China had read Coleridge or De Quincey, they carried with them a similar sense of the Asiatic in his torpor, but speaking in their own sober and firsthand tones did not exhibit the sense of being invaded or threatened. Commander Bingham wrote in his preface: "The Chinese are essentially a commercial people immured in darkness, and all bowing down before the shrine of Mammon" (1843, xiv–xv). He later said, "For China is intrinsically an immoral and sensual nation" (1:362). When Robert Fortune first arrived in Shanghai in 1843, he had the impression of the "great proportion" of the people being "in a sleepy or dreaming state" (Fortune 1847, xi); the Chinese seemed to hold the Westerner in a kind of "superstitious dread" (p. 106). A foreigner who went to a shop at that time, just after the Opium War, would be immediately surrounded by a crowd, who would "gaze at him with a sort of stupid dreaming eye" (p. xi). Statements like these portray the Chinese as being like opium addicts even without their opium.[27] As Reverend Arthur Evans Moule said, the Chinese "are so phlegmatic a race that it is hard to measure the depth or reality of their emotions" (Moule 1891, 155). The word "phlegmatic" was used at least since Linnaeus in the eighteenth century in racial classifications that became standard in the nineteenth and twentieth centuries.[28] The same word was used to characterize the Chinese disposition in its preference for opium over alcohol, which was the counterchoice of the supposedly quicker-paced European.[29]

With Chinese strangeness and inhumanity as commonly accepted givens, some writers at the same time took pains to assure readers that Chinese were human after all. After discussing the toil and sacrifice of overseas Chinese colonists for the sake of their relatives back home, Charles Gutzlaff affirmed "that their affection towards their kindred is very strong" (Gutzlaff 1834, 166). In counterbalance to his mention of the phenomenon of infanticide, Toogood Downing argued that "there is as much feeling shown by mothers towards their children in China, as in any other nation" (Downing 1972, 3:266). After observing a "charming" scene of people fishing, Robert Fortune once concluded "that the Chinese, however strange they may sometimes appear, are, after all, very much like ourselves" (Fortune 1857, 265).[30]

Searching for or happening upon the human side of China, these authors advanced their inside views of Chinese life and thereby further proved their expertise. Such inside views also took the form of defending the Chinese and even asserting their superiority. William Hunter described his adoption of Chinese sleeping methods on hot summer nights. During a stay back in New England in 1832, he was "subjected" to stifling nights "on mattresses and pillows filled with feathers . . . with the thermometer at any height you please." The same season in China was a treat. There he slept on a "clean, cool, hard rattan mat or mattress of bamboo shavings."[31] By 1832 Hunter felt at home doing business in Canton-Macao and was proud of adopting a simple but exquisite sleeping arrangement.

The contradiction between assertions of Chinese inhumanity and fondness for China figured in efforts to work through the issues of foreign domination over China. The open assertion of Chinese humanity could only lead to recognizing the Chinese as equals. But the opium trade and the Opium War were based on assumptions of Chinese inadequacy. Because of the heavy investment in trade and war (and, later, income from opium taxation), these assumptions could not be lightly abandoned. Hence the peculiar mix of assertions of Chinese inhumanity and occasional admissions of Chinese humanity or proofs of Chinese superiority. This mix is something I will briefly elaborate now in terms of the personal contacts between Chinese and Westerners in this period.

PERSONAL CONTACT AND RELATIONSHIPS

Taking specimens of skulls or feet and observing "antlike" masses or human/inhuman behavior were always compounded with experiences of personal contact and relationships extending over long periods of time. In these relationships Westerners wrote as if presuming that they would never be challenged by Chinese interlocutors who might feel misrepresented, embarrassed, or maligned. This sense of insularity is thematic among both Westerners and Chinese. At the same time, the Western visitor assumed that fairness and reciprocity would prevail in his attempts to associate with the Chinese. The assumption of reciprocity—a firm facet of the myth of the free intercourse of modern nations—allowed for both the foregrounding of the warmth and intimacy these visitors wrote of enjoying with the Chinese and the making light of the violence that recurred on both small and large scale throughout these times.

According to Downing and Hunter, the pre–Opium War period in Canton generated much nostalgia. There were warm relations between Europeans and Chinese, both of whom in many cases stood to make great sums of money from the opium trade, including Hunter himself. Nevertheless, "the heart warms as much towards an Indian or a Chinese, when you know them, as towards an Englishman," Downing intoned (Downing 1972, 1:90). He assured his readers that the impression of Chinese being all alike and "wanting in expression of countenance" is something that "soon wears away," for one finds "as much character in each individual here as elsewhere" (Downing 1972, 3:321).

William Hunter was one of the few longtime foreign inhabitants of Canton and Macao in the pre-Treaty days to leave substantial personal accounts. Having arrived in 1824 as a boy of thirteen from New York, he studied Chinese for eighteen months in Malacca until the end of 1826, after which he worked for Russell and Co. for most of the following years until 1842 (he died in Nice, France, in 1891).[32] In *The 'Fan Kwae' at Canton before Treaty Days*, he spoke glowingly of the "social good feeling and unbounded hospitality always mutually existing" in those times (Hunter 1882, 26). The trust between Chinese and foreigners was such that he "never knew of a formal *lease* being drawn up for any one of [the foreigners]" (Hunter 1855, 220–21). In some cases, in fact, merchants of either side forgave each other's debts.[33]

In all such transactions, the burden of responsibility for the behavior of foreigners and Chinese rested more heavily on the individual Chinese. Warm relations in part depended on Chinese wishes that foreigners behave correctly. Private friendships always depended in part on how things must appear in public, especially before official Chinese eyes. When Hunter was studying at Malacca, for example, he befriended a man from Sichuan, "Shaow-Tih," who was learning English and whom he later freely saw in Canton in the late 1820s. But when Hunter was present at an official affair in 1830, the man was to Hunter's surprise now performing the duties of official interpreter. "He was looking fixedly at me, and when our eyes met he carelessly indicated, by a motion and significant glance, the Mandarins, which signalling I understood to mean that I was not to recognise him" (p. 262).[34]

Chinese and foreign men ate and drank together (but in no accounts of this period appeared to smoke opium together), while upper-class Chinese women were present only in the background and were mainly seen only when foreigners visited their Chinese friends' homes. Foreign women were forbidden from residing at Canton in those times by the Chinese authorities. Hunter was "specially favoured" when, shortly after arriving at Canton in 1824 as a "very young Fankwae," he received an invitation to visit the family of one of the main hong merchant's sons during the Chinese New Year's holiday (Hunter 1855, 225–26). He wrote of the "great kindness and unbounded surprise" with which the women of the family received him and remarked on their "sparkling black eyes, splendid eyebrows, and teeth of ivory whiteness" (some also smoked "the long thin delicate pipe" with its silk tobacco bag attached, p. 226). They wore "numerous bangles on arms and ankles and . . . caused silvery sounds pleasant to the ear" (p. 227). Two years later, when he must have been fifteen or so and could "speak to them in their own language," he visited them again and was rewarded with similar treatment.[35]

Perhaps his youth allowed him greater entrance into and favor from this household than might be the norm. The faintly mesmerizing quality of his encounter evokes in miniature the writings of travelers to other places in the world in which foreign male visitors eventually formed amorous relations with female inhabitants (see Pratt 1992). Hunter and others could only go as far as to observe and chat with Chinese women during brief visits or, as in Commander Bingham's case, view them with his telescope, through which he once saw "many pretty little female faces" (Bingham 1843, 1:245–46).[36] Foreigners' (especially sailors') transactions with Chinese prostitutes were yet another type of contact.[37] Cunynghame heard about a well-known but unnamed foreign gentleman, of "great proficiency in the Chinese language," who had succeeded in making an assignation with a Chinese "flower-boat" lady, an appellation that presumably refers to the type of courtesan whose brothel was on a boat in the river at Canton (as seen in Shen Fu's late eighteenth-century *Six Records of a Floating Life*, which mentions opium smoking in these same brothels). They had been conversing only a short while, however, when they were seized, tied up together back to back, and "placed, *sans culotte*, on the summit of the boat" on a cold night (Cunynghame 1845, 233–34). The man was ransomed two days later for $3,000, Cunynghame was informed. "No wonder, therefore, that the people of Canton had no respect for us, and no small care will be requisite on our part to prevent their falling into the same error for the future" (p. 234).

As suspect or unnatural as such interracial relationships were considered, marriage between Chinese and Portuguese had long been common in Macao by the time of the Opium War, as a reference from Commander Bingham indicates (Bingham 1843, 2:183). Interracial marriages occurred in places even farther outside the rule of the Chinese empire, such as Malacca, where Hunter studied, or Taiwan during and after Dutch occupation (which ended by the mid-seventeenth century). Such relations were not common in treaty port China until later in the century.[38] An English counterpart of Cunynghame's story would be the English wives of Chinese men running opium dens in East End London, who were sensationalized in fiction of the last quarter of the nineteenth century. Two characteristic features of these works, as Barry Milligan shows, were demonic oriental men absconding with European women and these women becoming "Orientalized and assimilated" through their opium smoking (Milligan 1995, 87). I will return to this topic in the next chapter but cannot avoid mentioning the sensitivity both Chinese and British felt about women mixing with foreign men. No matter how militarily dominant the European was, many among the Chinese furiously opposed such mingling. Likewise, the opium den in London and the mingling of genders and races there were decisive in the eventual determination of laws against both opium and Chinese immigration. The phenomenon of competing masculinities and the role of the woman as someone to be protected from foreign contamination are subjects of major studies that have been written in the field of postcolonial theory.[39] What I have briefly covered here will provide background for the gendered and erotic aspects of opium smoking that I discuss later.

VIOLENCE BETWEEN CHINESE AND FOREIGNERS

As already noted, a certain Euro-American went to China assuming his natural right to have access to wherever he desired to go and to whomever he desired to relate. Unless he forced his way, however, he was obliged to accept the contact that he was allowed. Some therefore felt privileged and all the more delighted if granted friendship with Chinese or given the opportunity to view previously unseen realms. Since such access was granted or allowed at Chinese discretion and was not available according to the European fiction of free intercourse, the foreigner was always in a position of wanting and at times clamoring to push farther. In making such demands, he was always willing to enter the realm of violence, whether verbal or physical, and eventually engaged in conflicts of major scale starting with the First Opium War.

In most cases Euro-Americans engaged in minor infractions of Chinese rules, which put them into the realm of relatively minor-scale hostility. If they ventured beyond the assigned area of their factories in Canton, for example, they were subject to pestering from so-called ruffians. When Toogood Downing went one night to observe a festival, someone appeared and said, "I thinkee more better you go," after which a mob followed, throwing unripe or decayed fruit at him and his friends. In such situations, he continued, "we usually turned about . . . and made those behind us scamper away . . . by offering to bamboo them. This was the only way to deal with the Chinese; for if we had appeared at all afraid of them . . . they would very soon have taken advantage of their numbers, and placed us in an uncomfortable predicament" (Downing 1972, 2:304–5).[40]

Aside from assaults with cannons and guns, foreigners were aggressive in minor situations in which they were confident of obtaining their ends because of the proven deadliness of their rifles and pistols, whether they actually carried them at a given time or not.[41] As evidenced in Downing's remark, foreigners commonly felt that they should make a show of force; if they demonstrated weakness or submission, the Chinese were likely to be more aggressive and uncooperative.[42] As a general rule, the foreigners tried to give the impression that they were not "unruly devils" and that they meant no harm. But as Hunter wrote, using an already classic line from the poetry of William Cowper, in the final analysis the Fankwae remained "monarch of all he survey[ed]" (Hunter 1882, 115; 1855, 6).[43]

The confidence of the foreigner in testy situations was based on a perception of the Chinese as craven and weak. They were apathetic when they should not be and were therefore unaccountable and anomalous. Such weakness at times generated frustration in the British, who during the Opium War might have wished on occasion for somewhat bolder opposition. In the action at Woosung (near Shanghai), Lieutenant Alexander Murray of the Eighteenth Royal Irish wrote at one point that they "were delighted to see the Chinese make so good a resistance" (Murray 1843, 155). But in the end, as the anonymous author of *The Last Year in China* illustrated in his account, the Chinese were more apt to throw an "orange peel" at the foreigner and then vanish rather than put up a good fight (*Last Year* 1843, 102–3). Since the values of free intercourse regarded a man as a man only if rational and brave in the face of challenging circumstances, the Western visitor had no choice but to resort to virtually routine forms of aggression when the situation called for it.[44]

THE SINOPHILE

One last portrait of the foreigner in nineteenth-century China brings us to the sentimental sinophile. This is the voice, for example, that in occasional asides would grant the Chinese a measure of justification for their insolent, dishonest, or craven behavior. The sentimental traveler expressed sympathy with native inhabitants and guilt over the devastating effects of foreign invasion.[45] An important aspect of this protagonist is the tendency to assert a self-effacing innocence (Pratt 1992, 78). He was not an "aggressor" but, in the case of the naturalist or medical doctor, merely a curious and independent "onlooker" working for a humanist cause. In the case of the merchant or even the soldier, he could step aside from his involvement in illegal or war-like activities and become a fellow human observer who could at times even convert to the Chinese way of doing things. In face of either the ugliness of war or the imputed depravity of Chinese people, this fellow human legitimized his presence by asserting or implying that he was part of a "civilizing" mission. He thereby put aside the aggressive goals of conquerors and market seekers and foregrounded instead his own benevolent intent to lead the native out of darkness and immaturity. The sentimental traveler, moreover, believed that whatever his specific goals may have been, he was in China on a mission based on standards of reciprocity, as I mentioned above. The Chinese may be "craven," but the European admitted faults of his own. Supposedly, then, once various obstacles to free intercourse were removed and various misunderstandings cleared up, everyone would be on equal footing and would emerge into a form of transcultural companionship that might even include love and friendship.

The sentimental mode could also carry the writer to the lofty heights of elevating the Chinese above himself or imagining them as living in a world of their own, entirely justified to itself. The inspired writer is full of praise for the Chinese people, whom he usually saw separately from their mendacious leaders. Robert Fortune called them "a quiet and sober race" (Fortune 1857, 37) and "the most wonderful people on the surface of the globe" (p. 93); he doubted "if there [was] a happier race anywhere than the Chinese farmer and peasantry" (p. 99). John Scarth said that the Chinese were "models of propriety and quietness in their towns and daily avocations of life" (Scarth 1860, 116). He saw them as completely self-sufficient in terms of material want and thus "averse to all innovations" (p. 121). Instead of being a sign of lack of progress, such aversion to innovation was tied in with the portrayal of Chinese as sober and quiet, and as having evolved a perfect form of life, though one that must change.[46] What Scarth proposed, then, was that once they are "roused from their trance and take their place in the march of progress," for which he said they are eminently trainable (p. 127), then they will be "capable of almost any demand made upon their energy." He added, "What a vast field has yet to be opened here to European enterprise!" (pp. 129–30). Scarth's "roused from their trance" once again emblemizes the role casting of the lively European (who likes alcohol) versus the drowsy Chinese (who prefers opium). Again, the state of trance prevails even when opium is not under discussion and even when the author can praise the Chinese for their propriety and temperance.

In his last book on China, *A Residence among the Chinese* (1857), Robert Fortune appears more content than Scarth and others with the way the Chinese are already. When he takes his tea, he says, "Reader, there was no sugar nor milk in this tea, nor was there any Prussian blue or gypsum; but I found it most refreshing for all that it lacked these *civilised* ingredients."[47] He enjoys a chat with a high priest at a temple or entering a city and encountering people who welcome him: "The crowd appeared to be perfectly good-humoured, and treated me with the greatest deference and respect" (Fortune 1857, 44). Besides plants and insects, he also collects ancient works of art, especially porcelains, over which he befriends Chinese of similar interests, whom he admires for being "passionately fond" of what they collect (p. 83). He watches Chinese opera, whose female impersonators, he says, perform in a way that "is most admirable" (p. 258). Did he know about the common association between young boy actresses and their older male lovers (discussed in chapter 6)? In that setting opium smoking often played a major role as a medium of friendship and a device of seduction. Enjoyment of opium, opera, and boy actresses, in short, were strongly intertwined.[48]

For the sinophile, chatting with Buddhist priests or observing pleasant scenes of Chinese life was a kind of passion. In between retreats to Britain or the concessions of Shanghai or other cities, the China lover and hobbyist like Robert Fortune traveled into the real China, each time becoming more expert and further expanding his repertoire of experiences. William C. Hunter was another type of China lover, not a short-term adventurer but one who had a long-term and lucrative career in China and loved his life there. For him, "runs home" to the United States and back were nine months of listening to the "wild waves" (before steamships, approximately 125 days each way, Canton to New York), and three months of wandering around "unknowing and almost unknown" (Hunter 1882, 126).[49] On the other hand, some foreigners lived and worked in China while having little good to say of it. Lovers and haters alike pretended to an authenticity, however, an inside knowledge, whether glowing or cynical. They were all working on "intercourse." John Scarth traveled with a sketchbook, the "best weapon to travel with in China" (Scarth 1860, 71).[50] Robert Fortune paid little boys to gather insect specimens for him. A foreigner could just be himself and gain access to local gentlemen or officials. Each took pleasure in making contact. But the question is, Could he maintain that pleasure in successive contacts or would the relationship eventually change so that he would no longer be able to regain his initial euphoria?

NOTES

1. Marshall Berman's 1982 account of modernity and "development" according to the story of Goethe's *Faust* (though not focused on colonialism per se) is one of the best studies of this process.

2. See Tang Xiaobing 1996.

3. As Tang Xiaobing discusses, Liang Qichao and many others eventually critiqued this aspect of modernist discourse (1996, 1–10).

4. Cited in Gandhi 1998, 41, from Lyotard 1982.

5. I leave out for now the part of the argument about nationalism that notes its highly contradictory nature, mainly in the form of claims by various nationalisms to cultural uniqueness. Nationalism must rid itself of its "bad" particulars (backward customs, "degenerate" habits) in order to merge into the form of one nation among others. At the same time it must reinvent its past and lay claim to certain images and traditions that give it a distinctive–nonuniversal, nonabstract–and singular identity.

6. See Hevia 1995a, 5–7. Said's work contains numerous topics and locutions that have prime relevance here, European culture "setting itself off against the Orient as a sort of surrogate and even underground self" (Said 1979, 3), the "passive, seminal, feminine, even silent and supine East" (p. 138), the "childish" Asiatics (p. 247) who nevertheless possess "number and generative power" (p. 311), from whose "overwhelming influences" we must protect ourselves (p. 166–67), their "timelessness" (p. 229) and "sameness" (p. 230), and the untruthfulness of the "Oriental mind" (p. 38). Although Said has been criticized for too monolithic a polarity between "Orient" and "Occident," quotes like these find almost verbatim echo in sources by other nineteenth-century Westerners on China. These views had an undeniable relation with actual policy and action, especially those of diplomacy and war.

7. On Gutzlaff, see, for example, Waley 1958; Fay 1975, 8; Hanan 2000, 419–31.

8. The Scottish philosopher David Hume (1711–1776) wrote that "the CHINESE have the *greatest uniformity of character imaginable*," whereas the English were, in James Hevia's words, "distinguished . . . by their diversity of manners, by a well-balanced structure of authority, by the absence of autocratic power, by religious tolerance, and by liberty." Hume is cited in Hevia 1995b, 66–67, original emphasis. See also Said 1979, 172, 222–23, 229–30.

9. As Mary Pratt notes, travel literature had become a lucrative business by the eighteenth century and continued to be so throughout the nineteenth century, when the books I will cite were written. Well-known eighteenth- and early-nineteenth-century

travelers such as Mungo Park, Francois Le Vaillant, John Stedman, or Alexander von Humboldt were sensationalized for their journeys into the remote terrains of Africa and South America. In *Bits of Old China*, William C. Hunter states that one of the earliest and most prominent Protestant missionaries to China, the Reverend Doctor Robert Morrison, was originally to have accompanied the famous Mungo Park's expedition to central Africa in the 1790s. Instead he went to China and from 1807 on spent the rest of his life doing missionary work and acting as interpreter for British concerns (Hunter 1855, 161).

10. See Pratt 1992, chap. 5.

11. Although he first went as a missionary, he was also employed as an interpreter for both diplomatic and business affairs.

12. Voyage of 1831, Gutzlaff 1834, 74. It was an extremely rare chance to ride in a Chinese vessel, as was remarked at the time. See Hanan 2000, 420–21.

13. See Samuel Wells Williams regarding the importance of Gutzlaff's voyages, Williams 1874, 16; also see Greenberg 1951, 139.

14. See Fay 1975, 83–84, who says it had "200 or so subscribers" in China, "150 in the U.S.," and a "smaller number scattered from London to Calcutta."

15. Huc, for his own amusement, once pretended to be a mandarin official, and in this disguise fooled William Hunter during a lengthy interview in Macao. Not at all offended, Hunter was impressed with Huc's "determined manner and self-confidence," which indeed carried him farther than most if not all other European travelers of the time. Hunter's text says 1853 for their meeting, but this has to be a misprint because Huc left China in 1852 (having arrived in 1839). See Hunter 1855, 187ff.

16. In one item of paraphernalia Scarth did just as Medhurst recommended (though without reference to him) in "shad[ing] the natural colour of [his] barbarian eyes by a huge pair of tea-stone spectacles" (Medhurst 1850, 8; quote from Scarth 1860, 5).

17. Almost a century later, in a 1935 lecture in Shanghai, the Swedish explorer and adventurer Sven Hedin "visualized" the day when Atlantic and Pacific from Europe to China would be joined by motor road (Hedin 1935, 129). See Said 1979, 218, for a similar expression of geographical ambition from the late nineteenth century concerning linking Algeria to Senegal by railroad.

18. See Homi Bhabha for a quote from a missionary in India who knew the Bible was used for wrapping paper there. Thus Bhabha notes how "the founding objects of the Western world become the erratic, eccentric, accidental *objets trouvés* of the colonial discourse" (Bhabha 1994, 92).

19. As Mary Pratt has written, such "specimen gathering" had been conventional in travel literature since at least the sixteenth century, but with the advent of what she terms the "global classificatory project" launched in the eighteenth century, specimen gathering became by comparison major in scale (Pratt 1992, 27–28). As she says, travel writing was never the same again.

20. Another observer, Duncan MacPherson, M.D., discovered filth upon his examination of a young woman's foot, then proceeded with a careful and scientific analysis of the configuration of flesh and bone (MacPherson 1842, 40–45).

21. Cunynghame also reported that there were no Chinese women in "Sincapore," the two who had been there having been taken to London to "exhibit their feet" (Cunynghame 1845, 35). In William Hunter's 1882 *The 'Fan Kwae' at Canton before*

Treaty Days, a man on Hunter's first boat to China in 1824 had reportedly taken two small-footed women from Macao to England to show to the king but failed in his mission because of "great opposition in certain quarters" (Hunter 1882, 3).

22. On bound feet in the Ming and Qing, see Ko 1994.

23. That the Chinese were opposite the Europeans was widely assumed and was applied to Orientals in general, including those of the Near East, as Edward Said has discussed (Said 1979, 39, 255).

24. See Gutzlaff 1834, xxviii, from preface by Reverend W. Ellis.

25. About some of these writers, see Liu 1995, 58–59.

26. See Hevia 1995b, 73–74. For a similar reversal among Orientalists of India and Islamic regions, see Said 1979, 150.

27. In another example, a feeling of disgust comes through in Samuel Wells Williams's comment about crowds in China during the time he served as secretary and interpreter for the American embassy to China during negotiations for the Second Opium War in 1858 and 1859: "There was a dismal sameness and vacuity in their putty-like faces, for there really has not, in my opinion, been much beauty distributed among the Chinese" (Frederick Williams 1911, 93). Justifying the foreign use of force against the Chinese, he said, "They are among the most craven of people, cruel and selfish as heathenism can make them, and we must be backed by force if we wish them to listen to reason" (pp. 64–65, from his journal edited by his son Frederick Wells Williams [1857–1928]). On the timelessness and sameness of the Arabs, see Said 1979, 229–30. Williams admitted "pity for this weak, wrong-headed nation in the hands of mighty and jealous nations like England and France," which dominated the United States in these negotiations (p. 225).

28. See Pratt 1992, 32, 45, where Linnaeus uses the word to qualify Africans, and on racial categorization in general, see Said 1979, 119, 206, 232–33. See also Allen 1853, 30, attributing "sanguine, lymphatic or muscular temperament" to the "Indian and Negro," in whom the effects of opium therefore "partake more of an animal nature."

29. See United Kingdom 1894, 5, 180, 237, and subsection on the report in the next chapter. Many witnesses whose testimony is part of the report cited time as a factor for why Chinese liked opium but the European did not.

30. In discussing Chinese funeral customs, he said, "It has been asserted that there is little genuine feeling in all this," but he went on to state that he believed "there is as much genuine sorrow amongst the Chinese for the loss of relatives as there is amongst ourselves" (Fortune 1857, 54).

31. He does this in Canton, "where it was rarely over 96 degrees at midnight." Given the flow of this sentence, "96" seems a misprint and should perhaps be 86, the mean July temperature in Canton being around 83 Fahrenheit (Hunter 1882, 126).

32. On his language study, which included the *Four Books* and other classics, see Hunter 1855, 177, 259; 1882, 16. Russell and Co. was the major American competitor with Jardine, Matheson, and Co. and Dent and Co., all involved in the opium trade, among other things.

33. The elderly Thomas Beale, for example, who arrived in China in 1785, lived his last years up to his suicide in December 1841, in relative poverty in Macao. He was forgiven his debts by the Chinese there and at the very last, according to Hunter, was invited to live in his compradore's house in a village beyond the walls of Macao. See Hunter 1855, 74–78.

34. The man was later part of Lin Zexu's official suite in 1839, at which point it presumably became impossible for them to meet again as they had originally at Malacca and for a while at Canton.

35. In general, as Hunter said, "it did not fall to the lot of the barbarian from afar to see anything of the inner or family mode of celebrating a holy day, or even of its daily routine" (Hunter 1855, 225). At another time he visited the merchant Pwan-Kei-Qua's mansion, where he got "good glimpses of Pwan's numerous wives," who had "lustrous eyes and the prettiest hands and small feet of a *natural* size" (original emphasis). He continued, "They were quite as curious as we were, but walked about or sat in the open halls unconcernedly as we passed through" (Hunter 1855, 31–32).

36. He also wrote of meeting farmer women of "really good-looking" and "very interesting" appearance (Bingham 1843, 1:357, 363).

37. Lower status women such as the "tanka" boat women of Macao, for example, were types with whom foreigners may have associated fairly often. See Downing 1838, 1:27–29.

38. One prominent and relatively early example is Frederick Townsend Ward (1831–1862) of Taiping Rebellion fame, who married the daughter of a compradore of Jardine, Matheson, and Co. A later example is that of the British consular official E. H. Parker (1849–1926), who also married a Chinese woman (see his obituary in Werner 1926, i–vi.). In Shanghai and other treaty ports, foreign men visited both Chinese and foreign brothels (as is commonly mentioned in late Qing fiction).

39. See, for example, Spivak 1988 and Gandhi 1998, chap. 5 for a summary; and in Chinese studies, see, for example, Chow 1991 and Hu 1997.

40. In another such situation, having experienced the "greatest civility from the natives" in the north, Robert Fortune was surprised in the mid-1840s to find himself set upon and robbed by a group of men in what he later learned was a notorious suburb of Canton in which foreigners had several times been beaten, robbed, and stripped. Stones were thrown; he received a brick in the back; and he struggled with the "robbers for nearly a mile, sometimes fighting, and sometimes running, until [he] got out of their territory" (Fortune 1847, 147–54).

41. The assumption was that the Chinese were easy to overcome. As early as 1793 Lord Macartney had already remarked upon the weakness of the Chinese military, pronouncing the troops "effeminate" (Hevia 1995b, 201).

42. After the wreck of his ship during the Opium War in 1840, John Lee Scott believed that he might not have been taken prisoner had not the Lascars who accompanied him shown so much fear before the Chinese crowd (Scott 1841, 20–21). Robert Gully, who was killed in captivity in Taiwan in 1842, left a diary in which he asserted that, even in his state of imprisonment, a certain show of defiance, not submission, would gain him greater liberty during his confinement (Gully 1844, 38).

43. Pratt uses the expression "monarch of all I survey" in her discussion of a recurrent stance of travel writers in the nineteenth century (Pratt 1992, chap. 9). "I am the monarch of all I survey, my right there is none to dispute," is from William Cowper's "Verses Supposed to Be Written by Alexander Selkirk" (1782), Selkirk being the model for Robinson Crusoe. Thanks to Gerrit Lansing via Ken Irby for the location of Cowper's lines.

44. An idea of such routine violence can be gleaned from an account of John Scarth's. Speaking of Shanghai residents of the 1850s, he said, "if there is a coolie do-

ing something particularly vexatious, and an angry foreigner gives him a good punch in the ribs, the Chinaman will drop down and have his cry." He adds that "the southern people are different, and will even resist a blow" (Scarth 1860, 149).

45. See Pratt 1992, chaps. 5–6. In an example of such a perspective, after the British capture of Ningbo in 1841, an anonymous field officer reported that when walking in the outskirts of the city, the Englishman had better carry a stick to fend off possible attackers or even kidnappers, for the Chinese "are a most insolent race. Still," he went on to admit, "it is no doubt galling to have foreign barbarians strutting as lords, where a short time ago their only quarters were *cages*" (original emphasis, *Last Year* 1843, 103). He was referring to the recent capture and imprisonment in cages of Captain Anstruther, John Lee Scott, Mrs. Noble, and others in the region of Ningbo.

46. Scarth went on to say, "The Chinese have been jogging on so quietly for ages, without alterations in their institutions, that they have brought all the material appliances of life to perfection" (Scarth 1860, 120). He found that "the people contain all the elements to make the Chinese one of the finest nations on the earth," but that the "whole is neutralized by the deceit, the cupidity, and cowardice of their rulers" (p. 230).

47. Original emphasis; Fortune 1857, 32. These were ingredients that Chinese manufacturers added for the foreign market; see Fortune 1847, 201–6.

48. In the finale of his book, however, he still hopes that trade and commerce with China will increase and that China will be able to produce more than "two or three articles of importance, such as silk and tea." The day will come when China is "fairly and fully opened to the nations of the west," at which point "a boon of far greater value will be conferred upon the Chinese than anything connected with . . . commerce," that is, the "glad tidings" of the message of Christianity (Fortune 1857, 440).

49. At one point he asserted that "democracy in its strictest sense is the ruling feature in China," whereas that of the West is actually less truly democratic because ridden with strife and hostility (Hunter 1855, 122–23). See also Said 1979, 214–15, citing Lord Curzon's words to the effect that many of those who "have spent a number of years in the East . . . regard that as the happiest portion of [their] lives."

50. In 1841, the English Captain P. Anstruther "would hold a merry intercourse" with Chinese who "frequently gathered round him" as he drew in his sketchbook, but because of his insouciance in wandering about sketching during the Opium War hostilities was captured and held prisoner for many months by the Chinese in the Ningbo area. See Bingham 1843, 1:280–85; Fay 1975.

Chapter Four

Westerners on Opium and the Chinese

THE BEGINNING AND END OF OPIUM

Westerners' observations on China, as described in chapter 3, overlap with their observations and debates about opium in China. The sottish, emaciated smoker was both a symbol of a distant and ancient empire and an ominous and insidious threat in the present. He was the cool self-lover who had been there longer; he was going slower and liking it. These symbols and images eventually became interwoven with the Chinese production of opium, which by the 1880s exceeded foreign imports in quantity and was cheaper. Not long after this, the British and Americans began outlawing opium the narcotic, thus culminating an almost century-long debate on the issue of their involvement in that trade. Economic factors certainly played a role in this termination. Less profit was to be made; other opportunities—tobacco, for instance—were to be found. But the decision to outlaw opium had to do with what opium did to people, China being a centrally illustrative example. In this chapter we consider illustrations from the 1820s on that prefigure the end of the century, when opium was finally prohibited.

The horror of Asian images was already something De Quincey wrote about in his *Confessions of an English Opium Eater* in 1821. He told of the overpowering effect that the "mere antiquity of Asiatic things" had on him. "A young Chinese seems to me an antediluvian man renewed." He wrote of the "unimaginable horror which these dreams of oriental imagery and mythological tortures impressed upon me" (De Quincey 1994, 243). The demonic and horror-inducing element of the Chinese opium den later became formulaic in British popular fiction from the late nineteenth century through the early twentieth (Milligan 1995, 85ff.). These images had taken root in the writings of Coleridge and De Quincey and of visitors who witnessed opium smoking in China from around the 1830s on. Opium smoking signaled new and extraordinary depths of depravity. It constituted an invasive force that would sap the vitality not only of otherwise very trainable Chinese, as Scarth saw them, for example (1860, 127), but also European men and especially women, as late-nineteenth-century journalists, fictionalists, and moralists luridly intoned (Milligan 1995, 89–94).

The second quarter of the nineteenth century, especially from the 1830s on, saw intensifying debate and information gathering about the smoking and eating of opium. De Quincey's *Confessions* (1821) marked a giant step forward in the attention given to opium as a pleasure-inducing substance in Britain. The rapid growth of the opium trade at the very same time in China focused more attention on the issue as merchants, doctors, soldiers, and missionaries began spreading information about what they saw in their travels in the Middle East, South and Southeast Asia, and China. The *Chinese Repository,* founded in 1832, became a forum for debate over the European role in the opium trade and was a source in which numerous opinions and observations were published. The *Repository* also printed translations of Chinese official documents regarding opium, since the Chinese were debating the problem as well, especially in the years just prior to Lin Zexu's posting in Canton in 1838, and were themselves gathering information about opium and its effects.[1]

The travel books I discussed above also contain passages on opium smoking. These, along with the *Chinese Repository* and some nineteenth-century studies of the opium issue, are crucial sources for examining the types of observations made and language used beginning in this early period. An important later source is the *Report of the Royal Commission on Opium,* a rich collection of statements (1893-1894) by witnesses before English Parliamentary commissioners who sought evidence about the opium situation as these witnesses saw it in various regions of India, Southeast Asia, and China. As a continuation of the last chapter and its focus on the nineteenth-century expert on China, this chapter makes the point that the China expert also had to be an expert on opium. Such expertise immediately prompts the question, How far does one go to become such an expert and what type of expertise is "credible" or "valid"? Two doctors I will discuss, for example, smoked opium in experimental doses in order to gain supposed firsthand knowledge. Besides considering the ways Western visitors took account of opium smoking, it will be necessary to consider the very act of observing and discussing opium smoking and its effects.[2]

I have somewhat compartmentalized the Westerner and the Chinese by saving the Chinese sources on opium smoking for separate discussion. I want to concentrate on the perspective of each, in particular in this chapter and the last chapter, to bring out as fully as possible the presumptions of Western visitors to China and the peculiar nature of their representations of China and of opium smoking and addiction. But I still want to emphasize that all these sources are about opium in roughly the same time and space, and broadly speaking are in a dialogue by virtue of the interaction between all the Chinese and foreigners who take part in the daily commercial, diplomatic, domestic, religious, and other arenas of exchange of that period. In every such interaction, each individual is inevitably a representative of his or her nation/culture, someone who can potentially be taken to stand for every Chinese or Westerner. I am interested precisely in the stereotype, but I also take someone's report to be an informative correction or supplement to someone else's, regardless of the bias of social or cultural identity. The phenomenon of the remoteness from each other is also something I want to let stand between Chinese and Western sources, the nonmention or superficial mention by one of the other. This remoteness is an integral part of the overall simultaneity of their existence in the time and space of this opium period of history. Something said or done in the remote corner of a nineteenth-century Chinese novel is just as relevant as the sayings of a British expatriate in China who, as fluent in Chinese as s/he may be, may never associate with the kind of people so intimately written about in that novel.

THE HARMS OF OPIUM

Lord Jocelyn

In *Six Months with the Chinese Expedition* (1841), Lord Robert Jocelyn recorded his experiences with the British military sent to China during the Opium War and, in a passage quoted by many later writers, described an "opium smoking house" he saw in Singapore. His portrait served for these later writers as a sort of locus classicus on the subject of opium debauchery, and serves for us as a launching point for the great debate over whether opium should be allowed into the repertoire of intoxicants heretofore led by the troublesome but hoary god of alcohol. In other words, was the drunken British sailor worse than, as bad as, as ultimately harmless as, or still morally higher than the opium sot? A crucial feature of almost all of these foreigners' observations (the exceptions probably being the two doctors who tried opium themselves) is that they witnessed smoking—if they witnessed it at all—mainly in opium dens or similar settings in which few if any Chinese of a social level comparable to the foreigner himself ever gathered.[3] Opium smoked in the environs of a comfortable home or smoked, for example, by Chinese medical men, merchants, compradores, scholars, poets, artists, people like Zhang Changjia, or their wives, daughters, or other female relatives, remained relatively unknown or off limits to these Euro-American writers.

Allowing that the opium smoker was "not so degrading to the eye as the drunkard from spirits," Jocelyn found all the same that "the idiot smile and death-like stupor . . . of the opium debauchee has something far more awful to the gaze than the bestiality of the latter" (Jocelyn 1841, 38). "Pity" was for Jocelyn the feeling that came as he watched "the faded cheek and haggard look of the being abandoned to the power of the drug," while mere "disgust" was what he felt watching the "human creature" intoxicated with alcohol (p. 39). The anonymous field officer and author of *The Last Year in China to the Peace of Nanking* likewise viewed an "opium divan" in Singapore on his way to the operations in China. His specimen smoker "leered on us with meaningless, but very good natured smiles. The effect of excess in opium is more like idiocy, than ordinary intoxication. It steals away the brain like drink, but does not substitute fire, as the latter appears to do" (*Last Year* 1843, 29). The comparison between opium and alcohol was recurrent among writers, as seen in Reverend R. H. Graves and others I will discuss, and pro and con views often took issue. For Lord Jocelyn and the anonymous field officer, although they made no explicit reference to race or nationality, the implication was that drinking alcohol was the English form of intoxication which, disgusting and bestial as it was, was not so awful as the Asiatic form of self-abandonment.

Lord Jocelyn's description brings into focus the special repertoire of vocabulary that many writers used to isolate and particularize the opium-smoking Chinese: idiotic, emaciated, faded, haggard. Lord Jocelyn referred to the "infatuated" people "half-distracted" as they went to feed their "craving appetite." Lively and "wild" at first, they gradually "merged to the wished for consummation" in which they passed into the "state of bliss" that they so "madly" sought (Jocelyn 1841, 40–41). A word like "bliss" did not refer to anything like Christian heavenly bliss but the dreadful and horrific imagery De Quincey wrote of in his *Confessions*. Infatuation and craving turned the opium smoker into an uncanny and awful specter of a human being who twisted intoxication too far out of proportion for those only used to the bestiality of the drunkard.

Dr. Nathan Allen, Reverend R. H. Graves, and Others

Numerous books and tracts were wholly dedicated to China and the opium question, among them *The Opium Trade in India and China* (1853), by an American, Dr. Nathan Allen (1813–1889). This was one of the earliest book-length works dedicated to formulating anti-opium arguments with the eventual goal of effecting prohibition. He belonged to the medical arm of the prohibition movement, which, as Berridge and Edwards have discussed, was gaining strength as part of the professionalization of medicine and pharmacy then taking place (1981, 113). Although Allen's influence alone may not have been great, his effort signaled an energy that gathered momentum in the 1870s and after.[4]

In his discussion of the effects of opium smoking, Allen admitted the drug's worth when used under expert medical guidance. But he emphasized that the "evils growing out of its abuse, surpass, in magnitude, permanency and extent, those of all other medicinal agents combined, unless it be that of ardent spirits" (Allen 1853, 30). Opium's effects depended on many variables—quantity, frequency of use, race, age, temperament, habits, idiosyncrasy, "etc.," as he listed—so many that the nonexpert should surrender all decision-making powers, Allen implied, regarding the use of opium. A new realm had been entered that challenged the human being with a "temptation far more powerful than that of any other intoxicating agent" (Allen 1853, 31).

Of particular significance was the fact that "the greater the development of the nervous system, the more marked and diversified, the effects of the drug." Allen declared, for example, that different races experienced different reactions: "On the Indian and Negro . . . its effects partake more of an animal nature, but where there is a greater development and activity of the brain, . . . it operates more directly and effectively on the mind." He then added that "at the same time, its deleterious effects on the body are by no means diminished" (Allen 1853, 30).

In what was already becoming formulaic in discussions of opium smoking, Allen then detailed what was in store for intelligent people who might experiment with the drug. He used the word "ecstasy" to describe the opium high and provided what might be called a modestly nice, even somewhat intimate, rendition of opium's "first and most common effect": to "excite the intellect, stimulate the imagination, and exalt the feelings into a state of great activity and buoyancy, producing unusual vivacity and brilliancy in conversation, and at the same time," he finished, "the most profound state of perfect self-complacency." He also quoted a Mr. Tiffany's more lyrical sketch of the opium smoker who, for example, "floats from earth as if on pinions" when high but then ends when sober as "the same nameless creature that he has ever been" (Allen 1853, 31).

Having sketched the opium ecstasy, Allen, like other writers, returned to his emphasis on the harms of opium, taking on the tone of an expert citing facts and quoting sources. He made use of scientific language to prove, for example, the weighty point that smoking opium was more harmful than eating it: "When opium is inhaled into the lungs, it comes in direct contact with a far more extended and delicate tissue, and . . . contracts the air-cells of the lungs in such a manner as to prevent *the blood from receiving its due proportion of oxygen*" [his emphasis], which "must have a most destructive influence" (Allen 1853, 33).

The issue of smoking versus eating opium alarmed prohibitionists like Allen for two reasons. The British American eaters or drinkers were, with supposedly few exceptions, pursuing positive medical results, whereas the Oriental smokers were a priori engaging in an act of intoxication and were therefore abusing the drug (opium smoking was still rare or nonexistent in Allen's time in Britain and the United States). The assumption was that moderation in smoking was impossible.[5] The other point of alarm had to do with the inherently suffusive effect of smoke, which in Allen's portrayal cast the recipient, whether smoker or bystander, into a more helpless and involuntary state than experienced by the eater. Smoke contacted "a far more extended" and therefore less restricted range of receptors. Even if the opium eater intended to use opium for its euphoric effects, those effects remained within the eater. Smoke, however, created an atmosphere that intoxicated even the bystander. In later nineteenth-century descriptions of opium dens, those atmospheric effects reached the nonsmoking journalist-observer who reported, for example, that "the cramped little chamber is one large opium-pipe, and inhaling its atmosphere partly brings you under the pipe's influence," or in another account that "the fumes gather in intensity, and though we sit near the opened door, it is not without an oppressed feeling about the head" (quoted in Milligan 1995, 88–89). These portrayals verged into titillation in a way that became commonplace in late-nineteenth-century journalism and in fictional narratives.

Allen quoted numerous sources, both Chinese and English, to detail the harm upon the health, appearance, and social efficiency of the smoker. He cited, for example, a British surgeon who visited China in 1839 and referred to the "peculiar languid and vacant expression" and "sottish indifference" (Allen 1853, 35) of the opium smoker, resembling in tone Lord Jocelyn who, not long after 1839, wrote of the "idiot smile and death-like stupor." Allen then included a major portion of Lord Jocelyn's passage on opium in Singapore (p. 36). He also quoted a source referring to the effeminacy of opium consumers, in this case those of Assam, "who are more effeminate than women" (p. 44). Such blurring of gender would become a major theme in the late-nineteenth-century vilification of opium smoking.

Allen touched on another common theme—the natural bent of the Chinese for opium smoking—when he asked why China could not enforce its laws against opium: "The Chinese people have naturally excessive acquisitiveness and fondness for those temporary enjoyments which do not require great efforts of body or mind." Furthermore, the Chinese were never "trained to the rigid exercise of moral principle or decision of character" (p. 64). Although opposite to Dr. Nathan Allen in believing that opium was relatively harmless, Dr. James Henderson likewise viewed the Chinese as innately prone to opium smoking. In "The Medicine and Medical Practice of the Chinese," Henderson stated that the Chinese smoked opium because they were "of so passive a character as to be the slave of circumstances rather than the devotee of religion." He added that "of all beverages used by man, opium seems to be the most suited for the Chinese" (Henderson 1864, 61). In *The Truth about Opium Smoking*, an 1882 tract that cited pro but mostly con views about opium, the author Benjamin Broomhall quoted Reverend W. H. Collins: "The Chinese are all of them more or less morally weak, as you would expect to find in any heathen nation; but with the opium smoker it is worse" (Broomhall 1882, 18). Closer to nature and more bound by "circumstances," the Chinese were thus incapable of self-conscious reflection. Opium smoking was characteristic of them because it furthered them in the tendencies they already had.

Reverend R. H. Graves has already been quoted as saying that "the devil never made a wiser move than when he introduced opium-smoking among the Chinese." To them, "opium gives that gentle excitement and soporific effect which are enjoyed by ease-loving Asiatics who are obliged, by their poverty to labor hard, with poorly nourished bodies, or who have no compunctions of conscience as to self-indulgence or waste of time" (Graves 1895, 75). He also spoke of opium as "eat[ing] out the virility . . . of the individual." In discussing opium dens in the United States, he warned of the Chinese taking "advantage of the laxity of our police to open opium dens to entice the unwary whites" (p. 146). Another former missionary to China, the English Reverend George Piercy, warned in 1883 of the "retributive consequence of our own doings" and spoke of a "plague spreading and attacking our vitals." He was referring to the increase in opium smoking in England, which he saw as "prolific of evil, springing up amongst us" (quoted in Milligan 1995, 83).

As these religious men saw it, opium exerted an invasive effect—whether degrading, feminizing, or seductive—on the white person. In referring to the enticement of unwary whites, Graves resonated with one of the strongest chords of anti-opium and anti-Chinese feeling in the late nineteenth century.[6] The presence in particular of the English or American woman in opium dens in London or San Francisco was one of the most inciteful gathering points for the anti-immigration fervor of those times. But Piercy went further than Graves in viewing the spread of opium smoking in England not only as a sign of evil invasion but also, in Barry Milligan's words, of a "retribution for England's dishonorable imperial policies" in China (Milligan 1995, 83). He thus added another level of causality beyond the inherently seductive properties of opium, which after seducing the Chinese, according to Graves's logic, would eventually do so to "unwary whites." If we put Graves and Piercy together (both from late century), it is as if the Oriental taking opium to Britain or the United States were a knowing agent of a free market policy, the evils of which were merely following—or being advanced along—their logical course. To go one more step, opium as an agent of "imperialist policies" fulfilled all too well the purpose of controlling human bodies, threatening to become the control center itself and thereby usurping all human as well as divine presumptions of sovereignty.

Alcohol versus Opium

The comparison and contrast many authors drew between alcohol and opium illustrate how opium was identified as a greater usurper of dignified control than alcohol. Those who believed opium was worse than alcohol argued, for example, that opium was harder to overcome. Nathan Allen quoted a writer in the *Chinese Repository* of 1836 as saying, "There is no slavery on earth, to be compared with the bondage into which opium casts its victim"; opium, "when once indulged in," exerts a *"fatal fascination"* (Allen 1853, 32, original emphasis). An excerpt from "Macnish's Anatomy of Drunkenness, p. 51," cited in the April 1837 *Chinese Repository* stated, "The ecstasies of opium are much more entrancing than those of wine. There is more poetry in its visions–more mental aggrandizement–more range of imagination." Wine "invigorates the animal powers and propensities," but opium "strengthens those proper to man," that is, the higher "intellectual faculties." However, "in proportion as [the effects of opium] are great, so is the depression which succeeds them." Such suffering follows that "the drug is again had recourse to, and becomes almost an essential of existence," until "the person becomes the victim of an almost perpetual misery." Reflecting a common hyperbole of opium prohibitionists, the excerpt concluded by saying that the results of smoking "never fail to terminate in death, if the evil habit which brings them on is continued" (*Chinese Repository* 1837, 569–70).

Reverend Graves somewhat echoed the association of wine with animal propensities when he connected the consumption of alcohol with the "active, impetuous disposition." But instead of granting opium its association with higher mental faculties, as Allen and Macnish's "Anatomy" did, he connected it with the "ease-loving," self-indulgent disposition of "Asiatics" (Graves 1895, 75). Likewise, the anonymous field officer quoted above argued that "the effect of excess in opium is more like idiocy, than ordinary intoxication." Opium "steals away the brain like drink, but does not substitute fire, as the latter appears to do" (*Last Year* 1843, 29). Whether it brought idiocy or excitement of the imagination, opium was considered a more powerful and threatening intoxicant than alcohol. As Reverend Graves put it, both intoxicants were evil, but "alcohol leads a man to beat his family," whereas opium "may lead him to sell his wife and daughters as slaves" (Graves 1895, 76).

The anonymous field officer's reference to fire is a key metaphor in the contrast between alcohol and opium. After stealing away the brain, alcohol nevertheless substitutes fire, but opium in effect introduces cold, that is, something tending toward death and nothingness. The effects of opium translate in the sober person's eye into an abyss of coldness and distance.[7] Theft has occurred, but it is an unsettling one because no one can say or see exactly what is stolen. A drunk is still one of us, but someone smoking opium appears to be robbing us of some basic, minimum semblance of human company.

OPIUM APOLOGISTS

William C. Hunter, Merchant

The counteropinion that opium was not so bad as people thought always co-existed with the negative. In the alcohol versus opium debate, for example, the counterview generally began with the point that, in contrast to drunkards, opium smokers were nonviolent. Commander J. Elliot Bingham of the British expedition to China during the first Opium War argued that the "imbecility" of the opium smoker "lasts but for a short time, during which he is harmless and inert" (Bingham 1843, 139). This view was common in medical circles as well (Berridge and Edwards 1981, 108). The American doctor Harry Hubbell Kane, who studied opium smoking, smoked it himself, and had white addicts among his patients in New York in the middle to late nineteenth century, held that chronic alcoholism was the worse evil because it was more violent (but he still thought opium dangerous; Kane 1976, 74–75). A doctor already cited, James Henderson, was like many others in simply placing opium on a par with alcohol, for in every nation some "beverage" was used, he asserted (Henderson 1864, 61).

Another way the counterview expressed itself was to assert that the harms of opium smoking had been greatly exaggerated and that its excesses were restricted to a small minority. William C. Hunter marshaled forty years of "personal experience" in China to support this counterview. Besides downplaying the seriousness of opium addiction, he called the Opium War "one of the most unjust ever waged by one nation against another," thus extending the question beyond the focus on the effects of opium on the human body (Hunter 1882, 80, 154). At the same time, he left only piecemeal comments about his participation in and feelings about the opium trade, in which by his own confession he was happily engaged for many years until the actions taken by Lin Zexu in 1839. Since Hunter was a significant contributor to the literature about China in the early nineteenth century, it is worthwhile to focus on him briefly by assembling his various remarks as found in *Bits of Old China* (1855) and *The 'Fan Kwae' at Canton before Treaty Days* (1882).

He reported, for example, that the foreign merchants at Canton often debated the morality of the opium trade and the effect of smoking on the Chinese. In general he found that the inhabitants of Canton were healthy and industrious in a way that was "inconsistent with habitual smoking" (Hunter 1882, 80). Further, he asserted that "opium was never found for sale in Chinese shops at Canton, nor were there any signs by which one could judge where it was prepared for sale or for smoking" (p. 66). It was no doubt common among the wealthier classes, "but I myself . . . rarely, if ever, saw any one physically or mentally injured by it. No evidences of a general abuse, rarely of the use of the pipe, were apparent" (p. 80).

Such remarks are exceptional, considering the evidence of both Chinese and foreign observers of the 1830s, who admittedly in many cases went purposely looking for evidence of opium smoking and its harmful effects. Conceivably Hunter was attempting to exculpate himself, or he did not see much beyond a limited range of Canton despite living there many years, or else opium smoking was less visible in Canton because of the major official and foreign presence there. Hunter's contemporaries in Canton, who had no particular claim against opium, observed widespread use, though not necessarily "abuse," as examples below will show.

Hunter wanted above all to assert that "in fact, smoking was a habit, as the use of wine was with us, in moderation" (Hunter 1882, 80). Compared with alcohol, with its "evil consequences," the use of opium was "infinitesimal." He and others commonly wrote of the violent and drunken abandonment of foreign sailors in Canton; compared with them, the Chinese were models of propriety. By extolling the virtues of the Chinese, he made a case for the relative innocence of foreigners' engagement in the opium trade in China. Just as he promoted the use of a "cool, hard rattan mat" on stifling summer nights, so he favored occasionally opium-smoking but "essentially temperate" and industrious Chinese (Hunter 1855, 18).

Hunter observed and participated in the opium trade, as is known from information about the firm he worked for, Russell and Co., and as he indicated in a few passages himself. In his earlier book, *Bits of Old China*, he provided a two-page panorama of life on the river in front of the foreign factories, including this description of Chinese boats openly engaged in opium smuggling: "Occasionally, towards dusk, with a fair east wind, could be seen rapidly and resolutely approaching in profound silence save the unintermitting plashing of three score oars, a 'scrambling dragon' from the 'outer waters' having in her hold, to judge from her draught, bags of opium worth tens of thousands of dollars" (Hunter 1855, 19). "Scrambling dragons" was a name for the boats devoted to transporting opium inland from the "outer waters" where buyers and sellers gathered out of the way to avoid obvious defiance of official decorum.[8] It was in these outer waters that foreign ships anchored and unloaded their shipments of opium. In *The 'Fan Kwae' at Canton*, he described actual participation in the trade when he took a clipper ship up the coast in 1837 to an opium depot at Namoa. A mandarin came aboard and announced the rules against trading anywhere but Canton. After receiving a *cumsha* gratuity, he asked how much opium they were delivering and then withdrew. The Chinese buyers then came on board to conduct the transaction (Hunter 1882, 68–69).

The ease with which this pleasant farce was conducted largely explains Hunter's downplaying both a central factor behind his company's presence in Canton and a major issue in what he eventually called one of the most unjust wars ever waged. He reserved one short passage in *'Fan Kwae' at Canton* to admit some guilt in the affair when he said, "we were all equally implicated. We disregarded local orders, as well as those from Pekin, and really became confident that we should enjoy perpetual impunity so far as the 'opium trade' was concerned" (Hunter 1882, 143). What does putting "opium trade" in quotes here imply? Perhaps a distancing and a bracketing that suggest frustration that the "opium trade" became such a signifying issue.

Hunter's most profound statement about his involvement in the opium trade appears when he equates the business transactions in opium with drug use itself. Up to the time of Lin Zexu, opium "had indeed been an easy and agreeable business for the foreign *exile* [his emphasis] who shared in it at Canton. His sales were pleasantness and his remittances were peace. Transactions seemed to partake of the nature of the drug; they imparted a soothing frame of mind with three percent commission on sales, one percent on returns, and no bad debts!" (Hunter 1882, 72–73). Hunter had discovered, in other words, that although he lived in the hardship of so-called exile in China, opium was nevertheless the most pleasant and reliably profitable business imaginable.[9]

It is at moments like this that the opium sellers, buyers, and smokers, however disparate their interests may be, are most in sync in their nonchalance about what others were loudly condemning, and in their tacit confirmation of the persuasiveness of the opium euphoria. Hunter enjoyed his exile, his dinners with Chinese business partners, and his participation in the opium trade, all of which in his analogy partook of the leisurely and carefree pleasure of opium smoking. The consequence of his subversion of Chinese sovereignty was something he noted only after "one of the most unjust" wars ever waged, one of whose main outcomes, as he presents it, was to upset the peaceful and harmonious life of Canton before the Nanking Treaty. His memoirs were dedicated to his good memories of those days, which in retrospect formed a suspended and uncomplicated period that was now lost forever.

Dr. Duncan MacPherson: Experimenter in Opium

Observers who were never directly involved in the opium trade held similar views about the relative harmlessness of opium smoking. They arrived in China during and just after the Opium War and thus overlapped with Hunter's time there. The difference with them was that, because of the Opium War, they were far more attuned to opium smoking as an issue. They saw and reported more evidence of smoking than Hunter did but downplayed, or simply did not see, the seriousness of it. Whatever the motivations for their portrayals might have been, they overtly and assertively wrote in reaction both to what they saw as exaggerated reports of the effects of opium and to the imbalance in the vilification of opium as opposed to alcohol.

The testimony of British physician Duncan MacPherson stands out especially among those that avoided placing opium in such an odious light. As part of the British expedition to China in the Opium War, he was one of very few Euro-Americans in China openly to admit trying opium himself (others I have found so far in the period from the early to late nineteenth century include Robert Gully, James S. Lee, and Henry Lazarus, mentioned below). To be sure, like Harry Hubbell Kane in New York, also a medical man, MacPherson portrayed his opium smoking as part of a scientific undertaking. He kept opium strictly in the realm of "means" to an "end," that is, the medical use of opium, while in tone he adhered to professional decorum by utilizing the extra credible language of science.

In his chapter entitled "Opium and Opium Smoking," he begins the account of his experimentation as follows:

> I had the curiosity to try the effects of a few pipes upon myself, and must confess I am not at all surprised at the great partiality and craving appetite always present with those who are long accustomed to its use. From what I have myself experienced, as well as seen in others, its first effects appear to be that of a powerful stimulant. There are few who have not, at some period of their lives, experienced the powers of opium, either to soothe or mitigate pain, or drown cares and sorrows. But as with most other temporary stimulants, there follows a period of nausea and depression; the opium becomes partly digested in the stomach, and it deranges all the natural secretions. When introduced into the system through the lungs, this does not appear to follow. Its effects are then far more immediate and exhilirating, as well as more transient.

MacPherson did not want to make too strong a case but "confessed" that the Chinese love of opium smoking was not surprising. He then established that in terms of exhilaration, opium smoking was superior to opium eating, which he in turn said the reader had to admit was an experience almost everyone had. He then went on to provide a page-and-a-half description of the opium ecstasy, all the while never venturing far from the vocabulary of medical science. Continuing where the last quote left off, he wrote:

> The pulse vibrates, it becomes fuller and firmer, the face glows, the eyes sparkle, the temperature of the skin is elevated, and it becomes suffused with a blush; the organs of sense are exquisitely sensitive, perspiration flows profusely, respiration becomes quicker, the action of the heart is increased, the nervous energy is exalted, and a glow of warmth, and sensations similar to those which often attend highly pleasurable and agreeable feelings, overspreads the body.

He was not quite without a discordant note, because suddenly at this point he added:

> every organized tissue shares the impression, and the whole system becomes preternaturally excited, and assumes the characteristic of disease.

He then finished his paragraph by returning to the opium ecstasy, no longer using medical vocabulary. He echoed what many had already said about the marvelous effects of opium on the imagination:

> The perceptions become more vivid, the imagination more prolific with ideas, and these of a more brilliant and exalted character. Fancy is awakened, and creates new and bright associations, the pleasurable scenes of former life are again recalled, events and circumstances long effaced from recollection, facts long forgotten, present themselves to the mind, the future is full of delightful anticipations, whilst the most difficult schemes appear already accomplished, and crowned with success. Under its operation every task seems easy and every labour light.

Finally, however, in a new paragraph and after a few more words devoted to opium ecstasy, he concluded with his version of the opium crash:

> The spirits are renovated, and melancholy is dissipated; the most delightful sensations and the happiest inspirations are present when only partaken to a limited extent, and to those not long accustomed to its use. If persevered in, these pleasing feelings vanish, all control of the will, the functions of sensation and volition, as well as reason, are suspended, vertigo, coma, irregular muscular contractions, and sometimes temporary delirium, supervene.

From this and what he wrote next, MacPherson seemed to imply that these dire effects were something that humans could learn to diagnose and, if they wished, beware of and avoid. In other words, opium was perhaps not so drastically different in kind from alcohol.

MacPherson went on to make further counterarguments against those "led away by the popular opinion that the habitual use of opium injures health and shortens life." If opium did injure health, he continued, then

> we should expect to find the Chinese a shrivelled, and emaciated, and idiotic race. On the contrary, although the habit of opium-smoking is universal amongst the rich and poor, we find them to be a powerful, muscular, and athletic people, and the lower orders more intelligent, and far superior in mental acquirements, to those of corresponding rank in our own country.

In this last point, MacPherson was echoed by many others who noted the health, industriousness, and temperate manners of the Chinese people.

Commander Bingham, for example, who at one time spoke of the Chinese as immoral or apathetic, almost precisely echoed MacPherson in finding among the lower orders "an ease and grace in their manners that we might look for in vain amongst our own cottagers" (Bingham 1843, 1:363).

MacPherson then provided his medical opinion on the possible uses of opium, about which he was completely at variance with Nathan Allen, who was so emphatic about the dire effects of opium smoke on the lungs. MacPherson was "inclined in part to agree" with the Chinese regarding the moderate use of opium "as a preventive against disease."

> The particles, by their direct and topical influence on the nerves of the lungs, which carry the impressions they receive to the heart, brain, and spinal cord, and, through them, to all parts of the body, may thus, to a certain extent, guard the system against disease, and, by its tonic influence, strengthen the several organs; this opinion gains strength when we call to mind that a peculiar active principle in opium, the narcotic, has of late been employed with considerable success in Bengal, as a substitute for quinine. It may also be mentioned, that, at the time fevers prevailed so extensively among our troops at Hong-Kong, but comparatively few of the Chinese suffered, though exposed throughout to the same exciting causes.

MacPherson in effect recommended opium for the British to use themselves at a time when, as numerous accounts related, mortality for the British participants in the Opium War was extremely high. The causes of death were not combat wounds but such things as malaria and dysentery, diseases that MacPherson asserted could be alleviated precisely by means of that which many British saw as separating their active intelligent selves from the passive languid Chinese masses.

Opium was used to relieve ague in the Fen districts of England at that time, although primarily as a self-administered folk cure that was not generally sanctioned by the medical establishment. Still, in England opium was "one of the most valuable drugs in medical practice well into the 1860s and 1870s," having been used in such major instances as the cholera epidemics of 1831–1832, 1849–1853, and 1866 (Berridge and Edwards 1981, 72, 67). MacPherson and others also knew that the drug was used in malarial fevers in India, which is presumably what he meant by his reference to "success in Bengal." The British officer Robert Gully, a captive of the Chinese after a shipwreck in Taiwan in 1842, took opium pills for his dysentery. He reported, "in a quarter of an hour it began to make me feel quite happy, in an hour quite sick, and laid me on my back the whole day" (Gully 1844, 51). He had perhaps never tried opium before (although it is conceivable that he may unknowingly have been given it as an infant soother). He continued, "It is very odd the effect opium has upon me: I could not get up, nor could I go to sleep, but was in a sort of dream all day."

It is unknown whether the medical use of opium was openly proposed or considered in places like Hong Kong or Chusan and, if so, among how wide a circle.[10] Did people like MacPherson openly promote their views and, if so, only to confidants or in meetings with many present? Whatever may have happened, opium was the most pronounced issue of the so-called Opium War. It is difficult to imagine the British military suddenly purchasing large amounts of it and allowing hundreds of ill soldiers and sailors to lie in "a sort of dream all day," or risking that those soldiers, once recovered, might become addicted. Death in the line of duty was in effect the accepted and more consistent alternative. In short, the decision that opium smoking was not something the official British individual should engage in was already virtually final as early as the Opium War—much earlier than the prohibition laws and the international conferences on narcotics control many decades later.

MacPherson concluded his chapter on opium smoking with a final refutation of the accepted belief in the harms of opium:

These facts would certainly, on the whole, rather tend to shew that the habitual use of opium is not so injurious as is commonly supposed; its effects, certainly, are not so disgusting to the beholder as that of the sottish, slaving drunkard. True, like all other powerful stimulants and narcotics, it must ultimately produce effects injurious to the constitution; and the unhappy individual who makes himself a slave to the drug, shuns society, and is indifferent to all around him; and, when deprived of his usual allowance, he describes his feelings as if rats were gnawing his shoulders and spine, and worms devouring the calves of his legs, with an indescribable craving at the stomach, relieved only by having recourse to his pipe—now his only solace.

There is no disease in which opium may not be employed; nor do we know of any substance which can supply its place. Yet here we find its use abused, like many others of the choicest gifts of Providence. (MacPherson 1842, 245–49)

MacPherson's reference to rats gnawing the shoulders and spine of the craving addict, his citations of Chinese medical opinion, plus his own experimentation with the drug, demonstrate that he did a rather considered investigation of the use and effects of opium, probably interviewing or even smoking along with Chinese habitués. To have tried a "few pipes" necessarily entailed some form of contact with experienced smokers, presumably Chinese, since as I have described elsewhere the smoking process was by no means easily or automatically apprehended (about learning this process he left no details). His conclusion, echoed by others who formed a solid though ultimately dismissed minority, was that the harms of opium were from its abuse, not mere use, and that in this it was in no inherent way different from "others of the choicest gifts of Providence."

Duncan MacPherson, M.D., in the costume of a mandarin, from the frontispiece of his book, The War in China

Bingham, Cunynghame, Fortune, Scarth, and Others

Other opium apologists who participated in the British expedition made points similar to Hunter and MacPherson. They and later ones were soberly assertive in their views about opium. Only a relatively small minority was unusually sympathetic, however, as exemplified by one late-century author who found China a wonderful place, in the words of the title of his book: a "Mystic Flowery Land" (Halcombe 1896).

Commander Elliot Bingham wrote, "Although I saw many smoking in the opium-booths, I observed none of those horrid-looking objects that are described by others, and who, I therefore can only suppose, become so emaciated from an *excessive* consumption of the drug" (Bingham 1843, 1:409; original emphasis). He averred that "there was not a single Chinese at Toong-koo,[11] who did not make use of the opium pipe when he could afford it." He then cited the example of the "bumboat man" and his wife, who would lie in their cabin "enjoying the forbidden luxury," but who were always "ready and willing to go to work" (pp. 409–10).

Captain Cunynghame said, "From the experience I had in constantly watching its use, I am of the opinion that, taken as it almost invariably is, in great moderation, it is by no means noxious to the constitution, but quite the reverse, causing an exhilarating and pleasing sensation, and, in short, does them no more harm than a moderate quantity of wine does to us." He added that in excess, "opium is as bad, but I think not worse, than the immoderate use of spirits, which too frequently in our own country brings on delirium tremens, and a hundred other dreadful maladies" (Cunynghame 1845, 237). He also asserted that the "horrible" abuses of opium "are generally confined to the Malays," whom he in this case contrasted with the "highly civilized Chinese" (pp. 237–38).

Arriving after the conclusion of the Nanking Treaty, Robert Fortune likewise declared, "From my own experience, . . . I have no hesitation in saying that the number of persons who use it to excess has been very much exaggerated" (Fortune 1847, 242). Having often been in the company of opium smokers, he observed that instead of going into his "third heaven of bliss," as Fortune at first expected, a smoker commonly took "a few whiffs . . . quietly resigned the pipe to one of his friends, and walked away to his business."

Robert Fortune's illustration of an opium pipe and paraphernalia from his book, Three Years' Wanderings in the Northern Provinces of China

His opinion was "that in the great majority of cases it was not immoderately indulged in" (p. 243). Fortune then quoted Lord Jocelyn's lengthy description of the opium den in which the smoker did go off into the metaphorical "long sleep to which he is blindly hurrying."

A decade or so later, John Scarth declared in a similar vein that he had "known many Chinese who smoked opium for years, and never seemed to be the worse for it" (Scarth 1860, 297). Opium's "general effects among the Chinese" seemed to him "very similar to those of either wine or spirits in England." In his view there was more harm in the way opium had been introduced in China, the corruption it gave rise to, and the difficulties it caused people who were unable to afford it (p. 298). The journalist George Wingrove Cooke (1814–1865) condemned English involvement in the opium trade and thought Chinese opium smoking "sufficiently disgusting." Nevertheless he found opium dens to be "ordinary" and the smokers to be "neither emaciated nor infirm," but in fact "sturdy" and healthy looking (Cooke 1858, 178). In his 1864 article, Dr. James Henderson claimed to have treated up to fifteen hundred opium smokers, including some who had smoked for many decades and had "suffered little from its use." Those who did suffer were able to stop, which he did not think was "such a formidable thing as some writers say" (Henderson 1864, 61–62). In New York Dr. Harry Hubbell Kane went so far as to smoke opium himself, "often to decided excess" (Kane 1976, v), and described good and bad effects in detail. He likewise condemned the exaggerated reports of opium's harmful effects, not because he thought the effects were minimal, however. His position was that if the harms were exaggerated, novice smokers would discount such dire warnings because of the fact that in the early stages of smoking the unpleasant aspects of addiction are not apparent (p. 78).

Charles J.H. Halcombe, author of *The Mystic Flowery Land: A Personal Narrative* (1896), is the most positive of all the writers I have cited so far. "Many people wrongly suppose that, after smoking opium, a man becomes half or completely stupefied. Quite the reverse, the opium seems to have a stimulating influence; and when a man feels tired, he smokes a few pipes of opium, and rises refreshed and invigorated." He found that excess was "more the exception than the rule." And finally, "the ethereal, De-Quincey–like visions which are supposed to enhance his [the opium smoker's] slumbers are only familiar to western romancers," of whom there were already many in Halcombe's day. Writing about adventures in the "mystic flowery land," he denounced the Western romancers who, never having been to China, fantasized about what he thought was one of the most practical substances used there (Halcombe 1896, 29–30). Halcombe was another lover of China, in other words, whose times there were as if charmed.

The Drug Enthusiast James S. Lee

Another voice in favor of opium belonged to engineer James S. Lee (b. 1872), who wrote *The Underworld of the East* (1935) about his times in India, Malaysia, Sumatra, and China in the 1890s and early 1900s. He experimented with drugs and often smoked opium with Chinese companions, but, unlike Drs. MacPherson and Kane, not simply out of scientific curiosity. He provided detailed descriptions of his consumption of morphine, cocaine, hashish, opium in a pipe, and certain mystery drugs he never named. He warned of the dangers of each, especially opiates, and followed his cardinal rule of drug taking, which he learned from an Indian doctor who helped him when he suffered from a case of malaria. "Dr. Babu" told him

> that he used many kinds of drugs, each in turn; changing over from one to another, using them sometimes singly, and at other times in combinations, so that no one drug ever got too great a hold on him. (Lee 1935, 30)

Lee also wrote:

> All these narcotic drugs, which are commonly known as Dangerous Drugs, are really the gift of God to mankind. Instead of them doing him harm, they should really be the means of preserving health, and making his life a state of continual happiness. (p. 38)

In saying this, he was reacting to the antidrug laws that by 1935 had already been in effect for quite a while. Even in his youth in the 1880s and 1890s, opium and Western involvement in the opium trade were vigorously debated in England. An example is Benjamin Broomhall's 1882 *The Truth about Opium Smoking*, a collection of anti-opium views spurred mainly in response to pro-opium statements like Sir George Birdwood's that opium was "absolutely harmless" (Broomhall 1882, 5).[12] In 1895, on the other hand, the British government's Royal Commission on Opium provided a lengthy report that generally found the harmful effects of opium to be greatly exaggerated. For a while the anti-opium movement lost momentum, although popular novels and magazines continued to convey vilifying portrayals of opium smoking. People like James Lee meanwhile continued to incorporate drugs into their lives largely unhampered (but more freely when outside of England) until the laws against "dangerous drugs" came into effect in the early twentieth century. According to his report he then retired to England and lived the rest of his life missing his old drugs.

The Royal Commission on Opium

On behalf of the British Parliament, the Royal Commission on Opium summoned witnesses between September 1893 and February 1894, asking them to testify in regard to such topics as the history of the opium trade, the situation of opium production and consumption, and the morality of engaging in that industry, as well as the moral state of those who consumed opium. The central focus was on India, where the commission held sittings after first hearing witnesses in London. But China figured prominently as well, both in the testimony of witnesses who had lived there and in the general background of wide knowledge about British and Indian involvement in the trade in China. The purpose of the commission was to examine the production and consumption of opium in India and to determine whether opium should be banned except for medical uses. Anti-opiumists hoped the commission would be favorable to their cause: the immediate "end to both cultivation and the trade in opium."[13] The commission heard extensively from both sides of the issue, and in what many called a whitewash concluded that opium addiction was not such a serious problem and that British involvement did not lead to a worsening of the problem. Of the many points debated, one was especially sensitive. Anti-opiumists, of whom missionaries were the overwhelming majority, saw opium as something that tarnished the image of Britain and in particular hindered the cause of spreading Christianity. They testified that they as British were often singled out by the Chinese as the ones who, in Reverend Joseph Samuel Adams's words, "caused them [the Chinese] all their misery."[14] Against this stand, other witnesses went to great lengths to deny that Britain introduced opium into China or was responsible for the present state of opium use, which they also declared was not as severe as anti-opiumists claimed.

Both sides included prominent individuals. Among the anti-opiumists was the translator and sinologist James Legge (1815–1897), who agreed that opium addiction was an "evil" thing. He once traveled with Joseph Edkins to Qufu, the site of Confucius's ancestral home, where he was very sorry to see the poppy cultivated so close to Confucius's grave.[15] However, when asked at the end of his testimony whether there was any evidence of "national degeneration of health" in China due to opium, he replied, "No," although the problem was serious enough to keep missionary doctors very busy, he added (United Kingdom 1894, 1:17). Others, mostly missionaries, gave graphic accounts of the suffering of opium addicts whom they saw in their hospitals, of opium beggars dying in the streets, or of women committing suicide by swallowing raw opium because they were about to be sold by fathers or husbands who needed money for their opium habit. These witnesses were particularly adamant that opium could never be used in moderation, and that no Chinese addict they met ever defended the habit or failed to be ashamed of it.

Sir George Birdwood represents the extreme of those who dismissed the harms of opium. With fifteen years in India, he declared: "As to opium smoking, it is, from my experience of it, as innocuous as smoking hay, straw, or stubble."[16] Others who spent time in India denied ever seeing the "opium sot" there,[17] while those who spent their time in China, including Thomas F. Wade, testified that they did see such victims but nevertheless insisted that moderate use was the rule.[18]

Thomas F. Wade lived forty years in China and played a major role as diplomat for Britain and as adviser to the Chinese.[19] In his testimony of September 15, 1893, he specifically mentioned the "anti-opiumists" and their false accusations about the British role in China. He cited Joseph Edkins's book *Opium: Historical Note* (part of which was appended to the Royal Commission report) to rally the evidence that the Chinese already knew of the poppy from centuries back (United Kingdom 1894, 1:87). He insisted that opium smoking was not introduced by the British. He also testified that he knew people of every degree "using it with impunity," but had also seen "most deplorable victims of it in every degree just as I have in my own country of the use of alcohol" (United Kingdom 1894, 1:88).

Several witnesses freely admitted to trying opium themselves, one even suggesting that the members of the commission do so (Surgeon-General Sir William Moore, who had spent over thirty-three years in India; United Kingdom 1894, 1:73). Of these witnesses, the businessman Henry Lazarus, who spent 1878–1881 in Shanghai, met people of all classes who were unashamed smokers, "and I positively went in for it myself, just to see what it was like." But, he declared, the Englishman would never acquire the habit. "It is simply because it is too slow, it takes too much time." After three or four tries he decided he did not want to form the habit, his main reason being: "I could not afford to waste the time." The medical missionary William Lockhart, who spent 1838 to 1864 in China and who during his testimony expressed his great admiration for the Chinese people, made the same point in explaining why very few Europeans smoked opium. He also asserted that the British did not in any way force the use of opium on the Chinese.[20]

What Lazarus shared with Lockhart, Wade, Birdwood, and others was an aversion to raising opium smoking to the level of a moral issue for which a horrified Britain should take responsibility. Lazarus would say that if you hired workers in China, you should turn away those who were too addicted because they would be inefficient. He otherwise claimed that he knew a Chinese businessman and decidedly "excessive" opium smoker, Fong-kee, than whom "no straighter broker" could be found. In intellect and energy, none could "surpass him." Yet "his face was so wasted that you might almost have made your hands meet in the hollow of his cheeks." Lazarus was especially enthusiastic in his quotation of his Chinese "boy's" opinion of the missionaries: "that the missionaries and their ways are really the great trouble and the great drawback to the liking of Europeans all over China" (United Kingdom 1894, 1:110).

Missionary witnesses before the commission, on the other hand, claimed
that they came into "contact with very much larger numbers of the Chinese"
than British merchants and diplomats (so said Reverend T. G. Sclby; United
Kingdom 1894, 1:123). They said that they saw more poor and desperate
people, especially those who used opium or were affected by addicted family members.[21] They took greater pains than their adversaries to evoke compassion for the misery of those they described. Instead of finding inhumanity in the Chinese and addicts in particular, as numerous writers I have
quoted earlier did, these witnesses found inhumanity in the collective whole
of the British, including themselves.[22]

DESCRIBING THE DETAILS
AND EFFECTS OF OPIUM SMOKING

The Act of Observing Opium Smokers

Many writers and witnesses gained their knowledge about opium at least in
part by observing the opium-smoking process itself, including the immediate reactions to inhaling opium and what they saw as the longer-term effects
on the general livelihood of individuals and communities. The observation
of these close-up details is a demonstration of the fact that, as I said at the
beginning of this chapter, the expert on China did well to be an expert on
opium, for he appeared to be delving into one of the quintessential Chinese
ways of being. A problem arose in that the description of indulgence of any
sort always posed the question of the author's complicity with those whom
he described. The drier or more removed one sounded, the more impervious one appeared to be to the clearly tantalizing effects of opium—hence,
MacPherson's use of scientific-sounding language. Nevertheless, the observation of opium smoking and its sensational effects still projected avenues by
which the observer could potentially lose the ability to maintain an objective
stance and instead merge into the community of habituated smokers. For
one thing, opium seemed capable of drawing in masses of people of any
race, perhaps even bringing about universal subjection. The warnings of
both Chinese and Western prohibitionists implied such an eventuality. Moderation, they declared, was impossible. After all, the opium the Chinese
smoked begged these expert observers, for their information and pleasure,
to smoke it as well, for as several witnesses before the Royal Commission on
Opium testified, your accuracy was in question if you had never tried opium
yourself.

The first of these points—that opium seemed capable of seducing masses
of people—is prominent in numerous descriptions of opium smoking. If we
take a composite of prohibitionist points of view, three topics of description

appear repeatedly. The first is the method of smoking and the dosages taken. One pipe was enough for novices but did almost nothing for "old stagers." The second is the smokers' reactions after inhaling opium: talkative excitement, followed by stupor, for example. The third is the large number of people affected by opium smoking. Many people appeared unwilling or unable to quit. Opium smoking had an inherent tendency to spread and, at worst, to kill off whole communities, as observers reported about so-called opium villages in Shanxi and other provinces.

That the observer himself would become a smoker led from an imperative borne within the scientific method itself. For the sake of accuracy of observation, the scientist should logically have a firsthand knowledge of opium smoking. The doctors Duncan MacPherson and Harry Hubbell Kane were perhaps following this logic. Although MacPherson and Kane did not conclude that opium was powerful enough to entrap everyone within its reach, the emergence and then victory of the prohibitionist position on opium and other narcotics took the specter of mass subjection as one of its central, if not always acknowledged, assumptions. Individual writers did not necessarily display this assumption, nor did they necessarily go very far in articulating a prohibitionist position. But their descriptions nevertheless suggested that a certain kind of person smoked opium or that opium turned an individual into that certain kind of person, and finally that the opium smoker should be broadly defined by observations made upon the Chinese people.

The writers who personally observed opium smoking in many cases made special trips to opium dens–places where they were guaranteed to find opium smokers. Lord Jocelyn's visit to a Singapore den in 1840 became a locus classicus for many later writers. Nathan Allen cited "Reverend Dr. Smith," who spent the winter of 1846 in Amoy and visited thirty-odd "opium shops," noting the relative quality of surroundings and interviewing smokers to learn how they had fallen "victim" to opium (Allen 1853, 39–40). Decades later, in late-nineteenth-century London, "doing the slums" was a common, even fashionable, practice, magazine reporters and other curious individuals touring East End opium dens, often coming up with lurid descriptions of "vampirelike or animalistic" Orientals engaging in debauchery (Milligan 1995, 85, 88–91).

People like Nathan Allen and Joseph Edkins did considerable research and produced special studies of the history of opium use, the commerce in and production of opium, the method of smoking, and the effects. History books like *The Middle Kingdom* (1847; revised in 1882), by Samuel Wells Williams, contained a chapter or substantial portion of a chapter summarizing what authors like Allen or Edkins wrote about in greater detail (Williams 1895, chap. 20). Travel books and articles often described opium smoking in passing, providing details on the appearance and behavior of opium smokers in inns, boats, dens, or everyday domestic settings.

The Look, the Smell

One knew the look of the "confirmed opium smoker," for example, without even entering an opium den or witnessing someone smoking. He could be told "by his inflamed eyes, and haggard countenance" (Allen 1853, 35); "his skin had that peculiar glassy polish by which an opium-smoker is invariably known" (Fortune 1852, 51). One knew the smell of opium, which was frequently encountered wafting through the air outside or being consumed by someone nearby. Williams found "the smell of the burning drug [to be] rather sickening," as he wrote in *The Middle Kingdom* (Williams 1895, 382). Robert Fortune wrote: "The soft, sickening fumes of the drug found their way through the chinks of the partition" in a room he rented for a night during his journey in Fujian (Fortune 1852, 292). Smell, of course, depended both on the quality of the opium and the propensities of the smeller. Dr. Harry Hubbell Kane, who experimented with opium but did not become a "confirmed" smoker, found opium to have a "creamy . . . not unpleasant fruity odor."[23] Cocteau wrote many years later: "Picasso used to say to me: 'The smell of opium is the least stupid smell in the world" (Cocteau 1996, 64).

Dosage

One also knew the approximate dosage smoked by the novice or the "old stager," or either the temperate or intemperate smoker, these levels being arrived at by consensus of smokers interviewed. Lord Jocelyn said rather imprecisely, "On a beginner, one or two pipes will have an effect, but an old stager will continue smoking for hours" (Jocelyn 1841, 39). Nathan Allen wrote more precisely when he said that a beginner cannot smoke more than "3 to 6 grains at a time," while "some consume even 300 grains daily" (Allen 1853, 29). Sixty grains was a mace (or about an ounce),[24] which would fill twelve pipes (at one long whiff of a five-grain pea-sized pellet per pipe) and which S. Wells Williams reported to be the dose of a "temperate smoker."[25] "Two mace weight taken daily," Williams continued, was "an immoderate dose, which few can bear for any length of time" (Williams 1895, 383). Samuel Mervin reported that ten to twenty pipes a day was common (i.e., one to two mace), but wealthy people might smoke from forty to sixty (three to five mace; Mervin 1908, 66).

These figures varied depending on individual, period, locale, and type of opium. For example, domestic opium was generally less potent than imported, and the domestic and imported could be combined. Moreover, opium was often mixed with other substances or smoked in the form of dross that had already been smoked (good-quality opium could be recycled several times, with the more recycled ash going to less affluent and finally the poorest smokers). As Hsin-pao Chang reports, one 1840 account had it that "three or four mace was considered a very large quantity" (citing a "Resident in China"), but an 1879 estimate had it that "average smokers consumed two to five mace" and "heavy smokers consumed five to twenty mace each day" (Chang 1970, 35). Likewise, a midcentury novel has a heavy addict consuming ten to twenty mace a day of strong foreign opium (i.e., one or two *liang*); and an 1895 novel refers to twenty mace *(erliang)* as the dose of a heavy addict.[26] Such variation may again point to the difference between imported and domestic opium (or various mixtures), the latter being more common in the later nineteenth century, when smokers may have accordingly increased their dose.

How to Smoke an Opium Pipe

Although they presumably lacked the actual skills involved, writers knew generally how opium was smoked and gave lengthy descriptions, sometimes correcting other descriptions they found to be inaccurate. "The opium-smoker always lies down," Williams reported, "and the impossible picture given by Davis,[27] of a 'Mandarin smoking an opium-pipe,' dressed in his official robes and sitting up at a table becomes still more singular if the author ever saw a smoker at his pipe" (Williams 1895, 382; also cited in Allen 1853, 27ff.). Dr. Harry Hubbell Kane pointed out the inaccuracy of Dickens's description in *The Mystery of Edwin Drood* (Kane 1976, 49–50). The details that authors provided included the furniture and utensils that smokers used and the preparation for and method of smoking. In his 1881 article in *Harpers' Weekly*, for example, Dr. Kane wrote of "cooking" the "treacle-like opium," which in the process changed from "its inky hue" to "a bright golden brown," giving off a "creamy odor, much admired by old smokers."[28]

Duncan MacPherson provides an example of a detailed description of opium smoking from sometime in the 1840s. After listing the necessary utensils, he relates the step-by-step method of smoking.

> The smoker now lies down on his bed, and drawing the table, on which the lamp is placed, close to him, with the probe he takes from the box a piece of opium about the size of a pea; this he applies to the flame until it swells and takes fire; instantly blowing the flame out, he rolls the opium for a short time on the bowl of the pipe, and then reapplies it to the flame, and repeats the same process until it becomes sufficiently burned to be fit for use. It is now introduced into the small aperture in the bowl, and the lungs having previously been emptied as much as possible of atmospheric air, the pipe is put to the mouth and the bowl applied to the flame, and in one long deep inspiration the opium becomes almost entirely dissipated. The fumes are retained in the chest for a short time, and then emitted through the nostrils. This operation is repeated until the desired effects of the drug are produced, the period of which varies according as the individual has been accustomed to its effects. Some old stagers will smoke

whole nights without being completely under its influence, whereas, to the beginner or to a person not used to the habit, a very small quantity is sufficient to
stupify. (MacPherson 1842, 243–44)

As in his description of the opium ecstasy quoted previously (which begins
immediately after the above passage), he employed professional-sounding terminology, sometimes redundantly and verbosely, precisely as if he was writing
for that professional-sounding effect. The lungs, for example, had "previously
been emptied as much as possible of *atmospheric* air." Latinate terms were
prominent: "fumes" were "retained" and then "emitted." He also makes frequent use of the passive voice. The "operation is repeated until the desired effects of the drug are produced." "Old stagers," a term Lord Jocelyn used as well,
suggests the awareness on the part of Jocelyn and MacPherson of the existence
of a culture and way of life that were wide in extent and imparted a certain hallowed respectability. But the abruptness of his last words, "a very small quantity is sufficient to stupify," recalls his similar tendency elsewhere to insert brief
but ominous and dismissive notes in his otherwise rather evenhanded account.

Immediate Effects

Another subject of description was the smoker's reaction once he began
smoking. After his first pipe, he "lies listless for a moment . . . and then re-
peats the process until he has spent all his purchase," Williams wrote. "When
the smoking commences, the man becomes loquacious, and breaks out into
boisterous silly merriment, which gradually changes to a vacant paleness and
shrinking of features, as the quantity increases and the narcotic acts"
(Williams 1895, 382). However, as a mid–nineteenth century British official
asserted, "The pleasurable sensations and imaginative ideas arising at first,
soon pass away; they become fainter and fainter, and at last entirely give
place to horrid dreams and appalling pictures of death" (cited in Allen 1853,
38). Such a statement sounds as though the official was reporting what he
read in De Quincey rather than what he imputed from his observations in
China. Robert Fortune made a more muted reference to such nightmares in
one of his travelogues. He noted that Chinese smokers at inns would often
stay up late into the night talking and laughing (Fortune 1852, 292). In the
common sleeping room of a boat, one smoker was in an excited state as he
entered his "third heaven of bliss," then fell asleep but was "evidently disturbed by strange and frightful dreams" (p. 50). He had told others that he
took opium for medical reasons (p. 51), a common excuse of opium consumers defending their habit, as also found in Coleridge, De Quincey, and
in nineteenth-century Chinese fiction.

A short passage in Lieutenant Alexander Murray's report refers to Chinese soldiers during the Opium War who supposedly took opium for the

sake of "get[ting] their courage up to the fighting point." Instead of stupor or euphoria, the reaction Murray described was that of crazed madness:

> About twenty wounded men were taken into our hospital, where their wounds were dressed; but several died from the immense quantity of opium they had taken to get their courage up to the fighting point. Most of the attacking party were mad with excitement, produced probably by this abominable drug. (Murray 1843, 109)

Murray did not indicate how he arrived at the conclusion that these soldiers "probably" died from having consumed too much opium or that the opium was taken for the sake of getting up courage. But two attitudes toward the Chinese were again apparent: that to an embarrassing extent they were a weak and too easily defeated enemy, and that they were categorically separate from the British because of their reliance on an unnatural means of support.

Murray's report is representative of a kind of general British face that participated in the "expedition" to China. Murray conceived of a proper enemy as someone who showed natural courage and stood up to fight a man-to-man battle. Instead he found half-humans driven mad by an abominable drug. Although he did not say as much, by implication this was not a proper victory. But he was in China mainly on a punitive mission to make the Chinese have more respect for the British. As he noted, by 1842 they were very civil to "us" (Murray 1843, 219). For officers like Murray, the operation in China was something of a gentleman's outing. In between fighting and other intervals of duty during this easiest of wars, he and others would go hunting, as he wrote in considerable detail (pp. 91–95; he was disappointed that he never met like-minded Chinese sportsmen). At another time he was delighted to see the Chinese putting up a strong resistance in battle. He also noted the gruesome scene at Zhapu ("Chapoo"), reported by others as well, where Manchu men, women, and children died by their own hands rather than allow themselves to emerge alive from defeat. Among all these things— opium-crazed soldiers, the scene of mass suicide at Zhapu, a better fight than usual, and sporting activities devoid of Chinese counterparts—opium was one of many details, perhaps "abominable," but not of overwhelming importance.

Long-Term Effects and Massive Use

In addition to the techniques and process of opium smoking and the immediate reactions to it, writers also observed the longer-term effects on the appearance, health, and livelihood of Chinese they encountered during their travels or interviews, for example, as they toured opium dens. In these types of observations the authors begin to move into the portrayal of the massive use of opium and its degenerative effects on whole populations.

After a night on a boat across the Hangzhou Bay, Robert Fortune found a "strange" scene the next morning: the passengers still asleep "were lying in heaps, here and there, as they had been tossed and wedged by the motion of the vessel during the night." Fortune "almost fancied" that he "could read the characters" of each: "There was the habitual opium-smoker—there was no mistaking him—his looks were pale and haggard, his breathing quick and disturbed, and so thin was he, that his cheek bones seemed piercing the skin" (Fortune 1847, 352–53). On another occasion Fortune was awakened by his host, an old mandarin, making a "harsh moaning noise" at night as he slept in a neighboring room. There had been an edict against opium smoking that would not take effect until the end of the year, Fortune continued, so the man would smoke every evening at nine, telling Fortune, "I am going to smoke now; you know I shall not be allowed to smoke next year." Such a smoker not only smoked more than usual and "enjoyed it more" because of the edict, as Fortune opined, but would go on smoking as he had done before when the "new year arrived" and "the edict had been long forgotten" (Fortune 1852, 342–44).

In his description of Chinese chair bearers, Walter Medhurst reported that "opium is the main cause of their apparent elevation at one time, and the want of it occasions their breaking down subsequently" (Medhurst 1850, 30). Reverend A. Elwin, a missionary for twenty-three years in Hangzhou, reported in 1893 to the Royal Commission on Opium that in county districts he had the greatest difficulty "to find any coolie or chair-bearer who was not an opium smoker." He also stated that after starting in the morning these laborers would work for about three hours, at which point they "began to get weak and were hardly able to move." They would then stop for an hour to visit an opium den, from which they would emerge as if they were "new men."[29] Another missionary, Reverend Joseph Samuel Adams, reported to the commission the same failure to find coolies or chair bearers who did not smoke. When employed, they would refuse to move, he stated, until they had more opium (Adams was stationed in Jinhua, not far from Hangzhou; United Kingdom 1894, 1:24).

Regarding the "poorer classes," the general view of Western observers was that the expense of maintaining the opium habit was ruinous. Nathan Allen cited Reverend Dr. Smith, the one who visited dens in Amoy in 1846, who "questioned ten persons indiscriminately as he met them—most of whom were laborers—as to the formation, effect, and expense of the habit, etc." (Allen 1853, 29). He found that five of them spent "an average two thirds of their daily earnings to purchase the article!" The journalist George Wingrove Cooke similarly found that "no man" in a Ningbo opium house he visited "spent on an average less than 80 cash a day on his opium-pipe," and that one of the men, a "chair-coolie," earned an average of 100 cash a day. English physicians assured him that the "coolie opium-smoker dies, not from opium, but from starvation" (Cooke 1858, 179). Reverend A. Elwin averred that coolies and other smokers among the poor "literally live on the opium; it is their meat and drink" (United Kingdom 1894, 1:48). In *Drugging a Nation: The Story of China and the Opium Curse*, Samuel Mervin stated that "a pipeful of moderately good native product costs more than a labourer can earn in a day," making it such that the poorer classes smoked a "compound based on pipe scrapings and charcoal" (Mervin 1908, 16).

The common assumption of these last observations is that without opium the Chinese would have more money and could enjoy better lives. Medhurst almost leaves this mold when he notes that chair bearers break down when they suffer from want of opium. What he does not say is that the main employment for these men was chair bearing (or similar labor) and that opium was for them an aid to endurance in a task the likes of which probably no European or American—except certain immigrants and African Americans both before and after emancipation—would have to consider undertaking. The Reverend Joseph Samuel Adams summed it up this way: "they [the coolies] said that if they did not smoke opium, they would not be doing the work of beasts" (United Kingdom 1894, 1:24).

These same writers and observers would probably have been offered opium themselves, although only a few recorded this. Robert Fortune commonly found opium in inns for travelers, and he himself received an offer to smoke it; "I thanked him, but, of course, declined the offer" (Fortune 1852, 218). Traveling in poor areas of eastern Guangdong, John Scarth noted that "the houses had few comforts . . . except the opium-pipe and a bed in the best of them." Moreover, the drug "was openly smoked among the surrounding crowd in nearly every village we visited, and was offered to us as the chief act of politeness" (Scarth 1860, 69). Such a situation may have existed in poor areas, but unless there was some kind of mutual understanding, tea and possibly tobacco would be the more proper offerings to a respectable visitor by a respectable host in the nineteenth century, as evidenced in fiction as well as numerous Western traveler's accounts. Despite the openness of opium smoking, several factors kept it out of the category of things like tea or tobacco that were automatically offered to guests: the conniving that was involved in the opium business, the intermittent enforcement of prohibitions against it, the effects of opium itself, plus the fact that a great many people were against it or simply did not have the habit of smoking it. Further, opium was offered more freely in certain cities or regions, among certain types of people, and in certain periods.[30]

In a series of three travel accounts published in the *Journal of the North China Branch of the Royal Asiatic Society* in 1884, the British consular official E. H. Parker (1849–1926) wrote of trips by waterway and sedan chair through Zhejiang and Fujian in which, among other things, he made numerous observations upon opium cultivation, prices, and smoking habits.[31] He found that, depending on availability and local trade restrictions, in some places imported Malwa *(xiaotu)* and Patna *(datu)* were the main types of opium smoked (sometimes adulterated for sale in the "interior"; Parker 1884a, 40), in others both foreign and domestic were available, and in still others the only opium sold or known was domestic. In Pucheng, a city of northern Fujian near the border with Zhejiang, for example, the import and sale of opium from Wenzhou, Zhejiang, was prohibited, for "Fukien authorities hold salt, tea, and opium in iron grasp" (Parker 1884c, 89). In reaction to one area of Fujian in which he found opium dens "abound[ing] everywhere," he wrote that "as in Chekiang" opium seemed to "sap the wealth and life of the lower orders. The idleness, delay, thriftlessness and poverty induced by opium-smoking is much more apparent here than in Szechuan, for of course 800 and 1200 cash an ounce is a very different thing from 200 and 300—not to mention the different physical effects of the foreign and native drug" (Parker 1884c, 81). He remarked further that "the absolute want of everything else in the way of pleasure, comfort, amusement, quiet, privacy, and luxury is quite sufficient to account for the charm which this indulgence, coupled with that of gaming, exercises upon the Chinese imagination" (Parker 1884c, 81). In his article "Journey to Sungp'an," an area northwest of Chengdu, Sichuan, W. C. Haines Watson found that the people of the mountain districts were healthier looking than those of the plains. "In the towns, however, one observes a distinct falling-off in the physique of the inhabitants, both male and female, which can be traced to the usually more confined mode of life and the freer use of the opium-pipe" (Watson 1905, 64).

The Opium Village

When writers blamed poor living conditions on opium smoking, they said, for example, that addicts sacrificed every comfort for the sake of their opium. Zhang Changjia, the opium addict I will discuss in the next chapter, would not disagree. Or, like Parker, they pointed out that opium cultivation, which earned more money which was needed for high taxes, displaced the cultivation of wheat or other grain, causing the price of wheat to go up.[32] Chinese officials complained of the same thing, as Spence reports of Ningxia: "In 1878 the local inhabitants kept their best land for opium, saying that otherwise they could not pay their taxes" (Spence 1992, 252).

The most dramatic pictures of opium devastation came in the form of what authors described as "opium villages," places that were extremely poor already but, as Samuel Mervin wrote, were then "ravaged and desolated by opium." "All classes, all ages, both sexes" were victims (Mervin 1908, 58). According to Su Zhiliang, by 1906 Sichuan, Yunnan, Shaanxi, Shanxi, Guizhou, and Gansu Provinces produced over 80 percent of China's opium (Su Zhiliang 1997, 187). It was in these provinces, and mainly Shanxi, that many foreigners saw such villages. The Reverend B. Bagnall, cited in an 1888 article, reported that in Shanxi "nearly everyone seems to be a smoker," especially on the Taiyuan plain. "One meets complete wrecks of what were once wealthy families."[33] Francis H. Nichols was more precise in his book *Through Hidden Shensi,* devoting a chapter to a description of opium villages in Shanxi. He began by noting the poverty of "nearly all of the chain of villages that line the road . . . from the great wall [outside of Beijing] to Tai Yuan" [the provincial capital], the route he traveled. In Chinese villages, he asserted, there were no "poverty alleys," all people being equally poor, living at subsistence level, "very dirty, and . . . defy[ing] almost every known sanitary law." However, "they succeed in living and in maintaining an equality of conditions which prevents both the ambitions and the discontent to which we are accustomed in western civilisation" (Nichols 1902, 56). Nichols here reflects a perception common to Western travel writers in China: Chinese were not only cheerful and content living at subsistence level but, as Fortune claimed, were one of the happiest races on earth.[34] However, as Nichols continued, certain villages could not by any standards "be called happy or fortunate," these being the so-called opium villages, "shunned as far as possible by everyone and . . . referred to as a company of the lost." As he further learned from missionaries and provincial officials, every year a number of villages "succumb to the blight" as the "entire population becomes addicted to the habit simultaneously." One by one they become "charmed with the happy oblivion it gives to cold and fatigue and the dull monotony of their lives." Finally, they cease to care for their fields or for nourishing food, spend "all that they have in the world . . . to satisfy their cravings for opium," and then die "one by one," until all that is left is a "shapeless mass of crumbling walls and roofless houses." Nichols ended his chapter with a photograph of an "opium beggar" in rags, supporting a walking stick, and wearing a begging bowl around his neck (Nichols 1902, 57–59, 67).

EVERYONE ADDICTED

The complete loss of interest in anything but opium is something Zhang Changjia also explored, in part to warn about it, but mainly, as I will discuss, to elaborate on the supreme and unprecedented self-sufficiency of the opium world and at the same time to write of the profound desolation of the opium lovesickness. For him the spread of opium paralleled that of Christianity in marking Chinese weakness and helplessness in the face of Western domination. The arrival of opium smoking in the world paralleled the invention of steamships in carrying humanity to yet more rushed and brutish levels of existence compared with earlier, gentler stages in history. Nevertheless, according to Zhang, opium smoking was not the prime embodiment of China's

Francis H. Nichols's photo "An Opium Beggar" from his book,
Through Hidden Shensi

crisis as a nation. Opium smokers were not to blame for China's subjection
to foreign domination.

Still, wealthy families becoming poor because of one or more family members' indulgence in the opium habit had become a sensational example of the
so-called opium blight. Already in the 1830s a Chinese painter in Canton had
portrayed six stages of the "career of the opium-smoker, from health and af-
fluence to decrepitude and beggary." Named "Sunqua" in the April 1837, issue of the *Chinese Repository*, the painter is described as beginning with a young

fatherless wastrel who inherits the "whole family estate" and, having no other inclinations, "gives himself up to smoking opium and profligacy." Sunqua's opium "sot" eventually ends "seated on a bamboo chair, . . . continually swallowing the faeces of the drug," his wife and child seated nearby winding silk in order to earn a "pittance for his and their own support."[35] People of far lesser means drove their families into misery as well, as the example of Ning Lao Taitai's fisherman husband in *A Daughter of Han* demonstrated in the 1880s and 1890s. Whether rich or poor, the opium addict went from being the subject of this relatively local moral tale to being a symbolic cause of all China's ills. These images of the addict overshadowed factors of wider scope that Zhang Changjia only barely discussed. In Sunqua's painting in particular, the gendered relations of wastrel and wife would have been fertile ground for defusing the logic of opium as overriding factor. Instead, opium was used to simplify and reduce the complex of factors that produced or allowed "wastrels" who dragged so many others into destitution and that allowed opium to be such a highly invested commodity in these particular times.

Ruined wastrels and opium villages going into extinction, increasing areas of fertile soil devoted to poppy cultivation in order to pay taxes, officials using opium taxes to meet government quotas, China relying on opium income to finance military spending or repay foreign debt, and then distant Europeans alarmed about fiendish Orientals poisoning white women. Opium formed an associative chain with snowballing momentum that threatened to spread to everyone. In prohibitionist terms, opium could never be used in moderation or in a containable fashion. As Peng Yang'ou wrote at the end of *Souls from the Land of Darkness*, opium smoking would have to spread until everyone was addicted. In Peng's vision, all would be gathered in the underworld's opium hell to suffer the worst torments imaginable, after which they would finally quit all at once, not gradually. Seemingly, there would be no wisdom about opium until everyone had smoked it. Making a similar point but without the condemnation, Cocteau wrote that no one understands opium without entering its pact and becoming its addict (Cocteau 1996, 26). Although Cocteau was referring to the effectiveness of opium on the true versus amateur addict, he might as well have meant that all nonsmokers are amateurs in general, and for them to create stories about opium threatening to poison all humankind is another of their futile moralizations, the nature of which Cocteau captured succinctly when he wrote, "To moralize to an opium addict is like saying to Tristan: 'Kill Iseult. You will feel much better afterwards'" (p. 26). As I interpret Cocteau, moralizing to drug addicts in this way is like saying that they are adulterers who must relinquish their right to decide whom or what they may love, and the way in which they may love him, her, or it. The assumption is that these adulterers can and must renounce this thing to which they are most attached. The life that is waiting for them after renunciation is sure to be better.

In nineteenth-century England, opium consumption went from being a tolerable and relatively minor matter to becoming a symbolically invasive presence that threatened to sap the vitality of the nation's citizens. The idea that opium had the power to spread and infect became such a habit of thought in both China and England that it became impossible to think of befriending opium smokers, so to speak, of asking them why at this time in history there was such "mass addiction." The teeming masses of opium-smoking Chinese now had the capacity to spread and invade, and in this invasion opium was suddenly as powerful as gunboats and rifles. At first, of course, weak Chinese were an easy enemy for the British troops in the Opium War. Contradictorily, however, the British also expected the Chinese to be reasonable participants in the civilizing, modernizing dialogue. But opium continued to spread, essentializing a further if not the furthest degree of the Chinaman's aggressive imperviousness to Euro-Americanizing progression. Opium smoking-cum-being-Chinese was like an act of theft and vandalism against human presence, where the level of humanity was gauged by the degree of susceptibility to the new modernizing interests.

What was too easy to miss, in elementary terms, was that the opium smoker was not just a stereotypical Chinaman. As Zhang Changjia and his poet friends show, many smokers also wrote and reflected about the opium way of life and the unprecedented escape opium offered from the pre- or non-opium ways of life. Of course, as Zhang also showed, opium's escape had its own confining rules. Chinese fiction, as we shall see in chapter 6, helps define the way opium worked in Chinese social settings that the Euro-American was less likely to see, including homes, brothels, and opium dens in aspects other than the generalized and distanced ones presented from Lord Jocelyn on. In contrast to the emphasis of the last two chapters, the next chapters ask new questions about opium, for example, What intimate, intricate, and even routine roles did opium play? rather than, How did opium detract from all that humans should be?

NOTES

1. See, for example, *Chinese Repository,* volume 5 of 1836–1837.

2. Expertise on opium smoking is similar to expertise on China as a whole. The problem in general of presenting oneself as an authoritative interpreter of non-European cultures has been extensively debated among participants in postcolonial studies (especially in terms of "subaltern" studies). See Gandhi 1998, 2ff. for a review of this discussion.

3. One witness to the Royal Commission on Opium reported in 1894 that he would take visiting friends to view "opium shops" in the Straights Settlements. He had to remind them that those who gathered in such places were the worst looking and were not fair examples of opium smokers (United Kingdom 1894 5:174–75).

4. See Berridge and Edwards 1981, chap. 14, who do not mention Allen's work but cite similar viewpoints. Missionaries produced anti-opium tracts in Chinese (the earliest in 1835), as discussed in Howard 1998, 131ff.

5. A Chinese witness testifying in India before the Royal Commission on Opium stated that one smokes opium but does not get drunk. Brandy, on the other hand, causes one to be drunk (United Kingdom 1894, 2:146).

6. See Musto 1973; Berridge and Edwards 1981; Milligan 1995.

7. In *A Thousand Plateaus*, Deleuze and Guattari take the drugged body as an example of the "body without organs," "with its production of specific intensities based on absolute Cold = 0," and then cite William Burroughs (Deleuze and Guattari 1987, 153–54): "Junkies always beef about *The Cold* as they call it, turning up their black coat collars and clutching their withered necks . . . pure junk con. A junky does not want to be warm, he wants to be cool-cooler-COLD. But he wants the Cold like he wants his Junk–NOT OUTSIDE where it does him no good but INSIDE so he can sit around with a spine like a frozen hydraulic jack . . . his metabolism approaching Absolute Zero" (Burroughs 1960, 21).

8. "Scrambling dragons" is the translation of *palong*; *kuaixie*, "fast crabs," was another term used.

9. Recall William Burroughs: "Junk is the ideal product . . . the ultimate merchandise. No sales talk necessary" (Burroughs 1960, 16).

10. In 1893 medical missionaries testifying before the Royal Commission on Opium categorically denied that opium was a prophylactic against malaria or that the Chinese used it as such. Quinine was the only effective treatment, they stated. See Dr. Maxwell (United Kingdom 1894, 1:17); and Dr. William Gould (United Kingdom 1894, 1:60), who reported that he himself took it in liquid form for dysentery and had trouble with withdrawal. Both Indian and British doctors testifying in India agreed that opium was not a prophylactic, but commonly asserted its great usefulness for malaria and other diseases, especially among the poor who had no access to quinine or other drugs (see, for example, United Kingdom 1894, 2:69, 90, 115, 162–65, and passim).

11. A bay in the Canton Pearl River estuary about twenty miles northwest of Hong Kong.

12. At least two other works had almost identical titles: Brereton, *Truth about Opium* (1882), and Woodhead, *Truth about Opium in China* (1931).

13. For more details, see Berridge and Edwards 1981, 185–88, chap. 14; Lodwick 1996, 85ff., passim; and Brook and Wakabayashi 2000, 39.

14. United Kingdom 1894, 1:28; for similar testimony, see also Reverend Hudson Taylor (United Kingdom 1894, 1:31) and the famous anti-opiumist Benjamin Broomhall quoting Marcus Wood (United Kingdom 1894, 1:49).

15. United Kingdom 1894, 1:14–16. Edkins himself appeared in the report (United Kingdom 1894, 5:248–49), saying: "The extension of Christianity will elevate the tone of Chinese society and give the people moral strength," the lack of which is part of what he thought made opium attractive to them.

16. United Kingdom 1894, 1:78; see also Surgeon-General Sir William Moore, with more than thirty-three years in India (United Kingdom 1894, 1:71–73), who also tried it.

17. See Moore and Mouat (United Kingdom 1894, 1:71–75) and Griffin (United Kingdom 1894, 1:107–8).

18. See Horatio N. Lay (United Kingdom 1894, 1:86), Stewart Lockhart (United Kingdom 1894, 1:99), and Thomas F. Wade (United Kingdom 1894, 1:88). Lay and Wade were major figures in British–Chinese relations.

19. For example, he negotiated the Chefoo Convention, which in its final 1885 form included an article allowing China a much greater part of income from the opium trade but requiring it to yield its claim to total prohibition.

20. On Lazarus, see United Kingdom 1894, 1:109–10; Lockhart (United Kingdom 1894, 1:114–16). Numerous others used time as a reason to explain why Europeans would not smoke opium (e.g., United Kingdom 1894, 5:162, 187 [a Chinese witness], 201, 226, and passim). Some also stated that the European did not like the reclining position adopted in opium smoking (e.g., United Kingdom 1894, 5:152, 180, 226, and passim).

21. Treating opium smokers was one of the top priorities of Protestant missionaries at the time (Howard 1998, 139).

22. On missionaries and the anti-opium position, see Lodwick 1996, and on medical missionaries in particular, Howard 1998; chap. 4. As early as the late 1830s, missionaries focused on British culpability in the opium trade (Howard 1998, 123–24).

23. See 1881, 647, and 1976, 42, as cited in Wylie and Fike 1993, 257, 262.

24. A mace was one-tenth of a tael, sixteen of which was a catty, or one and one-third pounds.

25. He added that this term is like that of "a *temperate* robber, who only takes shillings from his employer's till, or a *temperate* bloodletter, who only takes a spoonful daily from his veins," his emphasis (Williams 1895, 383).

26. See Chen Sen 1986, chap. 18, 231; Zhan Xi 1992, chaps. 2, 10.

27. That is, John Davis, a student of Chinese since his arrival in Canton in 1813 and a major figure in British operations in China, for example, first governor of Hong Kong (see Chang 1970, 62ff.).

28. Cited in Wylie and Fike 1993, 260–61.

29. See United Kingdom 1894, 1:47; also partially cited in Spence 1992, 250.

30. As he stated in 1893, the translator and sinologist James Legge "found that there was no evil so much deplored by the respectable classes of people as this habit" (United Kingdom 1894, 1:14). But Alexander Michie, a merchant with forty years' experience in China, said that, "You can hardly go to a Chinese dinner without having the opium pipe" (United Kingdom 1894, 1:131).

31. His three articles were "A Journey in Chekiang" (made in 1883), "A Journey in Fukien" (made in 1884), and "A Journey from Foochow to Wenchow through Central Fukien" (made in 1883) (Parker 1884a,b,c).

32. Parker 1884a, 29. According S. A. M. Adshead, in Sichuan of the late nineteenth century, the poppy "did not seriously interfere with food production, except that the wheat export declined" (Adshead 1966, 97). On poppy cultivation in North Manchuria in the early twentieth century, see "Notes on the Agriculture, Botany, and Zoology of China" (Skvortzow 1921, 79–82). The poppy there was worth two or three times the value of wheat or other cereals and was often planted in the best soil. On grain supplanted by opium in the 1870s and 1880s, see Howard 1998, 202ff., and in the first quarter of the twentieth century, Su Zhiliang 1997, 253–56.

33. Cited in George Jamieson's "Tenure of Land in China and the Condition of the Rural Population" (1888, 92).

34. See also Smith 1894, chap. 18, "Content and Cheerfulness."

35. *Chinese Repository* 5 (May 1836–April 1837): 571–73.

Chapter Five

Zhang Changjia's *Yanhua,* "Opium Talk" (1878)

THE SIGNIFICANCE OF THE TEXT "OPIUM TALK"

Zhang Changjia's "Opium Talk" is unique in the literature of addiction as the personal testament of a Chinese opium smoker. Nothing else like it exists in China except poetry and sporadic accounts that do not match "Opium Talk" in autobiographical detail and length. Along with poetry, other nonfictional sources, and narrative fiction, Zhang's piece provides the kind of voice that is lacking in considerations of its political and economic aspects and obliges us to legitimize the perspective of the smoker of opium, particularly the articulate and elite consumer who discusses at length his own addiction and that of his friends and acquaintances.

Zhang Changjia presents opium as something utterly new in the world, possessing an attraction that nothing else is capable of encompassing. He and his fellow smokers know something no one else knows, which is that history has passed definitively to a new stage. Now that opium is present, nothing else is foreseeable. Since no "sages," no "canons," no "grandiose logic" can undo the fascination with opium, as the preface writer says, those sages and their canons have become useless; and since they are useless, there is no point in moralizing against opium smoking or expecting it to stop. It is this way "because fate must run its course, and even with heavenly intent it would be difficult to undo." The fact is that "the way of Confucius" will never "take effect in the foreign lands." Instead, Western Christianity is "on its way to transforming the ancient land of China" (no. 13). In this Confucian–Christian framework, opium is an allegory of the forcing effect of a huge transformation that is arriving in China and the world. For addicts in particular, opium smoking is the site of a giant abyss between Confucianism and Christianity in which they live out the impossibility of going back to one or adopting the other.

How do we place Zhang's text as a piece of literary writing in late imperial China? The work appears in a Qing collectanea edited in Shanghai by two well-known figures, Qian Zheng and Cai Erkang (fl. 1875–1897), the latter of whom wrote a brief note appearing at the end of Zhang's piece.[1] Qian Zheng was at the time editor of the Shanghai newspaper *Shenbao* and was son-in-law of the important figure Wang Tao (1828–1897), who among his many endeavors assisted Walter Medhurst Sr. (1796–1857) in a translation of the New Testament and James Legge (1815–1897) in his translation of the Chinese classics. Wang Tao was baptized a Christian in 1854. Cai Erkang was likewise baptized and became the collaborator of two famous missionaries, Timothy Richard (1845–1919) and Young J. Allen (1836–1907), who each spent many years engaged in educational and reformist efforts in China. As Paul Cohen writes, the Christianity of people like Wang Tao and Cai Erkang served in great part to "dramatize the fact that other world views—legitimate and respectable—were *possible*" besides the Confucian one.[2] Outside of what he reveals of himself in "Opium Talk" (he once refers laconically to having conversed with a "Westerner," for example, no. 19), Zhang Changjia himself remains a mystery. But his own version of alternate reality emerges from his presentation of traditional Chinese culture as having definitively receded. His "fall of the god of money" is analogous to the end of the sole reign of Confucianism that Wang Tao, Cai Erkang, and many others represented both in their professional pursuits and their Christian conversions.

How Zhang was associated with Qian Zheng and Cai Erkang is unknown. However, the publication of his piece by people who involved themselves extensively in nontraditional occupations such as newspaper editorship and the translation of Western learning, including Christian texts, identifies his work as part of a hybrid culture already well developed in treaty ports like Shanghai by 1878, the date of the preface to his work. As did many others like himself, however, he wrote in a classical prose that was full of ambiguity and dense with allusions to history and classical literature. The title *Yanhua* recalls the term *shihua*, one that poets and commentators had been using for centuries in similarly digressive and aphoristic collections of comments on classical poetry. His citation of contemporary poems on opium and his references in general to the experiences of other cultured smokers like himself indicate the existence of a substantial group of articulate opium smokers who, it seems, otherwise barely revealed themselves in published form. Such people lived, however, in daily even familial contact with nonsmoking people who served in government, military, business, education, and various occupations involving foreign interests (opium smokers themselves would have been involved in all of these occupations). This chapter is about their opium world as represented by one who was thoroughly conversant with the Chinese classics and belles lettres, but nevertheless crystal clear about the irrevocable shift that had taken place in Chinese time. Preceding by about two decades the concentrated introduction into China of the discourse of modernity, Zhang already indicates the sense of radical shift which is so central to that later discourse.

To read Zhang's "Opium Talk" is to witness an extended expression of melancholia at both a personal level and a level representing a broader Chinese self in the midst of a prolonged and often traumatic disruption in its cultural history. But it is never pure trauma or disruption. Zhang Changjia the opium smoker finds a place of belonging somewhere between his own opium smoking and that of other Chinese, including friends, whether he is actually with them or not. However devastating the effects of opium may be, and however much he may hate addiction, he finds a distinctive way of being because of the unprecedented world of effects introduced by smoked opium. From the place of opium he gains a perspective on all of human history, which as he presents it has progressed steadily and irreversibly to the present state of the use of fire in steamships, modern weapons, and opium pipes (also called "guns"), all simultaneous inventions of a new age. In his opium wisdom, as a hero of opium smoking, he renders steamships and pipes coterminous in that they equally define the same point in history, from which he occasionally looks nostalgically back on earlier times of less complex inventiveness.

Like many others, he recognized that the fact that millions of Chinese smoked opium, and Europeans generally did not, had inevitably become a centrally defining difference between the two. Businessman Henry Lazarus said that Europeans did not smoke because they did not have the time to waste. Medical missionary William Lockhart declared that Europeans had a "distaste" for the habit (United Kingdom 1894, 1:115). Others stated that if Europeans smoked "they would be putting themselves on a level with Asiatics" (United Kingdom 1894, 5:164), or that Europeans in general literally disliked the reclining position, their clothes being too tight.[3] Zhang's "Opium Talk" might just as well have confirmed this European distaste, and precisely in the voice of what to the European at first looked like an opium sot. In his slowness, reclining on his opium bed, Zhang framed the appearance of opium as a shattering but very young and new event in world history, in which the Euro-Chinese interaction was something relatively minor compared with the effects of opium.

Zhang does not appear to have been a traveler like the Europeans in China or like Wang Tao and an increasing number of Chinese of that period (1860s, 1870s, and later) who had journeyed throughout the world.[4] Many of these Chinese had already begun to write about how the Chinese had to relinquish their cultural solipsism and face the problems of adaptation and reform. To some, Zhang's addiction may give the appearance of evading someone like Wang Tao's more articulated attempt to address these issues. Wang

Tao's own brother was a heavy addict (dying sometime in the 1850s), and Wang himself reported taking heavily to liquor in his twenties and thirties during the first period of work with foreigners.[5] Wang Tao at first resisted accepting his own involvement with Western interests, but eventually became a famous journalist and active promoter of reform. But Zhang Changjia was also engaged in a dedicated articulation of the opium addict's particular fit into the current age of Western encroachment. Face-to-face with Westerners in China, he and company could perhaps no more quit opium than missionary Arthur Smith and company could quit preaching. He and his poet friends were actively engaged in expressing their thorough immersion in opium. In effect, Zhang was involved in a solid dialogue with Smith, responding to him by being Western–Christian in a strange way, that is, opium Westernized. Zhang was thus demonstrating to all that the uniform evolution of China according to European interests was impossible. He acknowledged the fall of the Chinese god of money, but his response, in Homi Bhabha's words, was still "half acquiescent, half oppositional" even mendacious, as scores of Western observers liked to affirm about the Chinese in general (Bhabha 1994, 330). Furthermore, although Zhang did not predict it, he was indulging in a vice that would filter "back" to Europe and thoroughly challenge the Western attempt to define addiction as something confined to the Orientals. "Western-seas medicine" was something "Asiatic," supposedly introduced by the "West," but was in fact assuming–or actually had already assumed–a global identity despite the attempts to confine it otherwise.

THE RUIN OF CHINA

In Zhang's presentation of the opium way of life, China was living out its end as it was known until then. "The beginning" of this end, as the preface writer states, can be traced back to Canton, where the poppy was first introduced. The common assertion among Chinese officials, literati, and others that the Western nations, especially Britain, used opium to drain China of wealth is not articulated in "Opium Talk," but the inevitability of China's opium–Christianization and Westernization is: "Once the Western lamp is lit, it shines in all directions. Those whose eyes it meets come like moths flying into a flame" (no. 18). The character for "smoke," *yan*, also commonly used to stand for opium, predicts "the present day of opium," Zhang says in his first entry: "it is made up of three characters, *huo*, fire, *xi*, west, and *tu*, earth." Fire refers to the method of smoking, new in Chinese history along with tobacco, another substance introduced from the outside; fire also perhaps refers to the gunships and weapons Westerners used to force their way into China. "Earth" was one of the common alternate terms for opium, *yapian*, and also translates as "mud" or "dirt." As if forming the three schematic points of a new cosmology, the three characters together may be translated as "Fire brings earth from the west."

What Zhang accepts as simply irreversible fate, other writers in gazetteers or memorials to the emperor portray invariably as a base plot on the part of Western nations to make money. A passage in an important 1836 memorial to the throne states: "The people called Hung-maou (Red-haired) came thither, and having manufactured opium, seduced some of the natives into the habit of smoking it; from these the mania for it rapidly spread throughout the whole nation." This passage is as translated in the *Chinese Repository* of 1837 (p. 393), thus demonstrating how the knowledge of this accusation was easily available to European readers as well, many of whom were in agreement. A concurring editorial footnote to the translation cites a "public Journalist in Calcutta" who wrote, "*One might almost fancy that trade arose out of some preconceived plan for stupefying the Chinese, to pave the way for conquering the empire*" (p. 394; original emphasis). A Mr. Hogendorp cited later in the same issue said, "Opium . . . is a slow though certain poison, which the Company, in order to gain money, sells to the poor Javans" (p. 568; from "Raffles' History of Java").[6]

Zhang spends no time accusing Europeans of using opium to seduce the Chinese or anyone else. This is because he sees his fellow Chinese going into opium smoking fully conscious of the "fate of drowning" that awaits them (no. 6). "They probably knew from the start what would happen and committed their mistake quite consciously" (no. 8). They are not mere automatons who respond so predictably to external enticements. "It is clear that it is not opium which harms people but people who harm themselves from opium" (no. 21). And in fact these people go gladly to their ruin and "feel no rancour or regret because of it" (no. 34). It is as if going to ruin is what anyone would do, so that blame is irrelevant in these cases.

The several ways Zhang and his friends have of expressing the ruin of China portray the empire in a latter-day state of decline. He expresses this decline in terms of China versus Europe, however, only in his reference to Christianity transforming China and in one short passage in which a "Westerner" once said to him: "In our country opium is a medical drug that we only use sparingly. In China people take it as if it were food and consume it daily in several meals" (no. 21). It is as if he is saying that the Chinese are foolish because they cannot act moderately; once one person starts a trend, everyone follows. But otherwise Zhang's prime way of describing China's latter days is not through juxtaposition with dominating Western nations but through the varied utterance of opium's supreme power over all former pleasures and mainstays. Moreover, he extends the beginning of the fall to a point long before the introduction of opium. Western nations may have hastened and abetted this decline, in other words, but they were not the sole contributors to it.

Although he lays responsibility on the Chinese rather than the Westerners or opium itself, Zhang still emphasizes the addict's helplessness. The power of opium is greater than anything else yet consumed by human beings. The present, by implication, offers nothing better to live for. "Opium is contractive in nature," he says, "and thus capable of making one put all other things aside," especially money, for it is fatally clear that "love of money is not as strong as love of opium" (no. 15). Thus, he concludes, "the rise of the opium demon has led to the fall of the god of money." In another passage he writes that opium to the smoker is like a perverse energy that takes over and replaces the "virtuous energy." This takeover, in turn, is like the entry into the imperial court of "petty sycophants" (no. 45) who in Chinese history (his example being the end of the Tang) signal the end of a dynasty, which he leaves unspoken must again be about to occur. What is not to be missed is that his trope of decline is not quite the old one of the eternal return of dynastic decline, ruin, and renewal. Again, he sees a takeover by some completely unprecedented force that has caused all former occupations and diversions to be put aside. In terms of tonics and drugs, "Since ancient times there has never been such a marvelous drug" (no. 22). In terms of wine and food, "how shallow" were all our former pleasures! "Looking back from today's perspective," which collapses the whole of the past that is never to be repeated, "all the tantalizing things from ancient times on absolutely pale before opium" (no. 16). Now even the "Creator of things cannot control the abnormal events of the world" (no. 16). "Even the most valiant of heroes fall into the trap; the wisest of wise are all the same taken in" (no. 41).

Such statements are various ways of expressing the enormity of what has come to pass, which in his imagery always shades between the effects of opium as an ingested substance and opium as a figure of "abnormal events" in the world. These events ruin everyone, though no one is an inherently inferior grade of human because of being ruined. The valiant and the wise are just as prone as those who might conventionally be considered inferior. Opium represents something insidious, and to live with opium and to know and experience this insidiousness is to re-become valiant and wise, although in ways now distantly removed from what once seemed the normal and unquestionable system. Opium addiction, in other words, is an entirely relevant and involved way of living the social and psychological disruption of this era of catastrophe.

FIRE, STEAMSHIPS, AND GUNS

The one image that runs through all Western things appearing in "Opium Talk" is that of fire, for example, tobacco, opium, the Western lamp, steamships, and guns. Zhang provides a history of human degeneration ac-

cording to the evolution of the use of fire, ending with the introduction of tobacco and opium. It is these two fire figures that exponentially hasten the
world's degeneration.

> In prehistoric times humans ate their food uncooked and enjoyed healthy lifespans
> of several hundred years. After Suiren drilled wood to make fire, lifespans gradu-
> ally decreased in length. When that method was superseded by the use of flint, hu-
> mans became even more violent and lifespans were further rushed.
>
> Still, food in those times was all boiled, pots and clay steamers serving as con-
> tainers. There was still an attention to healthy living. In recent times, however,
> once tobacco became popular, all everyone did was to consume fire, searing
> their lungs and harming their vital essence. If tobacco is this harmful, then
> opium must be worse by far. (no. 38)

Tobacco and opium mark a definitive break in the history of the use of fire,
which in an unbelievable and unprecedented way humans now take directly
into their lungs. Fire is something that quickens and brutalizes human life,
the ideal being the usual one of Taoist minimalism, in other words, that the
more sophisticated and processed the pleasure, the more decadent and
ephemeral the state of civilization.

In another passage Zhang compares a steamship being fired up in order
to set sail for a long trip with the opium smoker who goes from feeling
"shriveled and listless" to getting fired up with opium until he "brims and
bursts with energy" and "steams forth with indomitable heat":

> When Western steamships are sufficiently fired up, they are keen and invinci-
> ble and can sail a thousand miles in one journey. But when the fire is extin-
> guished, the ship rests in complete silence, all night long surrendering its ability
> to move. If you want it to go the next day, you must fire it up again. The more
> fired, the more it can move. Upon reaching full potential, it is ready again for
> another journey of moving without stopping.
>
> It is the same with opium smokers. When their craving comes on, their bod-
> ies feel shriveled and listless, their joints all stiff. They must rely on opium to
> fire themselves up. At the beginning of firing up, they wriggle like worms. A lit-
> tle more fired up and they begin to flow like a great river. Fired up for a good
> while, they brim and burst with energy, and quickened in every limb they steam
> forth with indomitable heat. By the middle of the night they have even more en-
> ergy to spare. (no. 36)

The consumption of fuel matches the "inevitable tapering off" of the opium
high, as Zhang continues, which in the end is "just like making flowers
bloom in winter. As soon as they bloom they begin to wither" (no. 36). Both
steamship and opium are marvels that represent artificial expansions. But as
for opium, "indeed there has never been such a bewitching thing in all human time" (no. 50), so that the steamship is perhaps minor by comparison.

Zhang likes to call attention to the "formidability of opium," to which "people become numbed . . . by habit of frequency." He finds the names for opium-smoking apparatus remarkable but too easily overlooked:

> Weapons are evil instruments which sage kings used only when they were forced to. For today's opium utensils the word "gun" is taken to refer to the smoking shaft, while "bottom of the sea" *(haidi)* designates the opening of the mouthpiece, and "gate of struggle" *(doumen)* the opening of the bowl. Such names indicate the formidability of opium. But people become numbed to this fact by habit of frequency and end up applying dangerous instruments directly to their own bodies. That one can be fully conscious and still make such a mistake is thus easier to believe. (no. 52)

How or when the word "gun," or *qiang,* began to be used for the pipe shaft remains a mystery, but it is not difficult to visualize the gun as an image that uncannily joins the gun-wielding Europeans with the opium-smoking Chinese. The image is one of Europeans shooting weapons into China and the Chinese responding, in effect, by sucking fire in through opium extract. We opium smokers, in other words, watch foreigners doing violence in order to win the right to deliver "their tribute of mud," but we ourselves then take these "earthly flames and turn into immortals" (from a poem in no. 58). Westerners might as well be equated with "the Buddha from the West who, opening the blossom of the poppy, supplies us steadily to this day" (from a poem in the preface). The coolies and chair bearers, meanwhile, refuse to move another inch until they have had their smoke in the opium den. Nevertheless, being full of both "bitterness and joy" (preface), Zhang still recalls smokers to the fact that "they apply dangerous instruments directly to their own bodies" as they pass opium smoke from the "gate of struggle" through the "gun" to shoot for home in the "bottom of the sea" (no. 52).

In the poems of Zhang's friends and in his own writing, the image of China is still that of an empire at some remove from other kingdoms in the world and to which those other realms bring tribute, however much in decline China may be. It is not yet the more self-conscious China among other nations that people like Liang Qichao begin to imagine a few decades later. Reaction to foreign onslaught does not yet take the form of the informed, active resistance that accompanies the more global self-consciousness. Opium-smoking China is something that foreign steamships or weapons cannot quite reach in ways the foreign operators of these devices expect. Foreigners bring "mud"; Chinese turn into "immortals." Even weapons, which are supposed to overwhelm and terrify, instead turn into opium pipes. The transformations intended by the advancing European do not turn out to be the anticipated ones. The Europeans "transform" the Chinese, but the Chinese answer this transformation with a form of self-mutilation. That answer can be interpreted in various ways: it signifies the artificial expansion with which both guns and opium pipes hallucinate the human being; it forecasts the self-mutilating use of drugs that promises to follow Western "progress" wherever it goes. If the words "promises to follow" imply too much intention on the part of the mass of Chinese opium smokers, then at least it should be said that opium addiction was established as a fully practicable way of life in this period and was a fully coevolving component of Western progress. By this I mean that opium smoking and addiction were not accidental or epiphenomenal things which could easily be brushed away in order for progress smoothly to continue. Progress, moreover, is something like Zhang's parable of the increasingly brutalizing use of fire, which humans now take directly but nonchalantly into their bodies (also in the form of pollution, radiation, and carcinogens, to extend Zhang's metaphor).

THE FLICKERING OF THE OPIUM LAMP

Fire is not always a violent image for Zhang and his friends, however. The light of the lamp is also the smoker's companion, creating an atmosphere in which an invisible lover abides for whom the smoker is sweetly but terminally lovesick. The preface to "Opium Talk" begins: "The dark silence settles as the lone lamp lights up. The sleepless sea creature, awake all night, suffers the pain of distant parting."[7] When smoking is finished, the lamp is alluring and difficult to part from; when smoking recommences, the lamp must be carefully tended in order to deliver the steady flame without which opium is impossible to smoke. "Noticing the flame tiny as a star, / I trim the wick before it goes out . . . I try to pull away, but it still pulls me back" (from poem in the preface). A friend of Zhang's who "detested opium" wrote a poem beginning: "All night love thoughts join in one breath. / Burning through lamp oil, who can equal you?" (no. 59). This is the love that replaces all other loves and is kept burning in the flame of the Western lamp, the one to which smokers "come like moths flying into a flame" (no. 18). When he tried to quit opium, Emily Hahn's friend of the late 1930s, Heh-ven, "missed the lamp most of all"; she herself "couldn't stay away from [her] opium tray, or Heh-ven's, without beginning to feel homesick" (Hahn 1970, 239, 229). Zhang's formula for achieving moderation in opium smoking, therefore, centers on "putting the lamp out right away" and "rising immediately" instead of doing what smokers would rather do: After they "finish their pipe they stay tossing and turning on the couch, moaning and groaning as the lamp glimmers away. They feel the greatest reluctance to part with their cherished friend. This then is the crux of their peril" (no. 46).

Opium smokers possess a certainty of the irreplaceableness of opium. They know, as the ghost of a dead addict says at the end of the novel *Souls from the Land of Darkness*, that even the famous ancient poets would smoke opium if they were alive now (chap. 24). Opium displaces all former interests of the healthy organic body. "In famine I would willingly put it before food," says one of Zhang's friends in a poem (no. 58). With the fall of the god of money also comes the fall of all thriving, which includes care for that "thriving." "Opium is the opposite of food. Food wants thriving, opium wants decline" (no. 37). But it is a decline that suspends the issue of health and ensures deliverance from illness and old age: "The sicker one gets, the more distant one gets from food, but the more intimate one gets with opium"; "the older one gets, the less one eats, but the more often one smokes" (no. 37).

Sexual desire is also part of that which is displaced. The young men who first smoke opium in the company of prostitutes in a brothel "smoke for pleasure, but the pleasure of smoking is still not their main goal" (no. 3); opium is their "ambassador for visiting the flowers," as Zhang says he once wrote in a poem (no. 62). But later, as Zhang describes, they abandon prostitutes for the sake of a room alone with opium (no. 3). Thus, although commonly used as an aphrodisiac, opium is also capable of bringing about an extreme indifference to sex:

> Of the things in the world that must go horizontal, like the so-called "union of fertile essences" spoken of in the *Book of Changes*, there is, we were sure, one and only one such thing. Little did we know that lately there has been added one more thing. For this reason I have written a poem on opium which includes these lines:
> "In the horizontal lies yet another true pleasure;
> the dream of the love couch is no longer alone." (no. 64)

The former ultimate pleasure and most significant human act, recorded and confirmed in the ur-signs of the *Book of Changes*, now has a rival as male addicts withdraw into their opium chambers and no longer feel tantalized by beautiful women. To repeat Claude Farrère's words, copulation now becomes "an inexplicable bit of clowning" (Farrère 1931, 202).

Opium smoking is a newly discovered way of becoming a hermit, the word for "addiction," *yin*, consisting of the "sickness" radical enclosing the character for "withdrawing" in the manner of a hermit or recluse. "In one bed, on a single mat, you can sleep with it, take nourishment from it, and perform all ablutions in it," Zhang writes (no. 17). As recorded in literature and history for centuries, the recluse from political turmoil withdrew in order to live more peacefully somewhere else, like the poet Tao Yuanming (372–427) on his farm. As with Tao Yuanming, drinking liquor was a pleasure many such recluses enjoyed with firm dedication. Another kind of recluse of ancient times withdrew in order to search for drugs of immortality, which he found in minerals and plants. Although many people died painfully from these drugs, the records also report the euphoria and release these drug users appeared to experience.[8] Many used the drugs publicly, especially the "five mineral powder," *wushisan*, and served in office or other public roles, but others withdrew or even tried to avoid unpleasant duty by deliberately making themselves sick from ingesting the drugs.[9] Zhang only barely alludes to this tradition, and does not himself use the esoteric and allegorical language of drug alchemy that had existed for many centuries. But the preface to "Opium Talk" contains a poem by Chen Shenghua of Shanghai with the line: "Nine times nine, the immortal drug is fired to perfection," a reference to one of the common formulas by which alchemical drugs (here used metaphorically to stand for opium) were prepared according to a process that lasted forty-nine days (or went through forty-nine "firings"). Another poem Zhang quotes has:"[opium's] marvelous effect is no second to the cinnabar elixir," cinnabar being the main ingredient of these ancient alchemical experiments (no. 58).

The paucity of references to both the earlier tradition of the hermit/recluse or to the traditional ingestion of cinnabar and other substances coincides with Zhang's declaration of the unprecedented effects of opium. Compared with other substances and objects of desire, opium is unique "because as long as we're even barely alive, we'll still want it," he says. "There is absolutely no giving it up in midstream—the day will never come" (no. 50). With opium one can become an ultimate hermit in one's own home anywhere, but only under the condition of being in a state of chronic long-term illness. Zhang Changjia gives little detail of his life, but from what he writes appears to be an addict who has gone deep into addiction—what he means by deep I will explain shortly—and who has then realized an alarming need to find a way of moderation. Alone, in other words, is too alone; and smoking just because the lamp still flickers is too addicted. The new hermit (as opposed to the ancient one), who withdraws in an unprecedented sweeping away of all former methods of withdrawal, writes an art of addiction which like the ancient *ars erotica* tries to explain how to avoid the self-destruction toward which one would naturally go without knowledge of the special methods of self-containment and temporal regulation (e.g., in the *ars erotica,* semen retention and the thrusting rhythm of "nine shallow, one deep").

WHAT OPIUM DOES

Opium Sage versus Wastrel Addict

As presented by his opium-smoking friends in the preface, Zhang is an expert of this "deep obsession" who, although he "regrets entering such a labyrinthine way," has found the perfect balance between frivolity and pedantry. "Wafting the smoke of wisdom from his very throat, / he is his own kingdom of thought," says one of his friends. His audience listens raptly, for

Zhang "describing it / gets at the wisdom within, / and lives out the joy of life," says another friend. They rely on Zhang to speak from his rich experience and thus "awaken scores of spring dreams." In other words, the opium smokers need a spokesman to explain to them and justify to the world their life of "all day lying on the couch."

Besides affirming the unprecedented pleasure and bewitchment of opium, then, Zhang will sympathetically describe what opium does to a person, including its harms, what it makes people do or act like, and the stages it drives them through. In all this he will also present examples of both good and bad addicts. Smokers are beyond the reach of both moralizing nonaddicts and former addicts, but will listen to another addict like themselves. They share the belief that every type of opium experience deserves to be articulated, whether in verse or prose, the goal being to give body to something nonaddicts and even addicts themselves all too easily dismiss as a wasteful and even an evil way of life. Zhang will lend a note of heroism to the life of being an addict.[10]

In the 1920s, Cocteau makes a point of distinguishing between the one who dabbles in opium and the true addict. "Opium spares [those who] do not take it seriously" (Cocteau 1996, 59), while with the true addict opium is as exacting as a jealous lover. Opium demands of addicts that they be completely loyal and reverent and that all conditions be perfect (there must be no bright lights, there must be a steady, nonflickering, nonsmoky flame, the perfectly cooked consistency of opium, etc.); otherwise it will deny its promised euphoria and instead deliver pain and discomfort.

Zhang never refers to the dabbler but provides his own versions of the nonreverent smoker in the form of the wastrel addict. The wastrel's abuse of opium, moreover, typically relates in some way to his association with other bad friends, which brings to light something that neither De Quincey nor Cocteau brings into focus: the distinction between the experience of the solo addict and opium smoking as a group activity. Laudanum drinkers like De Quincey and Coleridge seem to have consumed their opium alone; of those Westerners I have mentioned who smoked opium the "classic" Chinese way, only Farrère and Hahn (and to some degree Lee) made it clear that they smoked in company. Cocteau wrote: "Smoking à deux is already crowded. Smoking à trois is difficult. Smoking à quatre is impossible" (Cocteau 1996, 67). But whatever one's ultimate preference might be, at the beginning one probably smokes with at least one other in order to learn the difficult art of cooking the opium, setting it correctly in the pipe, lighting, and smoking it. As numerous nineteenth-century Westerners observed, smoking in company was for many Chinese and other peoples the most common way of consuming opium. It had been the custom from perhaps the beginning that whether sharing a single pipe or using one's own, one joined with others to smoke and talk. A smoker also shared with a nonsmoker in order to introduce him or her to opium. In the novel *Souls from the Land of Darkness*, it was said to be common for a smoker to be generous in sharing with a nonaddict, but once that partner became addicted, the sharer would stop sharing (chap. 21, 195). Smokers who were congenially gathered together were said to share the "orchid aroma" or to be joined in an "orchid room." In the locus classicus of this allusion, which appeared long before the existence of opium smoking, those of like mind were said to emit a fragrance like that of orchids.[11] Such an image signifies the union of refined friends of like interests. The aromatic atmosphere, moreover, brings about inner transformation and self-enhancement. As Zhang phrases it: "For every happy occasion, I have a room full of orchid guests. Fortunate to have such good friends, I have us gather side by side as we talk of old times" (no. 62).

In fact, a certain continuity exists between these opium smokers and their five-mineral-powder ingesting predecessors. In one old anecdote, two fourth-century friends of considerable status think fondly of each other whenever they have a euphoric experience. One of the friends takes the powder and, coming upon a beautiful scene, immediately thinks of the brilliance of his absent friend.[12] It was not necessarily that individuals took the powder together at the same time, but that people of like interests and status enjoyed the special effects of this drug and did so without embarrassment or sense of shameful indulgence. But outside the orchid room, the opium smokers of the Qing dynasty suffered the effects of opprobrium attached to the habit by both Chinese and foreigners. In contrast, although there were fourth-century critics of the indulgence in drugs, alcohol, and other uninhibited enjoyments, they represented contending views, not ones that arrived from a consolidated position of moral or state authority.

In one of Zhang's many descriptions of the stages of opium addiction, he takes the smoker from the early period of enjoying company with others to a later one of only tolerating solitude:

> In their early stages opium smokers take after Mozi. The seasoned smoker takes after Yangzi. By this I mean that new smokers enjoy company, not solitude. They usually invite friends over, those of the same interests as themselves, and everyone smokes together. They'll even gladly mingle with strangers and people of lower classes. If this is not an example of Mozi's "universal love," then what is it?

Then he turns to a depiction of the wise, moderate smoker:

> But the seasoned smoker, he likes solitude, not company. He usually hides himself away and shuts out noise. He sleeps alone in his own room. He scorns company with even the closest relatives and the most respectable people. If this is not a case of Yangzi-like self-serving then what is it?
>
> Now the true sage among smokers is one who associates with those he should associate with but does not overdo it, and he distances himself from those he should be distant from, but does not become aloof. Such a person is rare. (no. 19)

Zhang Changjia now appears in his didactic pose as he defines good and bad smokers, the distinction between whom is the main theme of his attempts to describe various states and stages of addiction. In such a pose he is writing an advice book about how to smoke opium, in passages like these attempting to cover the various pitfalls and carrying readers through a representative composite of both good and bad experiences. It is as if to say that, as something here to stay, opium smoking must now be incorporated into human life just like all other practices that have their potentially adverse consequences.

He especially detests the "rich young wastrels" "who fly about acting brashly and impulsively. There is no evil they will not commit. Fortunately," Zhang continues, "they take up opium and thus chance upon a medicine that is made precisely for those whom nothing else can save" (no. 15). In other words, the ruin they cause themselves is their just end, as portrayed in *Dream of Moon and Romance* and numerous other nineteenth-century novels that depict young men spending everything they have on opium and prostitutes. Opium is thus a new antidote to "wastrelhood."

As his prime example of a bad smoker, Zhang's young wastrel is not necessarily unintelligent. He likes to "play at getting the secret knack of things" (no. 6). He hears about the pleasures of opium but also knows of the fearful results of addiction. He nevertheless claims to know—to have the knack of manipulating—the precise turning point before which he can stop in order to avoid addiction but experience the euphoria.

> They insist, "Wait until I'm on the verge and then I'll stop." What I am trying to say is that if you're afraid of getting addicted, why smoke at all? If you want to quit, why wait until you are on the verge? In general, when you're on the verge of addiction, you are already in a situation in which you are proceeding step by step into the highest states of ecstasy. It is just like water rushing downstream in a torrent. The flow is so fast who could stop it? At this point, only someone who can hold back waves can avoid the fate of drowning. Such people are rare indeed. (no. 6)

The same young wastrel continues to prevaricate, arguing that he still controls the secret turning point. He shouts, "Forswear the meat cleaver and instantly become a Buddha! I have the discipline to control it!" Later on, when he "knows too well that there is no going back," he says, "In the end I have the fortitude to stick to a moderate dose and to avoid falling into a state of complete fascination and oblivion!" The final voice is that of the terminal victim who lands "into the most unbearable suffering" when "it is too late for regrets," and who "finally says with amazement, 'That one mistake can lead to such an end!' But how long is a human life after all? It is over now!" (no. 5).

Another type of bad smoker is the one who as a young man finds in liquor "the greatest pleasure in life," but later when he discovers opium completely abandons himself to it and never touches liquor again.

This makes me think of those nowadays who try to succeed by means of examination learning.[13] They start with the canons of the sages and biographies of the virtuous. Next they intone the words of the great old essayists. Later they take the dregs of the present times, the so-called model essays, which they croon and recite, and spend their lives mouthing complete babble. I would like to know whether they remember even half a line of the so-called canons of the sages, biographies of the virtuous, and the essays of the old masters? They think this is a way of gradually entering the realm of bliss. I say it is degrading yourself day by day. (no. 9)

Having said that the opium euphoria surpasses that of all other things known in history, Zhang nevertheless blames the wastrel for treating opium as a facile replacement of other pleasures. In other words, the new is not absolutely new; and the new trick (opium/current model essays) is not absolutely foolproof. The wastrel smoker is foolish because he takes opium as if it delivers him into a completely self-sufficient state of pleasure.

The Stages of Opium Addiction

It was important in a society in which opium loomed so large to have instructive sketches of the stages of addiction clearly laid out for everyone to see. Both moralists and smokers decided it should be this way, although addicts knew such maps were mainly descriptions, not deterrents. Addicts simply had stronger truths, certain as they were that opium was so good and so bad that it was impossible for nonaddict moralizers to say anything worth listening to about opium. Cocteau put it this way: "To say of an addict who is in a continual state of euphoria that he is degrading himself is like saying of marble that it is spoilt by Michelangelo" (Cocteau 1996, 70–71). Like other addicts, Zhang Changjia never denied the opium trap: "Life is either smoking or waking from dream; / it is like thirst, then like starvation" (no. 61); or "Endlessly caressing the lamp, scorching the lungs, exhausting the spirit, despairing all day and night, squandering time and ruining one's livelihood: this is the harm of opium" (no. 62). Zhang, moreover, had his own multistage portrait of the process of addiction like that of the painter Sunqua cited in the 1837 *Chinese Repository.* As Zhang wrote:

> When young men of privilege *(zidi)* first smoke opium, in the beginning it is a matter of the thrill of "fishing and hunting" for courtesans. They smoke for pleasure but the pleasure of smoking is still not their main goal.
> Later they seek a bright and tranquil room and the most exquisite utensils. They devote their thoughts to nothing else. This is one transformation. (no. 3)

This portrait is of a well-off solo addict—perhaps a mild wastrel—who starts with prostitutes and like-minded male friends but then withdraws and turns into an opium connoisseur. Nineteenth-century novels portray various versions of this type, ones whose propensities complement the considerable craft industry of the production of opium paraphernalia or, as Zhang says, "exquisite utensils." These items include opium trays with erotic scenes or opium containers with lids that sport a lion with movable eyes and tongue.[14] Major opium-selling centers like Shanghai and Amoy were famous for such products, other places having fewer if any craftspeople who went for such elaboration.[15] The rich addict might have "opium servants" *(yannu)* to light the lamp and cook the opium *(Souls,* chap. 7, 130); he might have summer and winter rooms for smoking his pipe *(Souls,* chap. 8, 135). If erotic scenes, lions with movable eyes, or opium servants were perhaps too ostentatious for the sage smoker like Zhang, he might still have had his own lesser version of fine utensils and certainly he would have wanted high-quality opium, which would have had a range of varieties comparable to those of tea, wine, or tobacco. Continuing, he writes:

> Then they wish for a place that is hidden and secluded where no one can discover them. In this stage of retirement from the world, they no longer make the effort to seek refinement. This is one more transformation. (no. 3)

The solo addict's room—whether the addict was male or female, or husband and wife if they smoked together—would shut out noise and light except that of the lamp, long-term smoking causing sensitivity to both.

> Next, they want good opium with clean ashes. They must have thorough enjoyment. Now they reveal all signs of their preoccupation and could care less about keeping it hidden from others. This is yet another transformation. (no. 3)

In Zhang's first stages, shame leads the smoker to seek a place in which no one can discover him (Emily Hahn spoke of "dread in the idea of being spotted"; 1970, 229). Later the smoker no longer tries to hide from others and finally roves about with his unmistakable look of an addict, as the next transformations describe.

> Next, smoking day after day gives rise to the problem of expenses, making them seek cheaper prices in order to maintain their daily supply. Appearances are now out of the question altogether. Thus another transformation.
>
> Following this their addiction is heavy, their bodies weak, and they fall into extreme poverty. They resort to taking loans in order to relieve their ever present urge. Even if the price is high, they don't dare bargain down. This is another transformation.
>
> Finally they haven't even a fraction of a cent to their name. No one will loan them anything. They wish they could break their addiction but can't bear the pain of it. So they put on an air of carefree idleness and go searching out former acquaintances, hoping for some kind of handout, no matter how demeaning the reception might be. This is another transformation.

At last they forgo all sense of conscience and turn into the ugliest of creatures. This is then their lowest level. (no. 3)

The mention of taking out loans signals not only the desperation of the addict who does all he can to maintain his supply, but also the existence of a market that preys infallibly and precisely on the addict, who will spend all he has no matter how disadvantageous the terms. Novels of the period portray characters who make a living through the framing and extortion of addicts. When the addict reaches the level at which he is "the ugliest of creatures" (no. 3), he goes out in public "with stomach barely full and body improperly clothed" (no. 8), with eyes watering and nose running, hair unkempt, and skin sagging and yellow, something like the picture, in other words, that many Europeans drew in their travel accounts, testimonies, and moral tracts, and the same picture that Chinese prohibitionists and satirists held up for condemnation and ridicule. Zhang and others also describe the addict of means, however, who maintains the decency of the levels before that of no longer observing scruples (recall Henry Lazarus's friend Fongkee). It is unclear whether Zhang attained that level or went further and later came back, for example. Zhang and his circle of friends could have composed both those who stayed within their means and those who did not, the latter of whom included a scholar he knew of "who fell into such extreme poverty that he resorted to selling opium in order to support himself" (no. 55).

The above long entry (no. 3) is his most elaborate description of the stages of addiction, but Zhang also captures finer moments of these stages.

If you want to tell whether a smoker is addicted or not, just look at whether he neatens his utensils before or after he smokes. Those who neaten up after smoking are definitely already addicted. Neatening up first and then smoking is a sign of one not yet addicted. Only those who have been through these things understand what I mean. (no. 11)

Perhaps neatening up after smoking means that the smoker anticipates the next smoke and readies his apparatus so that he may avoid delay when he has his next craving.[16] Such preparation might include shaping the bead-sized pellets of opium to be ready for prompt cooking at the next smoke. What if some delay prevented him from smoking at his usual set time? Opium smokers needed to smoke at set intervals, or the craving became unbearable. The readier things were, the faster they could relieve their craving.

Another distinction Zhang makes is between mild versus deep addiction, with the latter described in one entry using a term that was common among smokers, literally, "addiction of the heart" or "addiction of yearning," *xinyin*, where "heart" stands for the word *xin*, usually translated as "heart" or "mind":

Smokers who wish to smoke only after the onset of craving are still at a stage of mild illness. Those who wish to smoke before the onset of craving, however, are already deeply ill. In other words, in the case of someone who smokes when his craving begins, once the craving is over, its traces can be left behind. For the one who smokes before his craving comes on, although the craving is out of the way, "yearning of the heart" never leaves. There are techniques for curing the craving, but not for curing the "yearning of the heart." (no. 27)

The last chapter of Peng Yang'ou's *Souls from the Land of Darkness* also refers to *yanyin*, literally, "addiction to opium," versus *xinyin*, "addiction of the heart," the latter being harder to cure. Another of Zhang's entries refers to the same phenomenon when he recommends a technique of moderation by which, instead of smoking regardless of craving, the smoker waits "until the urge to smoke is at its extreme" before smoking again (no. 46). *Xinyin* in this case refers to a deep addiction that Zhang claims to have discovered a way to cure and may have been one he himself once suffered or still suffered.

In entries like the one on *xinyin*, Zhang portrays the ultimate stages of addiction in which yearning no longer has to do with pleasure or pain in the conventional senses. In another entry the final stage is one in which "whether one is smoking it or not: no fragrance" (no. 4). That is, in earlier stages, the smoker found opium to be fragrant, whether smoking it or not. Later he found it fragrant only when smoking it. At last it was no longer fragrant whether smoking it or not.[17] An original sense of pleasure gradually evaporated as it was supplanted by the newly established organ of pleasure, opium, which has now usurped all former organs and senses. In simpler terms, opium no longer induces euphoria when one is so heavily dependent on it. At the extreme, as happens with many addicts, avoiding the pain of craving supplants in importance the anticipation and attainment of the opium euphoria.

The use of the word *xin* also suggests that this stage of addiction be called an "addiction of lovesickness." Zhang, his preface writer, and poet friends repeatedly describe the tortured reluctance to part from the flickering love lamp, which in one entry Zhang describes himself "endlessly caressing" (no. 62). Elsewhere in Zhang and numerous other writers, "lovesickness" or "love yearning" is the word *xiangsi* itself. The title of a poem from about the same period as Zhang is "*Xiangsi tu*," by Yuan Yi, that is, "Earth of Lovesickness," where "earth" or "mud" is a term standing for opium.[18] Zhang quotes the poem of a friend who writes the line "morning and night, the taste of lovesickness" (*xiangsi wei*, no. 58). As a late stage of addiction, *xinyin* thus culminates the trajectory that began with the use of opium as aphrodisiac but now finishes with the endless longing that can never be satiated.[19] Addicts who know about *xinyin* cast a warning to each other announcing the dire state of endlessness that marks the extreme stages of addiction. The way has now been mapped from initial to final stages so that smokers can roughly know how far they have come.

The Physical Effects of Opium Smoking

Aside from mapping the stages of addiction, Zhang also describes the extreme physical effects of opium, often by means of some unusual metaphor. He compares those effects, for example, with a nation's use of its army:

> Why is it that opium smokers are always thin and anemic and their mouths always dry? In general, one's energy has definite limits. Nourish it and it is ready for action; stimulate it and it rises. Things have always been this way. Compare this with the nation's use of military. Training in times of peace is a way of maintaining resources so that they will be effective when needed. But putting an army to constant use will rarely fail to run it into the ground. Is one's energy then something one can so harmlessly keep stimulating? Restrain yourself then! Be prudent! (no. 39)

The addict is like a hegemon who, being constantly at war, ruins his army by attempting to conquer too many rivals. Smoking opium "stimulates" energy and makes it "rise" but provides no revitalizing nourishment. The opium energy is "something made out of nothing" (no. 36).

Another of Zhang's models of the effects of opium on the smoker recalls numerous other addicts' singling out of the feeling of renewal after they have quit opium.

> If one smokes opium over a long period of time, one becomes as if covered by a huge stone: rain and dew can't get in to provide nourishment, and the plant has no way to sprout and grow. There is only fatigue and emaciation.
>
> All we need do is look at someone who suddenly quits smoking. In not even a month the complexion has gradually enriched itself and the body has begun to fill in. Isn't this like taking the stone away and watching the plant bound into growth? This example gives us a good mirror of ourselves. (no. 44)

Although the "euphoria" induced by opium is "superior to that of health," as Cocteau says (1996, 24), the regeneration after quitting opium bestows a unique sense of rebirth that only the addict is privileged to understand. Opium smoking is like making flowers bloom in winter, Zhang says, but "in the end," as he continues, "it isn't as good as the beauty of the seasonal thaw arriving of its own, the whole earth turning to spring, and trees and plants blooming in all their glory" (no. 36).

The stone under which addicts smoke opium and the winter in which addicts make flowers bloom have something in common. They are signs of the "illness" opium the "drug" is there to cure. Opium is precious in times

of suffocation and winter depression. It also stimulates fast energy for ambitious hegemons who strive to conquer as many rivals as possible. The
thread running through these allegories is the hopeless cause or the action
counter to natural law. The force of Christianity transforming China is the
concrete historical version of this common thread of allegories of hopelessness. Similarly, the persistent sense of melancholy and catastrophe suggests
the resonance between the physical and psychic effects at the level of a personal self, on the one hand, and the level of a broader Chinese self in the
midst of irreversible historic disruption, on the other.

The Opium Fool

Zhang portrays the opium world under the rock as an alternate one that is
unto itself. But it is second best, not quite capable of outdoing or replacing
sober life, although making a valiant try. Like food, liquor, sex, music, gambling, and other things Zhang lists, opium makes the individual "feel transported" (*yiqing*, no. 16), but in a way that is hugely impractical in the heavy,
normative sense of the word. The addict continually proves to be a fool in
that normative world. The ineptness and ineffectiveness of the addict is the
butt of satire as the nineteenth-century novelist Peng Yang'ou portrays a fore-
man at a Shanghai textile factory arriving late one day because it took him an
hour to move his bowels. Constipation was the common plight of addicts,
who sometimes went several weeks without relief. Another addict, the di-
sheveled, black-toothed owner of the same factory, does not hear the female
workers mocking his pathetic appearance. He gets his loose clothing caught
in machinery that traps and mangles him to death (*Souls*, chap. 16, 170–72).
The addict is a fool because he is full of ambitions when euphoric, but after
the high is over he accomplishes nothing. Cocteau puts it gently: "Opium
chastens one's ambitions" (Cocteau 1996, 36). De Quincey says of the laudanum addict: "His intellectual apprehension of what is possible infinitely
outruns his power, not of execution only, but even of proposing or willing";
"he is powerless as an infant" (De Quincey 1994, 234). Zhang writes:

> Everywhere they look they try to make something out of nothing, seeking ever
> higher levels of refinement. Perhaps they chance upon someone else's accom-
> plishment which makes them recall the happiness at once having done that
> something themselves. They almost want to claim the other person's accom-
> plishment as their own. Nothing exceeds the rush of inspiration at such times.
> (no. 36)

The inspired addict Zhang portrays is like the glib leader with plans of
dynastic renewal seen in the preface to "Opium Talk." The "someone else's
accomplishments" are perhaps the steamships and weapons invented by
the Westerners. The opium fool is a figure of the China fool, as many Euro-

foreigners had already implied. While Europeans are moderate in their use of opium, Zhang Changjia smokes opium under a rock and has the most inspiring visions of all time. Such foolishness is a type of resistance, the futility of which nevertheless expresses the impossibility of submission and homogenization. Addiction and foolishness are states of survival beyond which there is as yet no better moral or more healthy future. The addict can of course cure himself or herself, but Zhang nevertheless persists in saying that cure is impossible. Although he does not specifically say cure is impossible "in this age," he says so in effect by having noted the moderate European use of opium and the irreversibility of the flow of Christianity.

To the extent that being addicted is not being Christian, the addict does not accept the guilt (or verdict of foolishness) imposed by Christianity. Moreover, the addict does not identify with or attempt to become the Christian—except by means of the trick of smoking the "Western-seas drug," which arrives at the same time as Christianity. The ships and weapons have already been invented. The conquerors are already on their way. To join them is only to be assigned the role of former Confucian, ex-Chinese, recuperated addict. Being addicted—though second best, not quite as good as sobriety—is the new in-between space, a type of void that is neither Confucian nor Christian. It is a sign of the incommensurable difference between Confucianism and Christianity and it marks a "cultural void," in Homi Bhabha's words, and constitutes a "strategy of cultural survival" (Bhabha 1992, 60).[20]

OPIUM CROSS-CULTURALLY

The lack of carry-through from opium enthusiasm to sober accomplishment identifies another common trait of opium smokers and eaters no matter where they are from. This appearance of commonality returns us to cross-cultural questions that I began to mention in chapter 1. How far should we go in comparing opium addiction in various cultural settings? How differently do opium and other drugs work in different times and places? It is very easy to read Zhang and find resonating statements in Burroughs, Cocteau, De Quincey, and other writer-addicts who lived in other times and places, and differed especially in belonging to the culture that Zhang saw as pushing back his own. Opium smoking and eating does in many ways produce traits and reactions that are both transcultural and transhistorical. However, the case of opium addiction can also be used to demonstrate differences in terms of cultural, social, gender, and other levels of personal or mass identity.

Before treating specific instances of comparison, I propose an overarching framework of Europe versus Chinese-other or China versus European-other that has to do with the concept of cross-cultural parity, which I will explain in the following particular way. Foreign "experts" asserted that

China had no "real" law (thus, for example, the foreign insistence on rights of extraterritoriality) and could not enforce its prohibitions against opium. Why China could not enforce laws and edicts against opium was a common topic of discussion among foreigners, who arrived at conclusions something like these: because Chinese—especially those in authority—are connivers or because Chinese laws and edicts are empty words. An implicit assumption was that the Chinese (addict-conniver) should be more like the European (whole person), but this was still a remote possibility. Being too much like the European would create a new problem: faced with an equal counterpart, how would the European then deal with his complicity in the opium trade (or his numerous other exploits in China) that he greatly profited from? If the Chinese became equals, they would naturally have more right to call into question this European duplicity. As it was, the Chinese had all along been accusing Euro-Westerners, especially the British, of treachery in their involvement in the opium trade. But the Chinese had not yet achieved the status of an equally sonorous and authoritative voice. From the Euro-Western perspective, it had always worked out well that the Chinese were the conniving and duplicitous ones, and thus the main ones responsible for their opium problem.

It is under this question of balance and imbalance of status that we must consider opium smoking in a cross-cultural way. Instead of parity or balance in legal or diplomatic terms, however, let us switch to the level of opium consumption and conceive of what it would be like if a Chinese "everyman" and a European "everyman" smoked opium together. Put simply, can they smoke "on the same level"? I have already alluded to this highly rhetorical question and would like to articulate it more openly as I consider factors of culture, social status, and gender in this chapter and the following ones. With few actual sources illustrating such a situation of intercultural smoking, I will nevertheless propose some crucial differences between Chinese and European addicts that parallel the situation of imbalance between the Chinese and European nations of the various treaty agreements of the nineteenth century and later.

Let us begin with one particularly telling difference: Zhang Changjia does not mention nightmares and fabulous or horrendous visions. This is not to say that Chinese smokers had no nightmares. But the reader of Coleridge, De Quincey, and Farrère comes away thinking the nightmare is central in the opium addict's experience.[21] Claude Farrère was the French author of stories about a self who spent many hours smoking opium in dens in Shanghai around the turn of the nineteenth century. He uses the word "Nightmare" to entitle the last of his stories in *Black Opium*, in which he writes, "Before smoking, I am dying from need of opium, and I die again afterwards, and while I am smoking, and always." He reaches the limit "where sleep is reduced to zero and nightmare is raised to a corresponding and inverse power—one divided by zero equals: infinity" (Farrère 1931, 261–62).

In not foregrounding the nightmare, Zhang and the numerous poets I have cited in part merely demonstrate that the nightmare was not a theme for Chinese writers about opium as it was for European writers (including nonaddicts) in the De Quinceyian tradition. In De Quincey's opium dreams, the Orient looms as a timeless, intimidating, even invading presence that destabilizes the enlightened and progressive British self. The Orient represents an "all-encompassing origin," in Barry Milligan's words, that threatens to tear "apart the very notion of British identity in the present" (Milligan 1995, 48); it is alien, horrific, and antediluvian. Zhang may have had nightmares and visions, but not in the manner of the isolated De Quinceyian persona who feels overwhelmed by the masses of fiendish Orientals. Zhang's representation of Westerners overwhelming China relates to something he sees concretely, not in the form of dream. He perhaps acquiesces in that "fate" has made it thus. Like De Quincey or Coleridge, he feels a loss of identity—Confucianism yielding to Christianity. But in terms of his history of fire, decline has already been occurring for ages; those who ate uncooked food are long gone.

Another point at which Zhang and De Quincey part ways is one I have mentioned before: solitude versus company. Horror and isolation do not enter Zhang's picture of decline because, as he and his preface writer portray it, everyone is going down together. De Quincey, on the other hand, claimed that he passed more of his life in voluntary solitude than anyone else of his age (Jack 1963, 305). In general, parties of laudanum drinkers were, so far as we know, rare or nonexistent (also recall Cocteau's horror of smoking in company). Once the opium den reached Britain, America, and other countries in the mid-nineteenth century, the style of smoking in company became common. But at the same time it drew almost immediate condemnation and eventual prohibition, and never rid itself of a highly vilified association with the teeming and degenerate Orient. In writing his guide to practical wisdom about opium, on the other hand, Zhang was secure in having numerous friends of the same "orchid aroma." As he says in his fondness for neat compressions of the good with the bad:

> I sent a letter to a friend in which I wrote, "For every happy occasion, I have a room full of orchid guests *(you shi sheng lan)*. Fortunate to have such good friends, I have us gather side by side as we talk of old times. This is the good side of opium.
>
> Endlessly caressing the lamp, scorching the lungs, exhausting the spirit, despairing all day and night, squandering time and ruining one's livelihood: this is the harm of opium.
>
> Today I have a short formula to give him: "No need to refrain from it, but you can't always be at it either." (no. 62)

As condemned as opium smoking may have been, opium smokers in China nevertheless could look around and see scores of others smoking openly and with relative impunity. A smoker who avoided or despised public settings such as the outdoors or opium dens, like Zhang, might have a coterie of opium-smoking friends who would smoke at home accompanied by a spouse, or would be waited on by their house servants, or would write letters or poetry to sympathetic readers.

The nearest Zhang Changjia comes to the nightmare is his "despairing all day and night," or capturing the fatal endedness of opium smoking in one concise entry about sleeplessness, another experience shared by opium consumers:

> Rest becomes impossible for the addict. Sleep becomes a small rest, death a big rest. (no. 26)

Although nightmares and invading presences (such as the sensation of insects crawling over one's body) were common experiences of consumers of opium everywhere, in the main Zhang puts his despair and bitterness into this and other varied statements describing opium addiction as a "chronic illness" (no. 43); it is like life under a rock; it is like making yourself go to war endlessly; or it is something that one can quit with only tremendous difficulty and not even then.

Even Claude Farrère's nightmares are not stereotypically De Quinceyian. He does not write of masses of fiendish Orientals. Instead of fearing the Chinese, he declares brother- and sisterhood with them. European and Asiatic are "reduced to a level," as he says. Men cease to be men, all differences are erased (Farrère 1931, 146). In short, as he presents it, the Chinese door has opened for him. For him, even though we do not hear from his male and female friends from "Foochow Road" in Shanghai (p. 145), the monoliths of East and West have somewhat disintegrated, if only for the hours they spend together with opium. Once they leave the den, they are constrained by traits of race and nationality, among other things, that link them with political and historical realities they can only escape with difficulty if at all.

Farrère's scene of European and Asiatic "reduced to a level" is precisely what he must have known other Europeans held in disdain. Lacking certain privileges Farrère had, would his Chinese counterparts have envisioned the same reduction? Neither they nor Zhang had treaty ports in England to which they could travel freely or emigrate for as long as they wished. Someone like Farrère may have acknowledged such political and historical differences, but perhaps also erased them through various types of imaginative role reversal. He could, for example, take the Chinese side or even pretend he was Chinese. He could suggest that the Chinese were more civilized in the end than the so-called modern Europeans. Chinese slowness, in other words, was wisdom; European speed was rash immaturity. He would prove this by his actions: through opium smoking he was slowing himself down and seeing things from a more Chinese angle. He still took opium smoking as a peculiarly Chinese custom. But in the East/West mise-en-scène, it was in fact a Chinese custom.

Any Westerner engaging in a deliberate search for commonality with the Chinese would find opium smoking one of the prime spheres for such an initiation. To cultural or racial purists, such smokers were engaging in cultural miscegenation. Such forays, moreover, would seem artificial and too deliberate. On the part of the Westerner, however, deliberateness is the only option. She will always be subject to the accusation of dabbling: deliberately coming over to Foochow Road and giving opium a try, experimenting with ego transformation. But there is no other choice; the dialectic of Easterner to Westerner in both space and time creates a symbolic rift between Western "realism" and its wise/sottish, pleasure-steeped Eastern obverse.

Aside from whether Farrère and his friends elided their differences or articulated and even tried to negotiate them, they shared ground in their excursion from sobriety and mingling of races. All opium smokers in China were in common defiance of the official, elite stance against smoking. The same prohibiting authority was also sensitive about Chinese who befriended or cooperated with foreigners. Such people were held in suspicion; in times of war they were punished for being spies and given the notorious label of "Chinese traitor," *hanjian,* which was punishable by death. Europeans in China who befriended Chinese may not have been such an anathema to other Europeans, but those who did, and even more the few who smoked opium or dressed as Chinese, were nevertheless peculiar in doing more than was prescribed and expected of them.[22] If they mingled in Chinese opium dens in Britain or the United States, they symbolized an insidious invasion from the East. Whether Chinese traitor or odd European, opium smokers represented a liminal way of life that took away from what was otherwise organic and whole, whether in China or Europe. As "Opium Talk" portrays it, addicts all lived in an opium present that was also a Euro-Chinese present. Opium was an originary bond between the two cultures, although a bond that many found disagreeable. Smoking was one place that symbolized their potential mixture and mutual transformation, not that many took the chance. Farrère knew, for example, that it was a place to go if one was interested. In terms of the ideology of opium prohibitionism, such transformations represented a dissolution of racial and cultural integrity. Farrère and Zhang were similar but not identical participants in this liminal way of life. Farrère welcomed such dissolution, which he rapturously envisioned; Zhang Changjia saw it as heavy and inevitable but not worth unending lament: even the gods could not undo it.

THE MALE SMOKER

Love-death

Continuing with the questions of cross-cultural commonality from above, let us turn to the level of gender by addressing the issue of the male opium smoker. By all accounts, Chinese or Western, the overwhelming majority of opium smokers were male. Their reports are not only of their Chinese or Western experience, but also of their particularly male experience of opium smoking. The use of the word "lovesick" *(xiangsi)* and the claim that opium displaces sex already direct us to these considerations of gender. Following some of Zhang's and his poet friends' thoughts, let us hypothesize that addiction to opium is like involvement in a love-death or a liaison with a dangerous lover. But the human other—a beguiling woman in the case of Zhang and friends—is no longer there. Interests have shifted in intensity and focus. To the addict, sexual desire is no longer so urgent. No longer focused on women, the addict appears and at times claims to transcend sexual desire if not also the differentiations of gender. At the same time, the addict appears emasculated by this opium "lover." Sex once transcended fails to deliver him into the sublime, instead leaving him with something equally if not more untranscendable.

In discussing the fire of the opium lamp, Zhang evokes the smoker's sweet but terminal love affair with opium, in particular as crystallized in the reluctance to put out the lamp. This state of lovesickness incurred by opium smoking emerges from numerous entries in "Opium Talk" and identifies another theme that is common to male Chinese and Western writers about opium. Zhang writes:

> I once saw a poem which had the following lines: "You associate with me, but I still will be myself. / Being haggard because of you in fact shames me." I think the words "associate with me" and "haggard because of you" can be transferred and dedicated to opium (no. 56).[23]

Opium is a teasing lover who promises nothing; the addict is in love but the love is unrequited, and the addict is therefore haggard. Zhang, in other words, is the teased lover who can't escape being teased. One minute thrown into ecstasy, he is "like the bright sun at the start of day" (no. 16). But then he wanes into despair and misery, until in such physical and mental pain that only one thing matters, smoking opium again. The addict is completely gutted by this love and full of "unforgettable hatred" because he can't escape it (no. 42).

The question follows, How or to what degree is Zhang still male in gender and sexual desire? Does opium itself take on gender-like qualities? Zhang claims that opium pleasure surpasses all others—the attractions of food, wine, and even women. He also says, however, "If we look among all the strongest attractions in the world and ask which one absolutely cannot be replaced, it is probably true that the power of women over men is the strongest" (no. 40). He refers in two entries to the phenomenon of the opium smoker in his earlier stages smoking with avid interest in visiting women in brothels but then losing that interest in favor of smoking opium alone in his room (nos. 3, 63).

The combination of these quotes suggests two states: one of solo satisfaction under the influence of opium, having no desire for women, the other of anguish as the smoker experiences a craving for opium similar to but worse than any desire he ever had for women. No gender change occurs in Zhang; his luck as a man merely changes for the extreme worse. Although Zhang never says as much, we might infer that opium to him is like another woman who utterly conquers the addict-man. In his state of solo euphoria, the male addict temporarily believes he no longer cares for women or any other pleasures. But soon opium turns the tables and teases him as he formerly teased women, never promising him anything. Zhang is like a polygamist; in having many wives he tries never to fall under the spell of any single one.[24] In opium, however, he finds a lover who spellbinds him more than he can resist and jealously bewitches him so that he cannot find other lovers to dispel the power of opium.

Cocteau says, "Opium is jealous to the point of emasculating the addict" (1996, 55). In a similar vein, Richard Klein paraphrases from a piece on cigarettes by the nineteenth-century French writer Théodore de Banville: "The cigarette is a woman, a terrible, ferocious, demanding, but absolutely, passionately desirable one, who allows no compromise and no alternative to her jealously required devotion" (Klein 1993, 43). That Zhang says the power of women over men is the strongest of desires perhaps means he still values sex over opium and regrets that opium is so strong, as he indicates in other entries.[25] It also may be interpreted to mean that opium is more of a woman to him than a human one and that desire enters a new register in which, as Cocteau and de Banville write, it is far more insatiable than ever before.[26] The situation remains that desire for opium displaces desire for women but in doing so it does not displace the effects of infatuated love. Lovesickness, in other words, prevails even when the addict severs relations with all humans. His "libidinal autonomy," or "narcissistic withdrawal," is only a mirage for nonaddicts resenting (or dreaming of while not admitting their own desire for) such supposed release. His sober, not sottish, reply is that the only release is death (as he allows in no. 51). Meanwhile, perhaps, his family members languish or fill with rage because of his addicted lack of care for them. (Zhang himself mentions no spouse or relatives except an "upright" younger brother who asks him why he has to be so fond of opium, no. 40.)

The discussion of Zhang in his aspect as male addict invites parallels between him and his otherwise cultural opposite, the Western male like De Quincey, Cocteau, or Farrère. As in Farrère's case, questions of both social status and gender arise in that the elite male addict initially enjoys a relative freedom and self-sufficiency, and by virtue of his status smokes opium differently from those who do not enjoy such privilege. The privileged addict suffers emasculation at the hands of his invading or teasing opposite, whether it be the masses of Chinese opium demons or opium as jealous

lover. But the coolie or the woman, especially the prostitute, who do not begin to possess such freedom and self-sufficiency, cannot experience the same
type of nightmare or addiction.[27] All addicts may suffer the itchiness that
opium and its derivatives induce (or other such physical symptoms), but they
will not share the same imaginary of nightmare, lovesickness, or emasculation. The imaginary will vary according to the role each subject plays in the
increasingly interpenetrating global-social repertory.

It is unfortunate that so far I have found next to no autobiographical
sources by female opium smokers in China; it is even less likely that I will
ever find sources by coolies or others of the lower classes. For the rather different perspective of women smokers, we are mainly restricted to accounts
like those in nineteenth- and early-twentieth-century fiction. Such representations, which I will discuss in the next chapter, suggest that women of
means enjoyed solo addiction as long as their marriages allowed them to live
comfortably and maintain their supply of opium. Non-elite female addicts
tended to be prostitutes who kept up their supply of opium by means of their
earnings or through the generosity of their clients. At worst, they kept up
smoking only by going further into debt to the brothels that housed them or
the keepers who sold them to the brothels. The brothel was one place where
the lovesickness of the man for the woman was something the prostitute
could rely on to maintain or increase her income. She could, for example,
introduce a young man to opium while flattering him into spending his time
with her for as long as he had money and had an interest in her. She would
abandon the young opium sot when she found a better customer or one who
would buy her out of prostitution. The female opium smoker could thus at
least defeat the individual opium wastrel. Her situation is distantly analogous
to that of the Chinese challenge to the foreign opium trade. Greater domestic opium production did not reverse overall Western domination, but it did
finally outsupply the foreigner's product. Opium thus becomes a means of
survival, a weapon even, for those whose survival is at risk because of the
particular disadvantages accruing from their status and from their personal
or social history. Opium is this weapon in part merely by default: the dominant persona experiences opium in a way that emasculates him before his
usual subordinates: demonic Chinese masses and jealous, insatiable women.

Self-love

Besides lovesickness for a real or absent lover, however, there are also self-
love and the love of smoking companions. Libidinal autonomy and narcissistic withdrawal sound too cerebral and demeaning for this phase of opium
smoking, even if it is only a phase that may alternate with states of nightmare
and lovesickness. The smoker is supremely self-content, "at peace with himself and all mankind," as "some very intelligent Chinamen" once assured

Doctor Harry Hubbell Kane (1975, 61). The smoker loves being by himself so much that he shuts himself up in a room and "scorns company with even the closest relatives and the most respectable people" (no. 19). As one of the poets of Zhang's preface wrote:

> Another universe,
> not a single hindrance or concern,
> all day lying on the couch,
> the taste of sleep country,
> letting the person be completely free.

These are descriptions of a state that rouses the ire of nonaddicts who look on and see nothing but sottish faces and undeserved, unworked-for self-contentment. Smokers enjoyed the pleasure of gathering to recline and talk about whatever came to mind. "I trim the wick before it goes out, / as we talk in low voices freely confessing our hidden feelings" (preface). Smokers together say things they would not say to anyone else, further creating a sense of belonging among themselves and of separation from nonsmokers.

In early-twentieth-century Shanghai and other cities of the surrounding region, "swallows' nest" was originally a term for a kind of den that supplied customers with lamps, pipes, and couches during temporary periods of enforcement of prohibition. Smokers brought their own opium. Like swallows carrying mud in their beaks to build their nests, smokers brought a bit of opium to the small and crowded nest of the den to smoke and talk quietly with other smokers, "discussing times ancient and modern" *(tan jin shuo gu)*. A late Qing poem put it this way:

> The little chamber is like a nest, in it lie many couches.
> Guests arrive late at night, the sound of talk is low.
> Just like swallows murmuring in the rafters,
> they carry their bits of grass and mud, taking no measure of time.[28]

Zhang writes, "Occasionally there is something they have no choice but to get up and do, and they feel in every bone of their body that they are not meant for this. When they return to their old nest, though, they again have a feeling of their proper place" (no. 23). He concludes that since smokers spend more time lying down than standing up, there is no way to know whether they are "humans or things."

QUITTING OPIUM

Every addict has to deal with the question of quitting, whether or not he actually ever succeeds in quitting or even decides to. A number of Zhang's entries deal with this question. A doctor tells him to gradually reduce his dose until he smokes nothing at all; sincere intent alone is the best cure (no. 46).[29] On this method, James S. Lee wrote:

> I have seen, in China [c. 1906–1907], opium smokers trying to give up the habit.
> They would start by getting a cylindrical pot made of hard wood, and three-quarter inch inside diameter and of just sufficient length to hold their day's supply.
> Every day they would file a little off the length of the pot.
> This kind of system is no good; the craving becomes intense, and few have the will power to carry it out. (Lee 1935, 105, 239)

In the 1890s and early 1900s, Lee first learned about drugs in India, continued to experiment with them in Malaysia, Sumatra, and elsewhere, and spent time with Chinese opium smokers both inside and outside China. He claimed to have cured himself of the morphine habit by counteracting the drug with cocaine and gradually reducing the injections of each until he "was able to stop using drugs entirely" (Lee 1935, 102–5). Still, he found the use of drugs "the only way to be really happy; to get away from the deadly sameness of life in this world," and repeatedly went back to them until antidrug laws, he reported, made it too dangerous and risky to continue (pp. 3, 106).

Zhang Changjia offers little hope of ending addiction to opium, concurring with Lee that the method of gradual reduction is too difficult (no. 46). Why?

> He who abstains for one day must put his heart into it for that whole day. If he abstains for one year, he must put his heart into it for that whole year. Even if he has abstained for a very long time, he can never for an instant let his heart stray from the task. (no. 47)

Zhang concludes: "But in fact no one is in the least capable of such effort."

In another passage he states that quitting opium is like a woman trying to maintain chastity (no. 48). Martyring herself is far easier because it only takes an instant to execute her self-mutilation, after which she attains honor forever. A chaste widow, however, only attains honor after years of hearing spring birds and watching autumn moons, as Zhang imagines. In using the model of female chastity, Zhang feminizes himself through comparison with the chaste widow, turning opium in this instance into the temptingly handsome man the young widow tries to resist as she stands by her door watching him walk by. Honor and respectability pale before the irresistible lure of opium and the pain of quitting it. Who can stand such pain that lasts for weeks on end, Zhang asks, in addition to the temptation that continues forever?

Nevertheless, he "playfully composes a list of ten prescriptions for quitting opium," that is, ten ways to divest oneself of opium addiction (no. 51). He starts with sex, then lists gambling, interesting conversation, reading, travel to beautiful places, and wine, all of which are types of pleasure he has else-where said that opium completely surpasses. In his seventh item he arrives at "making oneself busy," although with what he does not say except "en-gagements," which must be numerous enough to leave him no interest in opium. Eighth on his list is sleep: "in extreme boredom escape to sweet darkness." The boredom that follows quitting opium is colossal (as James Lee also wrote); let the addict at least sleep and forget it. Or else he is refer-ring to the dullness of life in general, against which sleep, like opium, pro-vides a temporary reprieve. The two last prescriptions are the gravest. Ninth is destitution, that is, becoming so poor and emaciated that one has no more energy or will even to steal in order to get opium. "Then finally one is forced to quit." Some people end this way because they keep spending their money on opium until they run out. They may be bewildered and devastated, but Zhang at least "playfully" suggests that perhaps it is good to end in this man-ner. His last item is death: "All opium smokers arrive at this point and thus meet their end."

Quitting opium involves transferring one's allegiance to another diver-sion. In order to dispel the power of opium, one finds another lover: sex, gambling, wine, work. Elsewhere Zhang mentions obsessions with bamboo shoots or flowers. One must pursue all of these with extreme devotion in or-der to avoid returning to opium. But perhaps a few months or years of ab-stinence would be enough, an ex-addict might say. It would be all right to go back to opium after that. Or, finally, it would be enough merely to retreat from large doses of opium and somewhat moderate one's smoking. One at least wants to arrive at having a sense of control sometimes, where that con-trol corresponds to modulating the dosage (twenty pipes today, ten for the next three days, thirty on the fourth day), regulating it (only so much per day), or gradually reducing or eliminating it altogether. Whatever one does, as Dale Pendell writes in *Pharmako/Poeia,* "You've got a monkey" (Pendell 1995, 137).

Zhang's list of diversions does not include what some twentieth-century reformers would consider the most important: the cause of working for cul-tural and political renewal and national resistance to foreign powers. But in listing these diversions, Zhang thematizes the way opium addiction exerts a monopoly over other allegiances. Nothing can challenge this allegiance ex-cept–the reformer hopes and asserts–a cause that adequately addresses the loss and disruption suffered because of the opium–Christianization of China. Something new has to be invented in order for it to be worthwhile to quit opium. Zhang's list includes only what the political or moral reformer would call personal concerns, which would be resolutely labeled "petty bourgeois" under the socialism that eventually triumphed for a while in the next cen-tury and finally brought about a virtual end of classic opium smoking in China.

NOTES

1. I first found the work in A Ying's *Collection of Opium War Literature* (1957), an anthology produced as part of a nationally promoted effort in the 1950s to collect and publish documents relating to the great tragedy of the Opium Wars, the unequal treaties, and the mass addiction that followed for almost two centuries in China. The collectanea, *Xieyu congtan* (Third Collection), is in the Shanghai Municipal Library. A Ying omits a few sections, which I have added back into the translation in the appendix below.

2. His emphasis, Cohen 1978, 884–85. Wang Tao did not note the baptism in his diary and later continued to write critically of Western efforts in China and of Christianity itself. See Zhang Hailin 1993, chap. 3.

3. See United Kingdom 1894, 5:152; 5:180, 226, and passim.

4. Wang traveled to Europe in 1867; Zhang 1993, 105ff. See also Yeh 1997.

5. He liked visiting prostitutes and wrote extensively about them; see Zhang Hailin 1993, 47; Henriot 1997; and Wang's fictional work, *Hou Liaozhai zhiyi*.

6. Thomas Stamford Raffles was lieutenant governor of Java when it was under British control from 1811 to 1816; see Rush 1990, 11.

7. This is an alternate translation of the one in the appendix.

8. See, for example, *Shishuo xinyu* 2:14; 4:101; and 8:153 (Xu Zhen'ou 1984, 40, 149, 271). For a brief but informative discussion of drugs in ancient China, see Li Ling 1997.

9. E.g., *Shishuo xinyu* 10:23 (Xu Zhen'ou 1984, 313).

10. Richard Klein writes of the heroism of cigarette smoking (1993, 143).

11. In Zhang, worded as *you shi sheng lan*. See part 1 of the *Xici* appendix to the *Yijing* in Gao Heng 1979, 520, in which the words are *tongxin zhi yan, qi xiu ru lan* ("the utterances of people whose hearts are aligned are like the fragrance of orchids"). Also see *Kongzi jiayu*, part 6, where the idea is that one becomes a better person when one associates with virtuous people. There the words are *yu shanren ju, ru ru zhilan zhi shi* ("residing with virtuous people is like entering an orchid room").

12. *Shishuo xinyu*, 8:153 (Xu Zhen'ou 1984, 271).

13. That is, succeed in climbing the traditional ladder of imperially sponsored exams; passing these exams leads to high rank and office.

14. For the first, see *The Vanity of Flourishing Life*, chap. 10, 380, and the second, *Dream of Moon and Romance*, chap. 3, 17.

15. In *Dream of Moon and Romance*, Yangzhou of the 1840s did not have such lids (chap. 3, 17).

16. Chris Connery (Santa Cruz) and Bill O'Connor (North Haven) both suggested this interpretation to me.

17. Fragrant is *you wei*, also meaning pleasurable or flavorful.

18. Yuan Yi's poem is found in the poetry collection *Qingshiduo*, edited by Zhang Changling 1983, 1009. See also a poem collected in an 1876 Shanghai guidebook, Ge Yuanxu 1989, 62.

19. In his written report to the Royal Commission on Opium, Joseph Edkins rendered what a "Peking informant" described to him about the phenomenon of "lamp craving," that is, *tengyin* (in *pinyin, dengyin*). "Some smokers have what is called *tengyin* 'lamp craving.'" Some sleep soundly after smoking, some for brief intervals only,

these latter being the ones who have "lamp craving." "Smokers who have the *tengyin* may be seen to look at the lamp and doze for a few minutes with their eyes open and presenting a glazed appearance. If the lamp is removed or suddenly extinguished they wake immediately." See United Kingdom 1894, 5:248.

20. Bhabha refers to a similar notion of in-between cultural space that he calls "time-lag." In his words, time-lag is "an iterative, interrogative space produced in the interruptive overlap between symbol and sign, between synchronicity and caesura or seizure (not diachronicity)." A break occurs in the synchronic order of symbols, an order in which the ego found its former comfortable subjectivity. The disruption caused by colonialist violence is a disruption of that symbolic order both for itself and for the colonized other. He discusses time-lag elsewhere as well, e.g., Bhabha 1994, chaps. 9, 12.

21. For Coleridge and De Quincey, see Hayter 1988, 123–24, 199ff.

22. General William Mesny spent his time "largely with Chinese," dressed in Chinese clothing, and was once addicted to opium, as he all too laconically reports (United Kingdom 1894, 5:247).

23. "Associate" can also be "mix with, socialize with." These lines originate in a passage in the *Shishuo xinyu*, 9:35 (Xu Zhen'ou 1984, 284), in which Huan Wen asks Yin Hao, "How do you compare with me?" Yin replies, "I have socialized with myself for a long time. I'd rather just be me." "Opium Talk" only partially quotes these lines, which could also be translated: "Having [long] socialized with myself, I would rather be myself." "Long" only appears in the original lines. "Being haggard . . ." originates in the Tang classical tale, "Yingying zhuan," from a poem by Yingying at the very end after the lovers have already been separated.

24. See McMahon 1995, 136–37 and passim: "Of chief importance is that the man avoid intimate attachment to any of his wives." "Having multiple wives instead of just one or two is precisely for this reason then: to keep the man distanced by keeping the women diffused."

25. See no. 28 of "Opium Talk," in which he writes of how opium has erased his desire for a woman but how he still feels a "sense of a throb" that underlies the opium addiction. Then in no. 30 he writes of a somewhat successful attempt to "rekindle" his "appetites for food and sex," and of his regret that he had "reversed priorities" to such a degree and chosen opium over sex.

26. De Banville "acknowledges explicitly that to give oneself to cigarettes is 'to put one's unique concern into creating a desire that cannot be satisfied'" (Klein 1993, 45).

27. The question of Cocteau's homosexuality introduces another set of variables in terms of his social and gendered identity, but the metaphors of opium as spellbinding love object and of opium as emasculating force still apply. For Cocteau, the choice of love object is doubly troubled in that both his male lovers and his opium are "forbidden." Opium and homoerotic love are central in the mid–nineteenth century novel *Precious Mirror of Boy Actresses* (discussed in chapter 6).

28. See Shanghaishi wenshi guan 1988, 196–97.

29. Zhang's doctor may have been a medical missionary, most of whom regularly treated opium smokers. On methods of cure (e.g., sudden versus gradual withdrawal), see Howard 1998, 152ff. On the ultimate pessimism of medical missionaries in their hopes to cure opium smokers, see Howard 1998, 160–61.

Chapter Six

Eaten by Wild Dogs: Opium in Late Qing Fiction

FICTIONAL PORTRAYALS OF OPIUM SMOKING

Zhang Changjia's "Opium Talk" concentrates our focus on the individual smoker and his state of being in the great opium present. Let us return to the larger social scene that we saw in foreign descriptions of opium smoking, using sources written in Chinese, novels in particular. One outstanding example, Peng Yang'ou's 1909 *Souls from the Land of Darkness* (in Chinese *Heiji yuanhun)*, is comparable to "Opium Talk" in focusing solely on opium. The other Chinese sources I use–except poetry, which is far shorter in length–refer to opium only in passing.[1] Peng Yang'ou addresses one of the most insurmountable questions by attempting to tell why and how opium started and became so widespread in China. The novel recreates the history of opium smoking, starting with a fictional first addict and his son's invention of the opium pipe at the end of the Qianlong period (the late 1700s), and continues through five generations of this family and beyond to the late Qing days of industrialized Shanghai and what the author portrays as the pan-addiction that is the central cause of China's degeneration. In the last scene of the novel the ghost of a young wastrel, who died when attacked by wild dogs while resting destitute by the side of a road, returns to earth to steal opium. He is then caught and stabbed by hell runners who take him back to hell.

Peng Yang'ou writes at a time during the late Qing when the movement of opium prohibition linked with an emerging discourse on nationalism to effect a significant, though brief and far from thorough, decrease in opium production.[2] Many writers, leading figures, organizations, and publishing concerns, especially newspapers, united in the energetic condemnation of opium smoking.[3] Literature and eventually cinema joined the effort, along with Western missionaries and Western and Chinese medical experts.

Opium in many of these representations became the symbol of China's failure as a nation. Many Chinese people knew that foreigners commonly saw the Chinese as an addicted and a degenerate race (Su Zhiliang 1997, 199–200). The governments of the late Qing in its last few years and the Republic in its first few years responded with legislation and enforcement that, along with international treaties on narcotics control, resulted in a more successful effort at prohibition than ever before.

In taking opium as an essential problem of China, Peng Yang'ou puts the problem in narrative form and keeps the explicitly propagandizing voice to a relative minimum.[4] Many other Qing novels, both earlier and roughly contemporaneous, also contain stories and scenes of opium smoking: the early nineteenth-century *Tower of Elegant View* (*Yaguan lou,* c. 1820, the earliest to contain references to opium smoking); the midcentury novels *Dream of Moon and Romance* (*Fengyue meng,* 1848) and *Precious Mirror of Boy Actresses* (*Pinhua baojian,* 1849); and the late Qing *Flowers of Shanghai* (*Haishanghua liezhuan,* 1892), *Love among the Flower and Willow Girls* (*Hualiu shenqing zhuan,* 1895), and *The Vanity of Flourishing Life* (*Ershi zai fanhua meng,* 1907). None but *Love among the Flower and Willow Girls* strongly condemn opium,[5] and none pretend to as broad a scope on opium as Zhang's "Opium Talk" or Peng's *Souls in the Land of Darkness.*[6] Collectively these works represent the pervasive acceptance and commonality of opium, in effect demonstrating what it is like when the proverbial "everyone" is addicted. They also allow us to focus on areas that Euro-Western observers and Zhang Changjia and his friends either viewed more distantly or virtually ignored: (1) the common language of opium smokers and scenarios of their smoking together, (2) the criminal activity and conniving that pervaded the opium society, (3) the distinctions between those who smoked opium and those who abstained, and (4) addiction among women.

Drawing on the collective portrait presented by these novels and other sources, in this chapter I address the daily life of opium smoking–the arena in which opium works as a dynamic, integral presence in a society in which great numbers of people smoke opium. This so-called daily life of opium smokers never lives innocently, as if apart from the judgment that laments or condemns it. By this I mean that when Peng Yang'ou explains why and how so many Chinese came to smoke opium, he assumes the existence of culprits, both foreign and Chinese, who set this scourge in motion. Within this framework of culprit and scourge, he and other writers describe those who smoke anyway, that is, those who smoke despite the fact that a certain eye sees them as living wasted lives. While using their power as authors to administer poetic justice to their opium-smoking characters, these authors explain and motivate the characters, granting them, so to speak, the attractiveness of opium and their need to use it. These portrayals allow us to ask questions about such things as the occasions of opium consumption, the rituals and conventions that smokers observe, their motivations for and manner of smoking it (e.g., skillful versus clumsy), and the communities they belong to as well as relationships they are likely to form. Having read these works, we must also ask how opium functions between men and women in terms of their separate experiences of addiction. Fiction helps decenter the focus, which has so far been overwhelmingly on male smokers. They are the most visible to Western observers because of the traditional customs of female sequestration, and are more central in Chinese sources because of the predominance of both male smokers and writers. Fiction particularly enhances the discussion of opium smoking because it concentrates on scenes involving the use of opium in sexual and marital couplings that few other sources are as likely to address.

FICTION IN ITS GENERIC CONTEXT

Granted that fiction is useful because it enters domains that we might not see otherwise, it must also be recognized in light of its specific historic and generic features. Authors of vernacular fiction do not write about opium in an unabashedly positive manner. A contrasting instance is found in Shanghai guidebooks from the 1870s to the 1890s, which contain short passages boasting that Shanghai's opium halls are the cleanest and most exquisite in the world.[7] The authors of novels, however, seem to follow an unwritten agreement that indulgence in opium smoking is not something that should be portrayed in a worthy character. A consideration of fictional descriptions of sexual activity clarifies this point. From early on, the Qing government explicitly mandated what could and could not be written about, sex being one of the prohibited areas. Fictional works were frequently listed and banned if they violated these mandates. Many authors—almost all anonymous—wrote about sex anyway, did so in an unabashed manner, and did not hesitate to describe respectable characters having sex. Affirmative evocations of opium euphoria, on the other hand, only occur in short poems and passages in Zhang Changjia's "Opium Talk" and elsewhere. Even Zhang Changjia stops far short of merely foregrounding the opium euphoria, while the Shanghai guidebooks also contain passages about the ugly side of addiction.[8] My point is that if authors wrote favorably about sex and other prohibited topics anyway, they could also presumably have written similarly about opium. But they did so only in poetry. When it came to narrative, the collective assumption was that opium smoking was for less than heroic characters.[9] Those who were socially most respectable did not smoke opium. Nor did respectable characters smoke opium even for a while and then reform themselves.[10]

In general, fiction that reflected the epochal changes of the nineteenth century did not appear until the 1890s, when fiction underwent energetic and rapidly innovative transformations.[11] Opium in particular did not become part of an explicit political platform among fiction authors until those last two Qing decades. Only minor examples of anti-opium stances can be found in earlier works, such as the midcentury *Trace of Flowers and Moon* (*Huayue hen*) and *Tales of Romantic Heroes* (*Ernü yingxiong zhuan*), which I will discuss below. Authors throughout generally portrayed opium smoking as something degenerate, although in at least one case, *Flowers of Shanghai* (1892), the author portrayed opium in a more or less neutral way. He took no pains to condemn it in authorial asides or demonstrate its evils in some heavily weighted way.

What this shared generic sense means, regardless of period, is that in terms of character portrayal no one like Zhang Changjia appears. Virtuous and refined characters steeped in the classical tradition cannot be opium smokers, even in *Flowers of Shanghai*, nor can characters who are self-consciously modern and reformist. If we were to hypothesize a novel that treated opium more affirmatively, it would be one, I think, in which the opium smoker was in some way linked with the tradition of great drinkers in Chinese history such as Tao Qian or Li Bo. Such, at any rate, is the link suggested in the poetry of opium euphoria. The same logic applies in portrayals of sexual heroes in both Qing fiction and poetry. They are people of the finest learned and innate capacities, including sexual capacities. If my hypothesis is reasonable, it is because, compared with alcohol and sex, opium smoking was a latecomer, lacking tradition and canon. It was too entwined with the arrival of Western domination and loss of Chinese cultural integrity. As a result, it tended to become overdetermined as a causal and emblematic factor in China's "decline."

Another outstanding feature of these works has to do with their literary past, especially earlier Ming and Qing portrayals of the character types of the polygamous family that I briefly discussed in chapter 1. When, for example, the author of *Precious Mirror of Boy Actresses* engages in explicit depiction of sexual arousal and intercourse or of an operation on a venereally damaged penis, he cannot be read outside the context of an extremely large body of erotic literature containing similar locutions, clichés, paraphernalia, and even other close examinations of the failing or prevailing penis. The participants in such scenes will have been met in some form before: rich philanderers (sometimes handsome and sensitive, sometimes grotesque and brutish), sexy courtesans or concubines, and young male lovers. Particularly central is the wastrel, who in the last half century or more of Qing fiction adds a new feature to his makeup: he is an opium wastrel who in numerous portrayals, both fictional and otherwise, becomes an emblem of the failure and decline of Chinese culture as a whole. In numerous works from the early Qing up to the 1890s or so, his virtuous opposite is a man of classic countenance who is temperate in all tastes and indulgences, whether he is monogamous or polygamous. By the time a new core of authors appears in the very late Qing (about the last two decades), such a virtuous opposite has become less easy to portray.[12] The world of classical sensibility and the route itself of classical education have become anachronistic, and only some kind of thoroughgoing change is possible.

Along with this evolution in character portrayal goes a transformation of readership. New venues such as newspapers and literary magazines appeared in the last decades of the Qing. Authors and readers alike departed in varying degrees from traditional careers and formed or experimented with new interests, as can be seen in the great breadth of subject matter in late Qing fiction after the mid-1890s. Shanghai in particular was a place of intense innovation, as the publishing context of "Opium Talk" has already shown: the publishers Qian Zheng and Cai Erkang both followed nontraditional paths in journalism and translation in the modernizing city of Shanghai.[13]

In sum, the rough history of the works to be discussed is as follows: those up to about the middle of the Guangxu reign period (1875–1908) still portray the man and woman of classical self-sufficiency.[14] The late Qing works signal a shift. By this time, authors of novels have begun to assume a publicly proclaimed mission of mirroring the nation to itself and of engaging in a thoroughgoing castigation of the moral bankruptcy of China in those times. Peng Yang'ou's attempt to encapsulate the history of opium smoking reflects the thoroughgoing nature of this mission. In earlier works of the nineteenth century (including a few I will discuss below in which opium smoking is almost or completely absent), China has not yet been marked as terminally corrupt. Opium smoking may be widespread, but a virtuous and traditionally minded upper class still has the strength to lead China in a healthy (i.e., sober) and prevailing way. In late Qing fiction, however, social evils such as opium smoking can no longer be so easily overcome or overlooked. Thus, when Peng Yang'ou explains why Chinese people smoke opium, it is as if he is standing on ruins describing what went wrong. He declares that China is in mortal danger and that opium smoking is no trivial or epiphenomenal issue. Now everyone must look at it; no one is permitted to pretend it hardly exists.

THE HISTORY OF PAN-ADDICTION

Why Chinese People Smoke Opium

Souls from the Land of Darkness enacts in novelistic form the totalizing allegory of opium addiction that I introduced in chapter 1. That is, the author takes opium as a figure of the essential problems of China. The novel is a composite "portrait," which Peng refers to using the term for photograph, *xiaozhao* (photography being relatively new and highly popular in Shanghai and other urban centers of late Qing China; chap. 1, 110). As such a totalizing allegory, the novel tells the history of pan-addiction: the story of how the proverbial "everyone" became addicted.

Reasons for how and why such a habit began and spread can be structured as follows.

1. To smoke is fashionable. The narrator begins by saying that people found opium to be a good medicine that stimulated energy and cured colds, for example, and "therefore" it came to be called "the Western drug," *yangyao* (107).[15] Opium had been part of the Chinese pharmacopeia for centuries,[16] but in its novel smokable form took on another aspect and assumed new names. It soon went from being a marvelous new drug to becoming "fashionable" *(shimao).* Not to smoke it was considered "foolish and impractical" (chap. 1, 108).[17] Unfortunately, Peng continues, opium was only effective as a cure when used occasionally. Once a smoker "became addicted" *(chishangle yin),* the drug's good effects were lost (chap. 1, 108).[18]

2. In Peng's fable, the opium habit also spread because it was inherited. His addict progenitor, Wu Lian, experiments with this *yangyao* ("Western drug") that he hears of, drinks a liquid solution he makes of the extract, and becomes addicted in two months, although he does not yet know what addiction is. He dies from an overdose, thus proving the danger of consuming raw opium. His son keeps the opium and, after lengthy experimentation, invents the opium pipe and all its apparatus. From father to son or from mother through the womb to unborn child, as Peng later dramatizes, opium addiction thus passes from generation to generation. But the man who invented the opium pipe is the most blameworthy of all, he declares (chap. 3, 116).

3. Opium smoking was something one person urged on another. A new clerk at a local government office is left alone when everyone vanishes to smoke opium. Over time, in his boredom, he accepts the occasional offers of friends until he becomes addicted himself (chap. 21). Similarly a young man in *Dream of Moon and Romance* visits a brothel and takes a liking to an addicted prostitute. She offers him opium; he says he "doesn't know how" (chap. 7, 50). Many chapters later he "now also needs his several pipes a day" (chap. 16, 112). The same happens to the main male character in *Tower of Elegant View*: the prostitute takes out "a set of utensils," which to him are completely mysterious, but he smokes and "felt as though he'd entered an orchid chamber overwhelmingly sweet in aroma. A sudden surge of energy swept through his entire body" (chap. 8, 5b–6a).[19] A young wife in *Souls from the Land of Darkness* tries to keep her addiction secret from her husband, who finally finds out and becomes addicted himself. In keeping their addiction secret from his prohibitionist father, they ally themselves with his mother and get her addicted along with them (chap. 19).

4. Smoking opium quiets wastrels, shrews, and other troublesome or undesirable people. Parents prescribed opium to their spendthrift sons;[20] hus-

bands did so to their troublesome wives.[21] Wastrels and shrews came upon opium themselves and, as Zhang Changjia says of wastrels (no. 15), found a medicine made precisely for them. In the 1895 novel *Love among the Flower and Willow Girls*, the argument (which the book thematically opposes) is phrased in this way: "Isn't it better to smoke opium and preserve one's wealth rather than go to ruin because of money spent on prostitutes and gambling?" (chap. 28, 124). A proverb of those times had it that "As long as there is opium, the ruler need not fear disorder" *(yan busi, zhu buluan)*. A Chinese merchant testifying before the Royal Commission on Opium said that the rich like opium for their children who will thereby stay out of mischief (United Kingdom 1894, 5:187). In the same spirit, Peng Yang'ou portrays smokers against prohibition who say that the nation would be peaceful if everyone imitated them.

The logic of opium as a pacifier thus works from the perspective of the one who achieves the pacification of others by getting them addicted as well as the perspective of the one addicted who is eager to demonstrate his harmlessness to society. The pusher and the user briefly share the same goal, as we saw in William Hunter's statement about the pleasures of the opium trade in the pre-Treaty days at Canton. If we hypothesize Zhang Changjia's perspective on opium pacification, he might recall to everyone the formidable qualities of opium as indicated by words like "gun" for the shaft and "gate of struggle" for the opening of the pipe bowl. Instead of being a pacifier, opium wreaks violence as smokers scorch their lungs with fire, thus taking human evolution one step further in the brutalization of life. From an opposite point of view, however, Zhang quotes the poem of a friend: "Foreign ships from afar deliver their tribute of mud. / From such earthly flames we turn into immortals" (no. 58). We could interpret this to mean that the foreigner (pusher) only knows how to make money, while the opium smoker transcends such banalities to become a loose-robed immortal on earth, leaving the tight-clothed "Red Hairs" toiling in transactions.

Why Chinese smoked opium was not a question Zhang Changjia asked. It would be like asking why humans love sex or special delicacies. Peng Yang'ou delved into the pseudo-historical origins and social reasons for opium smoking with the twin goals of deracinating it and repurifying the Chinese people. By Peng's time, the notion of "Chinese people" had changed from twenty or thirty years before in that China's humiliation was now a topic of nationalistic significance. Reformers evoked a sense of national collectivity, which could provide for strong and concerted action. In this newly defined global sphere, opium smoking, along with practices like polygamy and bound feet, signified racial and cultural inferiority. The drive then arose to deny that these attributes of inferiority were fundamental to Chinese identity by treating them as if they were detachable and disposable.

Chinese Inventiveness

Opium as an agent of controlling other human beings begs the question of European complicity and Chinese gullibility. The view of many Chinese leaders, officials, and literati was that the British and other Western foreigners lured Chinese into opium in order to soften them and drain their wealth. Peng Yang'ou reacts to this idea with a satire suggesting that the Chinese actually prevailed in the face of European seduction. The Chinese were truly ingenious once they discovered the marvelous qualities of opium, he exclaims. Granted that Westerners made more money and thus outwitted the Chinese in this transaction, the Chinese nevertheless demonstrated "scientific" originality as they forged "new knowledge and new ideals" in their "discovery" of the unique method of consuming opium through the opium pipe (chap. 2, 111). Peng uses the newly adopted word "science" *(kexue)* to refer to Chinese inventiveness in what he proudly satirizes as one of the greatest failings of his fellow Chinese.[22] His satire suggests that China had the opium pipe instead of the telephone, or the opium pipe while someone else invented the car.[23]

Since the opium pipe was a unique, subtle invention, Peng creatively details the steps of experimentation in its development. Although he does not say as much, the all-important achievement was the liberation of opium from the tobacco-opium mixture in order to get the purest smokable extract possible. The problem, as Peng's story demonstrates, was that the taffy-like extract did not smoke well in the existing forms of pipes. Peng's fictional inventor first put opium in the bowl of a water pipe. But when he lit it, he could not get air through the mass of opium. One of the first moments of discovery occurred when a hole was poked in the bead of opium, thereby allowing air to pass through. Still, once lit, the melting opium dripped into the bowl and clogged it. Later, with a dry pipe, he was more successful, but the opium eventually stopped it up as well. Triumph finally arrived with the invention of the special bowl (shaped somewhat like a hollowed-out doorknob with a small opening in the outer shell) that retained the dross and clogged up less easily.

Peng's inventor also discovered the reclining position for smoking and the opium tray for utensils, which protected one's bed from being dirtied (chap. 2, 113–14). Filtration of opium both before and after smoking was another area of inventiveness, as was the refinement of the utensils. Different stores specialized in each item of the apparatus (chap. 3, 116–17). As Peng later relates, smokers also had to be resourceful when away from the secure nest of home or the opium den or hall, where they could go at regular intervals to pass their craving. Thus there was the homemade pipe for travelers, who used a crude piece of bamboo for the shaft and the shell of duck eggs for the lamp.[24] Along remote roads in Shanxi Province, people of both high and low ranks would lie by the road and smoke opium using these devices (chap. 17, 176). In another scene, Peng describes a candidate in the examination hall who hid his eggshell and pipe, the shaft of which was "made of rubber man- ufactured in the West" and could be folded up and concealed if necessary (chap. 19 185). The inventiveness of smokers is in fact proverbial. In his opium journal Cocteau writes of the "Annamites" in Marseilles, "where one smokes with implements calculated to confuse the police (a gas pipe, a sam- ple bottle of Benedictine with a hole in it, and a hat-pin)" (Cocteau 1996, 76).

In the social landscape of Peng's novel, the addict is everywhere, and is young, old, male, female, low, and high. Peng's method throughout is to cre- ate the most vivid portraits of the ridiculous extremes to which addiction makes one go. Everyone will become addicted because, as he says, "You know the nature of the Chinese: each follows the other in the same old rut until all go together to the dogs" (chap. 4, 120). In his anti-opium logic, the extreme will arrive when all are addicted, even the unborn baby. Everyone will be sent to the special level of hell for addicts, where they will suffer the worst agony before being forced to quit in one fell swoop. Then and only then will opium addiction be put to an end. In contrast to Zhang Changjia, Peng foregrounds only the negative and thus does what Zhang opposed thirty years before: totalize opium addiction into the essential problem of China.

In doing this Peng was like others of his times—Liang Qichao among the most prominent—who were proposing nothing less than a complete trans- formation of the Chinese mentality. Since the 1890s the idea had spread that China was an atrophied nation in need of rejuvenation. Opium prohibition- ism, which had existed in some form for over two centuries, found a new mandate as it was absorbed into this rhetoric of renewal. In Peng's joke, the Chinese had true genius but used it to invent the opium pipe. Farmers in In- dia earned a living planting opium; the English taxed and sold it and used the money to support their military, Peng writes. At the end of this line of transactions, the Chinese consumed the opium, "independently and on their own developing the science of opium consumption" (*chiyapian kexue*, chap. 2, 111). The mentality behind this effort needed complete extermination in the depths of hell.

THE EVERYDAY LIFE OF SMOKING

Everyone Addicted

In other novels, opium is similarly pervasive but functions in a contingent, not totalized, capacity. Most significantly, these novels collectively represent the daily life of opium smoking, including the satirical hyperboles of "everyone addicted" and the ordinary particulars of specialized terms or common knowledge and experience. What follows is a collection of examples with commentary of what these novels and other sources show it is like when the proverbial everyone is addicted, including scenes and dialogues from everyday smokers as these novels present them.

The "proverbial everyone," as I have coined it, includes two types of people whom the prohibitionist deems should not be addicted: men in positions of responsibility and dignity, on the one hand, and mothers and children on the other. The rich addict Wu Rui'an (fourth-generation descendant of the opium pipe progenitor), for example, buys the post of county magistrate and one day in his opium oblivion mistakenly burns an important official document. In alarm he sends for his secretary, who is in his own room "passing his opium craving" *(guo yin)*. He takes so long that Wu finally goes there himself. His secretary's advice is to confess, resign, and go back home (chap. 7, 132).

All work of local government is delayed, according to Peng, because everyone from the top down smokes opium. Since smokers sleep late, anyone with business at the *yamen* (the local government office) can only go late in the day (as Reverend Arthur Moule also discovered a few decades before).[25] When sent on missions, *yamen* runners procrastinate or neglect their duties while they stop off to smoke opium. They take advantage of their connections with the *yamen* to smoke in dens without paying or paying less than the designated price (chap. 23). Even teachers of young pupils smoke. One of them reclines in front of his class, takes a draw of opium, tells a boy to recite, takes another draw, hits this one, scolds that one, then finally gets up to hit at them all with his opium pipe (chap. 23, 206). When people smoke with such little restraint, as Peng depicts it, even the rats become addicted. One day a stench emerges from a deceased addict's opium room. His family then discovers a mass of dead rats that had become addicted and then died when they ran out of opium (chap. 13). However contrived and hyperbolic Peng's portrayals may seem, the element of truth would be recognized by readers who had examples of their own. In a poem from the mid-nineteenth century *The Bell of Qing Poetry* (*Qingshiduo*), rats in the rafters sniff opium smoke every time the smoker lights his pipe; the next morning the smoker finds rats fallen onto the floor.[26] In reference to French-occupied Annam, Cocteau wrote of the "dogs and monkeys that became addicted like their masters." "All animals," he said, "are charmed by opium. Addicts in the colonies know the danger of this bait for wild beasts and reptiles" (Cocteau 1996, 75).

The harmful effects of opium on fertility and on both born and unborn children was a common point among observers of opium smoking. Reverend Moule quoted a doctor at the Mission Hospital in Ningpo: "Opium-smokers beget few and unhealthy children."[27] A passage in the 1895 anti-opium novel *Love among the Flower and Willow Girls* declares that the bones of the offspring of opium smokers are "all soft" (chap. 20, 84). The same novel also portrays a man who is unable to beget because of his heavy addiction (chap. 25). In *Souls from the Land of Darkness*, one man tells another of the harmful effects of starting opium too early in life: the body will fail to develop properly and one will be unable to have children. Babies born to addicted mothers will be addicted too, the man warns, and will suffer from craving unless someone blows smoke over their faces for them to inhale (chap. 17, 174). The man who is told these things returns home to find his new baby daughter addicted at birth. Someone puffs opium at the baby, who finally stops crying, which makes everyone laugh with great mirth (chap. 18, 180). In another late Qing novel, *The Vanity of Flourishing Life*, a woman watching opera at home while smoking opium feels a pain and without warning or foreknowledge suddenly finds herself having a baby (chap. 15).

The implication in these portrayals is that it is especially dangerous for women and children to become addicts. The male wastrel is bad enough, but when the woman becomes a wastrel, the rupture of the social fabric is complete. Peng's demonstration of pan-addiction culminates at the end of the novel, when he suggests that everyone in China will have to become addicted, at which point "God" will create a special hell to punish them all (chap. 24, 211). When these ghosts are reborn, they will no longer be addicts and will thus eliminate the possibility that anyone will become one again. Again, the only solution is complete eradication.

The Community and Language of Opium Smokers

Many opium smokers employed common terms, used common objects, and had certain smoking experiences in common as well. Descriptions of these commonalities need to be compared and cross-referenced before specialized language, methods of smoking, and objects can be understood. Especially in regard to highly crafted paraphernalia, the terminology assumes either personal expertise or familiarity on the part of the reader. I have concentrated on deciphering the process of smoking but have not gone into the connoisseurship of paraphernalia, which except for drawings, photos, and occasional basic utensils, I have not been able to examine.

The main designation for "smoking opium" in Chinese is *chi yan*, to "consume" or "eat smoke," which can also refer to someone smoking tobacco. Simply saying "he or she is a smoker," *ta shi ge chi yande*, most likely signifies that the person is a smoker of opium, not tobacco, although not necessarily a deep addict. If there is a need for clarity, someone might add, "he or she smokes the 'big' smoke," *ta chi dayan*. "Big smoke" always means opium. "To inhale" is the word *xi*, with other words also appearing, for example, *chou*, "draw" or "suck" (*Tower of Elegant View*, chap. 8, 5b), *chui*, "blow" (*Dream of Moon and Romance*, chap. 3, 17), and *xiu*, "sniff" or "smell" (*Dream of Moon and Romance*, chap. 3, 17). Another common way to refer to the act of smoking is *guo yin*, to "get through," "pass," or "satisfy one's craving." In mid- to late-twentieth-century Chinese this term lost its opium connotation, now usually meaning to get a big charge out of doing something or to enjoy something immensely. Someone who has already smoked his or her fill and has passed from craving to relief might say to someone else: "I have satisfied my craving," *wo guoguo yin le* (*Dream of Moon and Romance*, chap. 7, 42). Someone who smokes in advance of a long day during which opium will be unavailable "must make sure to satisfy the craving to extra repletion," *yin xu guo ge shifen zu*, as does a young bride early on her wedding day in *Souls from the Land of Darkness*. Her female servants help her smoke two "guns" at once—two pipes set up side by side—in order to consume as much opium as possible in a short amount of time (chap. 9, 138–40).

When "opium craving comes on," *yanyin laile*, a smoker must satisfy it in order to avoid pain and discomfort. A man whose craving has come on arrives at a brothel that he frequents and asks someone to "hurry light a lamp and let me pass my craving" (*Dream of Moon and Romance*, chap. 11, 79). If there is no time to smoke, and a smoker is afraid of later "breaking out with craving," *yin fa*, then like a male character in *Souls from the Land of Darkness* he might take some "raw opium," *shengyan*, and mix it in hot water; this is called "opium extract broth," *yan'gaotang* (chaps. 11–12, 150). During the wedding day, the young bride's servants in *Souls from the Land of Darkness* slip her opium pellets, *yanpao*—raw opium cooked and rolled into a round pill-like form ready to smoke—or, in this case, directly swallow if necessary (chap. 9, 139). The man in jail in *Dream of Moon and Romance* has a friend who brings him opium pellets that the friend places in boiled water, stirs in with his finger, and gives to the prisoner to drink (chap. 24, 168).[28]

The pellets do not necessarily relieve one's craving. An addict in *Love among the Flower and Willow Girls* is about to enter the cell in which he will take the civil service exams. Because there is too much wind, he can't get his pipe lit well enough to smoke it. Then he, like others around him, begins "swallowing pellets" *(tun pao)* but feels no better. During the exams he resorts to "swallowing extract" *(tun gao)* without tea or water to wash it down. *Pao* in this case refers to opium that has been cooked and prepared as pellets; *gao* is opium in the taffy-like consistency the smoker buys before cooking it. The man keeps swallowing *gao* until his tongue feels "as if covered with scales." Still unrelieved, he swallows more until he begins "writing dream talk"; then his feet feel "as if he were stepping on cotton and his whole body began to heat up." At last he leaves the exam cell, but just as he is about to smoke his pipe alongside other examinee-addicts, he drops his opium canister and it breaks on the urine-soaked ground where other examinees have been relieving themselves. He smokes the spilled opium anyway and becomes nauseated from the stench of urine transmitted into the opium (chap. 5, 18–19).[29] His desperation is due to his fear of *tuo yin*—having a severe case of craving, like the one a man experiences later in the book when his wife must blow opium into his mouth because he is too weak to smoke himself (chap. 5, 19; chap. 13, 52).

Smokers typically recline when they smoke, facing one another on either side of the lamp, that is, "passing their craving on either side of the gun," *dui qiang guo yin.* Style and skill are crucial in determining who is the master smoker. In a scene in *Dream of Moon and Romance* an experienced smoker teaches an inexperienced one, a young dandy who is interested in new sensations. The process goes like this:

> Wu Zhen twisted off the lid of the opium canister and placed it in the tray, then invited everyone to smoke. . . . Lying on the right side of the *kang* with Lu Shu . . . on the left, he dipped the iron needle into the opium in the canister and began cooking it over the flame of the lamp. When the opium swelled and drooped about an inch, he twirled it on the needle and rolled it into a ball against the second finger of his left hand. He gathered more opium onto this bit from the opium box, cooked it, and rolled it into another ball, repeating this process several times until he had the right size opium bead. Taking the pipe, he brought it near the flame and fixed the bead into the cavity of the bowl, fitting it there snugly with his finger. Then he took the needle and pierced a hole through the opium, still holding it near the lamp. He took the first turn to inhale, then wiped off the mouthpiece and handed the pipe to Lu Shu. (chap. 3, 17)

A novice like Lu Shu lacks the feel for drawing in the smoke. With Wu Zhen holding the base of the pipe, Lu places his mouth over the mouthpiece and takes a draw but inhales *(xiu)* so strongly that the vent hole clogs up. They repeat the process of recooking the opium and having Lu try to inhale again until "they finally finished smoking this one pipe." When a clumsy smoker in *Precious Mirror of Boy Actresses* inhales *(chou)*, "saliva drooled from his mouth and dripped down the side of the pipe. He wiped his mouth with his fur sleeve and tried again to inhale, but only succeeded in clogging up the pipe." After a serving boy cleans the pipe for him, the man "took the opium needle and clumsily dipped up some opium, but only managed to burn a hole in his sleeve, which made everyone burst out laughing" (chap. 34, 424).[30]

An expert smoker in *Precious Mirror of Boy Actresses*, Xi Shiyi, himself a trader in imported opium, has consummate technique, as the following passage shows. He is known as someone with a "heavy opium addiction," *shi ge yapian dayin*, who smokes one to two *liang* a day—ten to twenty mace. Because he likes the strong Bengal opium *(heitu)*, the prostitutes in the brothel he visits do not want to smoke with him. "Completely overcome" *(zuidaole)* by the stronger type, they only like the milder Malwa opium *(baitu)*. He finally finds a woman named Juhua who doesn't mind smoking his kind of opium, although she smokes in lesser amounts.

This Xi Shiyi fellow liked to take big long draws when he smoked. As Juhua cooked the opium for him, she started with too tiny a bit for one draw and had to go to six times that amount before she had it just right. But she was still an expert at preparing opium. She knew just the right balance between overcooking and undercooking it. Xi Shiyi especially liked what was known as the "opium noodle," for which he took a needleful of opium and cooked it evenly all around until he could draw it out in strings of about five inches. He fixed the bead around the smoke hole and sucked it all in with one long draw, then closed his mouth tightly and didn't let the slightest bit out. This was his proudest and most consummate skill. (chap. 18, 231–32)

The method of smoking "opium noodle" *(miantiaoyan)* is portrayed with greater detail in a scene from *Souls from the Land of Darkness* in which an old male habitué of opium dens demonstrates his skill to a younger addict:

Stretching out his hand he took an opium needle, scooped up a large globule of opium and began cooking it. "My, you have fine opium. See how far it draws out when you cook it, a good five inches. Say, do you know how to smoke 'opium noodle'? Let me show you." He cooked and rolled it twice more until he got it to string out even more. Next he picked up the pipe and with a circular motion took this noodle-like string of opium and set it around the smoke hole like the mound of a cow pie, which he smoked all up in one long draw. (chap. 19, 187)

Peng Yang'ou evokes a seeming commonplace of opium dens: the role of the elder smoker who advises the younger. The man demonstrating the technique of "opium noodle" is nicknamed Baixiao, literally, "Knows Everything." He spends his time going from den to den and other places gathering news and gossip that he divulges to those who share their opium with him. Before supplying the younger man with the desired information, the elder smokes several pipes of opium. After finishing the young man's purchase and seeing that the latter now ignores him, he arises and "cheerily ambled away, quite pleased with himself" (chap. 19, 187). In another chapter of *Souls from the Land of Darkness*, a monk smoker lists the benefits of going to opium dens: "1) to relieve boredom, 2) to hear news, and 3) with so many smoking friends you never get lonely. Moreover, if you're having some trouble or difficulty, you can search out older smokers in the dens who can help you figure out some plan" (chap. 13, 154). These so-called lawyers, he continues, all get their leads from associating with people in the opium dens.[31]

Zhang Changjia does not mention opium dens and only speaks of meeting his opium friends more privately. The men portrayed in *Precious Mirror of Boy Actresses* mainly smoke together in their homes, but also in a monk-addict's apartments or in a special room adjoining a gourmet restaurant. Both exquisitely and miserably furnished opium dens existed (the better ones can be called "halls"), some attached to or combined with other enterprises, some relatively permanent, others mobile as they located themselves wherever they could to accommodate smokers on the road, for instance, or to avoid official harassment. Zhang Changjia's declaration that smoking is better in solitude or selected company than in haphazard groups may reflect a distaste for vulgar opium dens, but it may also have to do with factors he hardly mentions: the risks attending the semilegal and morally condemned status of opium smoking and the fact that such risks increased in the mixed company of some opium dens. Again, he writes his "Opium Talk" as living proof of the virtuous use of opium, although his virtue is not quite as good as flowers and trees blooming in spring. Avoidance of dens notwithstanding, poems and digressions on the experience of opium smoking include advice to younger smokers and exchanges of information and observations with other smokers of all ages. In between digressions one goes back to chores in the other world of standing up and walking.

Extortion and Conniving

Both the periodic enforcement of prohibitions against smoking and the general condemnation of opium production and use created a world in which smokers were liable to be pressured about indulging in an officially condemned yet widely available drug. Smokers were subject to threats and loss for which they had little or no recourse to legal protection. People could extort them by threatening to turn them in for smoking opium. If smokers were rich and powerful, they were less subject to the petty extortionists who were everywhere, but even they were cheated or robbed at many junctures both inside and outside their households. For these wealthy smokers, the deception started in the household, as servants took advantage of a master's opium state of mind to gain favors or steal money and property. Cases like these demonstrate how differently smokers behaved depending on social status. Servants and prostitutes also smoked opium, for example, but did not lose sight of advantages to be gained from smokers of higher status.

A rich addict in *Tower of Elegant View* (c. 1820) has a special building constructed in which to enjoy opium smoking. The builders overcharge him, and the handsome boy servants he hires, "knowing of his addiction to opium" (chap. 9, 5b, 6a), serve him his opium in order to turn his attention to themselves instead of his wives. In *Precious Mirror of Boy Actresses*, visitors who insist on seeing the famous boy actor, Qinyan, are turned away by the boy's owner-manager, at which point the visitors break in, take the manager's opium pipe, and threaten to turn him in to authorities (chap. 16). The same manager, Cao Changqing, later directs his boy servants (also dressed as *xianggong*, "female impersonators") to divert a vulgar but rich opium addict who wants to see the famous boy actor. Here, as in other scenes when boys serve opium to men, they climb into the men's laps, hug them, and share draws on the opium pipe (chap. 27, 337). In another chapter, a boy persuades a young man to part with a valuable bracelet by engaging in a lengthy seduction: the boy passes liquor from his mouth into the man's (a custom practiced between what are portrayed as vulgar boys and men in *Precious Mirror of Boy Actresses* and also described in brothel scenes between men and women in other novels), then massages the man and has him lie down to smoke opium, which he likewise serves to him by passing smoke into the man's mouth. After more hugging and rubbing, the boy succeeds in obtaining the bracelet (chap. 51, 652–53, 22b).

Besides servants and opium servers who take advantage of their masters and clients, others obtain money and opium for themselves by searching out better-off addicts whom they cheat and blackmail. In *Souls from the Land of Darkness*, Peng Yang'ou writes of a kind of "lawyer" or "pettifogger" *(songshi)*[32] who, himself a smoker, is in cahoots with *yamen* runners and owners of opium dens in which he targets rich addicts whose wealth he contrives to manage. He pretends to protect his clients and helps them sue those who cheated them, all along appropriating large amounts of the rich addicts' money (chap. 13, 157–58). This cheat is a more sophisticated version of the kind Walter Medhurst described in the 1840s as "vagabonds" and "rascals" who "are frequently to be met with, wandering about the country, who, under pretence of searching for smuggled opium, require travellers to open their baggage." After learning what the travelers have, they plot either to rob them or extort them "by the threat of bringing them before the mandarins" (Medhurst 1850, 22).

Smokers may be robbed of their opium by people who either resell it or want it for themselves. In *Souls from the Land of Darkness* a heavily addicted young bride secretly brings to her husband's household a large store of fine opium that is stolen one night. Since opium is her "life" and she cannot expect her husband's family to buy her more, she must have it back (chap. 10, 142). After a lengthy investigation, during which both the robbers and minor *yamen* officials and runners smoke and appropriate her opium, she and her husband pay a bribe to obtain less than half of the original amount back (chap. 8).[33]

Another category of exploitation is the extortion of money from brothel keepers, prostitutes, and their customers. The novel *Dream of Moon and Romance* contains detailed enactments of this type of opium crime, the perpetrators resembling the lawyers and vagabonds just mentioned. Opium addicts like the so-called lawyers in *Souls from the Land of Darkness* approach a brothel keeper and ask for a loan or demand money to pay an opium debt, are refused, and later contrive a lawsuit. To prevent this, the brothel keeper must pay a greater amount than was originally sought. The prostitutes must give up more than the usual portion of their earnings to meet the extortioner's demands. The brothel keeper, moreover, must secure his own coterie of addict friends who have connections in local *yamen*s or know people who know the ones suing. One of these troublemakers in *Dream of Moon and Romance* is a heavily addicted young student. Having spent all his money on opium, he now relies on extortion to maintain his supply, exacting "four silver dollars from each brothel" (chap. 9, 62–63).

Periodic edicts against opium also trouble the smoker, including a man in *Dream of Moon and Romance* whose enemy deliberately frames him.[34] The enemy colludes with a *yamen* runner, who arrests the man and puts him in jail, a particularly awful place for an addict if there is no access to opium (chap. 23). The man's friends eventually bribe the jailer with opium, however, and take opium solution to the prisoner, to whom the drink is like "sweet dew, which he drained in three short gulps" (chap. 24, 168). The author of *Dream of Moon and Romance* describes extortion and frame-ups in detail, demonstrating his own familiarity with such practices and the network of conniving, and presuming that readers would be familiar as well. In an actual recorded example (1831), a cook colluded with two ward runners and a local constable to blackmail the cook's opium smoking master for 600 taels; other cases like this were common throughout the nineteenth and twentieth centuries (Spence 1992, 243–45).

THOSE WHO DID NOT SMOKE

The Respectable Class

If opium smokers were in some sense a race, who did not blend with this race? How were people marked or not marked as opium smokers? As numerous Chinese and Western observers affirmed, opium smokers included people of all levels. Yet not everyone smoked, and those who did not smoke also included people of all levels, especially women. At the extreme, the abstainer moved in a completely different social sphere, associating if possible with virtually no one who smoked. In portraying such people, nineteenth-century novels in some cases nearly excluded the existence of opium smoking. What was this non-opium way of life like in light of its contiguity with its opposite? How, where, and by whom were the lines drawn between those who smoked and those who did not?

Western and Chinese observers offered wildly varying estimates of how many Chinese had the opium habit, a number and percentage which, along with population growth, increased through the nineteenth century and into the twentieth.[35] Among some groups (e.g., coolies and prostitutes) and in some areas of China (e.g., Shanxi or Gansu), the percentages seemed very high, according to Chinese estimates, up to 80 percent of men in the last quarter of the nineteenth century (Spence 1992, 237–38). Others, whether

Western or Chinese, gave from about 20 percent to 40 percent of men in the 1890s, and usually estimated women smokers to be far fewer (e.g., 1 percent).[36] James Legge and William Lockhart gave an even lower estimate, 10 percent of men overall in the 1890s.[37] Many admitted that all estimates were necessarily imprecise and that smokers were not at all uniform: some smoked heavily, others hardly at all; some smoked for a certain period and purpose, then later no more. Those who opposed opium, moreover, might have wanted estimates higher. Those who were not so distressed saw high numbers as well but argued that moderation was the rule. Perhaps they wanted to see the continuation of the system that generated such large revenue from opium production, transport, taxation, and sale (or could see little alternative to that system). All agreed that the numbers of nonsmokers or rare smokers was very high—higher than the total of regular smokers—however these latter were defined in terms of extent of use.

In the social universe of nineteenth- and early-twentieth-century fiction, as I previously mentioned, no one like Zhang Changjia or his friends appears whom I have yet found. No refined, upper-class characters smoke opium. This fact matches what James Legge said to the Royal Commission on Opium in September 1893, "there [is] no evil so much deplored by the respectable classes of people as this habit."[38] These nonsmokers, moreover, tend to move in a social sphere in which no one else smokes, including household servants and nonliterati friends. Such is the case in all the novels mentioned so far and in novels in which opium hardly figures at all, for example, *The Trace of Flowers and Moon* (*Huayue hen*, preface 1858, with the last chapters probably completed in the 1860s), *Tales of Romantic Heroes* (*Ernü yingxiong zhuan*, first published in 1878, probably begun in the 1850s), and *Dream of Courtesan Chambers* (*Qinglou meng*, c. 1878). Like *Dream of Moon and Romance* and *Precious Mirror of Boy Actresses*, these three novels precede the period of rapid and intense transformation that fiction underwent in the last decades of the Qing. Characters of classical sensibilities still prevail in these novels, and authors still write with minimal registration of the effects of such things as the Opium War and the situation of a China repeatedly forced to concede territory and rights to Western powers. The relative lack of reference to opium smoking, however, is not necessarily an avoidance of historical realities. *The Trace of Flowers and Moon* is significantly marked by the disruption of the Taiping Rebellion.[39] All three can be read as radical, even heroic, enactments of the refusal to be perturbed by the opium evil and to be dislodged and depressed by foreign encroachment. Such heroism seems overly fantastic in retrospect, especially in contrast to numerous late Qing novels, but in its own context represents a devoted attempt to extend the world of classical themes and sensibilities.

If anyone smokes in these three works, it is a vulgar, villainous character or else someone who is portrayed as unfortunate and fallen. In the other novels I have already cited, smokers play much greater roles and include decadent members of the literati, prostitutes, wealthy merchants, their male and female family members, government clerks or officials (i.e., those who bought their posts instead of earning them through meritorious perform-ances in the civil exams), or professionals or other associates of Beijing opera. However, a refined or pure member of any of these or other non-literati groups, especially the courtesan or the boy actress, may also be an ab-stainer like the literatus.

An example of the villainous smoker appears in *The Trace of Flowers and Moon*, in which the brothel madam Niu is an addict "who lies in bed all day" passing her craving but holds on as tightly as she can to her property and moneymaker, the courtesan Qiuhen (chap. 24, 202). The madam later dies in a fire started when she leaves an article of clothing too close to her opium lamp (chap. 44, 368). She is one of two addicts portrayed in the book, the other of whom is a courtesan who later reforms by quitting opium and join-ing the effort to suppress the Taiping Rebellion. The courtesan Qiuhen's vain hope is that her literatus-lover will rescue her from prostitution. Like him, she is an absolute abstainer and writes for him a preface to a proposed set of poems on the scourge of opium (chap. 31, 270–71). She knows, as she writes, that "virtuous" women sometimes smoke opium, but a great number of prostitutes typically do. She thus distinguishes herself as an exception.

Like *The Trace of Flowers and Moon*, the *Dream of Courtesan Chambers* is also about sensitive literati and their love affairs with talented courtesans. Opium appears in at least two instances in this novel: when the hero Yixiang dis-plays his special hatred for a villainous opium addict (chap. 8, 53), and when one of the courtesans he loves, Aiqing, swallows opium in an attempted sui-cide.[40] Yixiang and Aiqing are significant for what they are not: opium ad-dicts, the male of whom is a wastrel who spends all he has on prostitutes, the female of whom smokes because that is the way of prostitutes in this period, as Qiuhen wrote in *The Trace of Flowers and Moon*. But opium is prominent enough in their lives for Aiqing to swallow it to commit suicide when forced into a hopeless situation,[41] and for Yixiang to recognize the odor of opium that issues from her nostrils after she loses consciousness.

Other than these minor episodes of opium involvement, these two novels are virtually devoid of opium smoking.[42] The same is true of *Tales of Roman-tic Heroes*, which portrays people from city and country of both heroic and vil-lainous character. Opium appears tangentially in an exchange between an un-justly cashiered official, An Xuehai, and an elderly and illiterate countryman, Deng Zhenbiao, who was formerly a strongman and bodyguard for travelers and transported goods. At eighty-seven, Deng is a vigorous and sometimes temperamental elder who commands respect from even a member of the ed-ucated class like An Xuehai, who seeks a favor of him. In order to meet Deng's approval and win his cooperation, An visits him. When offered tea, he asks instead for something else that he refrains from mentioning and "fears" Deng may not have. Deng "looked at him in consternation, 'You don't possibly mean that someone like you smokes opium, do you?' To which An replied, 'Nothing of the sort. What I like more than anything in life is a sip of Shaoxing wine. Would you by chance have some, dear sir'" (chap. 15, 283). As An had previously been told, wine is precisely the way to Deng's heart. After they begin to drink, An is able to enlist Deng's help. Opium appears obliquely in one other scene, which features the activities at a temple fair. The many stalls selling goods or services include one selling the tool for scooping out opium extract. At this, An Xuehai does not even raise his head but scurries past without looking (chap. 38, 926).

Tales of Romantic Heroes offers the example of nonsmokers of both moral and physical purity. An Xuehai is the traditional instance of the Confucian exemplar, although even he says of himself that he is too "stiff and impractical" (chap. 13, 236). The uneducated but genuine countryman Deng is an upright man who can still fight and procreate: at his advanced age he takes a concubine who soon gives birth to healthy twins. Although anti-opium sentiment is not a major theme, these examples of true virtue are the author's stand-ins for what the world would be without opium. His replacements of opium are liquor and tobacco, the former of which is the hallowed favorite from early times, the latter a recent introduction which, though opposed at first by Chinese rulers, finally became a staple.[43] Tobacco appears throughout the novel as a custom among both gentry and commoner, virtuous and villainous, male and female. An Xuehai himself, however, only likes liquor. He declines to smoke several times when he is offered tobacco, including when he first drinks with Old Deng, who is also a nonsmoker. Deng's habit is to roll "iron balls" in his hand, *tieqiu*, a custom of self-styled hardy male elders. Liquor is what the author promotes as the choice of the truly wholesome and virtuous man.

The Use of Tobacco in *Tales of Romantic Heroes*

Tales of Romantic Heroes can in general be read as a purified correction of earlier novels featuring characters who indulged in nonmarital sex (explicitly described), women who were jealous and shrewish, and men who were irresponsible and philandering.[44] Though it is hardly mentioned, opium is also corrected in this novel. Tobacco, moreover, is a highly visible and recurrent item that at times serves as a possible metonym for opium. In this case, the metonymy indicates both a good and bad stand-in. In other words, tobacco is sometimes a decent replacement or alternate custom; at other times it represents a filthy habit indulged in by villainous or lowly characters. Either way, tobacco smoking was extremely common in Wen Kang's time and is entirely appropriate in his fictional representations.

Scenes in which tobacco could almost be a substitute for opium include the young hero, An Ji, being offered a dirty public pipe at a travelers' inn (chap. 4, 72); a vulgar and shady woman squatting on a stool as she noisily smokes her pipe (chap. 7, 134); an old pedant smoking a filthy pipe that he never cleans, always using old ash to mix with fresh tobacco (chap. 37, 878); or a commoner woman at the temple fair (who looks like she could also be a prostitute) with a pipe hanging from her mouth (chap. 37, 922).

These few scenes contrast with the many in which tobacco smoking is a custom in the daily life of the central "virtuous" characters. A mother and daughter smoke after a meal, each using her own tobacco pouch and pipe (chap. 9, 174); women smoke and talk together on the *kang* (a heated brick bed), An Xuehai's wife among them (chap. 20, 412); and when guests arrive, "it goes without saying," hosts serve them tea and tobacco (e.g., chap. 24, 512). Tobacco smoking is also part of serious situations. During an important mission of persuasion, for instance, while her daughter does the talking, a mother sits alongside smoking her pipe with a worried look on her face (chap. 26, 555). When the hero An Ji's two wives are unhappy with his overly playful behavior, one wife sits silently smoking, the smoke issuing from her nostrils as she wears a knowing smile on her face. Meanwhile, the other wife, Thirteenth Sister, who is a nonsmoker, cleverly prepares to put the hero in his place (chap. 30, 666). At another time, an anxious young maid smokes alone as she leans against a door frame with one foot resting on the raised divide at the door's threshold (chap. 40, 1013). She is about to be given as concubine to An Ji, who is to be sent to a distant post. She would be honored to be his concubine, but, not yet knowing what will happen, she feels uneasy and at a loss, comfortable with neither lying down nor sitting.

Again, the prominent men of the novel, especially An Xuehai, his son An Ji, and Old Deng, do not smoke, nor does the main female heroine and woman warrior, Thirteenth Sister, who abstains from drink as well. Other women and men, both gentry and commoner, smoke tobacco; in one instance, the guards at the examination hall take snuff (chap. 34, 789). Other novels roughly reproduce this division by class, but with upper-class women tending to abstain from tobacco as well.[45] Tobacco parallels opium, but it is considered safer and more proper, and in the case of *Tales of Romantic Heroes* serves by default as a corrective to opium.[46] Parallel to but better than opium, however, tobacco is still somewhat dirty, in some cases filthy. As especially seen in *Tales of Romantic Heroes*, nonsmokers are the purest and highest in the social hierarchy. They are the good officials, the righteous strongman, and the woman warrior who, though she eventually becomes wife and mother, still retains features of her original superchastity.[47] She never fully joins the crowd of women smokers, who include both her co-wife, her co-wife's mother, and her mother-in-law.

Smokers and Nonsmokers in *Precious Mirror of Boy Actresses*

Precious Mirror of Boy Actresses does not draw the line between virtuous and villainous as clearly as *Tales of Romantic Heroes*, but the literati who do not smoke opium form a distinct group with only one area in which they cross into a lower class. The young men socialize with boys who are female impersonators in Beijing opera. Association with such lowly people is something that the strictest households would normally forbid their sons, who should be gearing themselves for the civil exams. These young men, however, have their special boy actress friends and at the same time prepare for and take the exams. The boy actresses in *Precious Mirror* share the refined sensibilities of their literati patrons and are likewise absolute abstainers. However, the owner and manager of the most famous boy actress is an opium smoker, as are some of the boy servants the manager employs. As for the women of the novel, none related to the literati males smoke, but as will be seen below prostitutes and a concubine of Xi Shiyi, the most profligate smoker in the book, smoke opium by themselves and with others, both male and female.

The nonsmoking literati who live in households devoid of opium smoking sometimes cross paths or associate with other men who in separate settings gather with friends to smoke. The literati nonsmokers do not consider smoking; they want to avoid even the smell of opium, which makes them feel "overcome" (chap. 50, 636). When together, these young men drink alcohol and chant poetry; if they drink excessively, they take a special herbal pill that reverses the effects of intoxication.

The following situation demonstrates the clean divide in this novel by which all opium smokers are in some way tainted because of their status, occupation, and moral behavior. The key character is the opportunistic and at times unscrupulous young Wei Pincai, who is a lesser peer of the main hero and handsome literatus, Mei Ziyu. Wei likes to climb the social ladder and thus seeks employment as secretary to a wealthy official's son, Hua Guangsu, who spends his days in pleasurable but refined pursuits with his wife, maids, friends, and troupes of boy actresses. No opium smoking occurs in Hua's household, he being a nonsmoker himself. When Hua discovers the famous boy actress Qinyan, he wants to acquire him for the private ring of talent that he houses in his palatial compound. He sends Wei Pincai as go-between to pressure Qinyan's owner, the opium smoker Cao Changqing, to release Qinyan to Hua Guangsu. When Wei Pincai appears at Cao Changqing's home, Cao at first judges Wei Pincai to be "someone of no great importance." But when he learns that Wei works for Hua Guangsu, one of the greatest patrons of boy opera singers in Beijing, Cao Changqing transforms himself into a gracious and fawning host who, after serving tea, brings out the opium lamp. With this gesture of hospitality, the visit takes on a new quality of engagement and duration as he now asks Wei to lie down and smoke. Wei declares that he is still a novice and does not know how to light the pipe, at which point Changqing lights it and hands it to Wei, who "takes a draw" but then hands the pipe back, saying, "I am an outsider to this art; pardon me if I don't return the favor." Wei finally tells him the purpose of his visit, at which point Changqing becomes agitated because he does not want to part with such a profitable talent as Qinyan, although he also knows that Hua is powerful and insistent. As Wei presses harder, Changqing "takes a dozen or more draws of the pipe" and continues vainly trying to fend Wei off (chap. 26, 322–23). Eventually, through underhanded means unknown to Hua Guangsu, Wei further pressures and frightens Changqing and finally brings about Qinyan's transfer into Hua's household.

Opium in this scene is something a host offers to a respected guest, possibly loading and lighting the pipe, whether or not the other is a novice. Wei Pincai may or may not be a true novice. In this and other novels the lack of familiarity with opium smoking includes the inability to achieve a successful draw on the pipe and may result in a potentially laughable display of clumsiness. Whether the draw he takes is genuine or pro forma, he cannot possibly appear to be on the same level with or lower than Changqing and thus will not smoke seriously or attempt to "return the favor." As for Changqing, he is already lower in social rank than Wei Pincai, who might, he hopes, be drawn closer to him by this offering of opium. As Changqing becomes agitated, he smokes more intensely, as if to draw energy and wits from the opium in order to fend off this representative of the powerful Hua Guangsu.

As imperious as Hua may be, he is not unscrupulous like Wei Pincai, who has two interests: (1) to avenge himself on Qinyan, who has previously insulted him, and (2) to gain the better favors of Hua Guangsu. Once Qinyan is housed in Hua Guangsu's compound, which he is not permitted to leave without approval, he becomes safer there than at Changqing's. In terms of opium, Qinyan is in potential danger wherever there are opium smokers and whenever he is with anyone who smokes opium. At his manager Changqing's, he is vulnerable to Xi Shiyi and others who covet his company and barge their way in. Hua, on the other hand, never forces himself physically on Qinyan and finally regrets having imprisoned him. Later in the novel, Wei Pincai displeases Hua, who then terminates him as secretary. By now, however, Wei has accumulated enough money to have a place of his own where he stores a supply of good opium and where he holds gatherings of men who smoke and gamble. Instead of Hua Guangsu, he now associates with Xi Shiyi and others who combine opium smoking with sexual liaisons with female and male prostitutes, especially boy female impersonators.

In the scenes of that world, wherever there is opium there is conniving, vulgarity, and lechery. In Zhang Changjia's terms, these would be the intemperate users of opium–the young male wastrels. The use of opium that Zhang considered most immature and most easily left behind was, according to his novelist contemporaries, the most prevalent use aside from utter self-ruination. Opium according to them was only conducive to mutually exploitative relationships between mainly two types of people: the male or female prostitute and those who owned them or bought their services. The exploitative use of opium crystallized into the main way opium was seen to arrive in the modern world. Drugs in general have been overwhelmingly defined in the context of misuse, excess, and exploitation and continue to carry that past with them up to the present.

FEMALE SMOKERS

Prostitutes and Concubines

Opium halls and dens catered to men. If women were present, they were there to entertain, serve, or act as mediators for prostitution and other transactions. Where were the women smokers? They were in the same dens in which men were solicited for sexual liaisons that took place elsewhere, among the madams and prostitutes in brothels, or at home as daughter, wife, or mother.[48] As for how to find out about women smokers, as I remarked in the last chapter, for the most part we must make do with secondhand material presented by male writers. A Qing source of the eighteenth century, for example, cites an "old prostitute's" comments about the deleterious effects of long-term opium smoking on both men and women.[49] Material exists from interviews with women, such as Ida Pruitt's *A Daughter of Han* or Maria Jaschok's research on young women sold into concubinage and prostitution in southern China (both referring to the late nineteenth or early twentieth centuries). In one case, the go-between for such sales was a smoker; in another, so was a woman who went from prostitution to concubinage.[50] From these and the sources I use below, we must extrapolate about what women smokers may have experienced.

Opium had been a fixture of brothel situations since at least the late eighteenth century.[51] The mid–nineteenth century *Dream of Moon and Romance* features women smokers who because of various misfortunes have fallen into contractual bondage with brothel keepers, some of whom rent these women from their families.[52] One such character is Fenglin, an addict who is forced to engage in prostitution in order to sustain herself, her addict husband and his mother, and the brothel keeper who houses her. The highest goal available to her, like that of other female characters in *Dream of Moon and Romance* and other novels, is to find a dependable man to help her purchase her freedom and grant her legitimate status as wife or concubine, to *cong liang*, in other words, "redeem herself into virtue." To do so, she must navigate through her own and various other types of dependencies: on opium, on her income as sexual partner, and on attachments of emotion and obligation.

Her story is briefly as follows: her widower father, a drinker and gambler, sells her at seven as a child bride *(tongyangxi)* to a family whose female head, Fenglin's mother-in-law, trains her to sing and play music, and at thirteen to begin doing "carnal transactions" *(zuo hun shengyi,* chap. 7, 51). But her uncle and her husband, both heavy addicts and gamblers, ruin the family business and Fenglin has to be pawned into a brothel in Yangzhou.[53] There she eventually meets an educated married man named Jia Ming, who rents her exclusively for himself. During a period of prohibition against opium and prostitution, her brothel closes down and Jia Ming finds her a separate place in which she and he spend days smoking, passing time, and devoting themselves to each other. When he falls ill, she nurses him. In gratitude he presents her with poems of appreciation, after which she vows devotion to him. He falls ill again, this time with an eye disease that she cares for by licking his eyes until they heal (chap. 28, 201). Jia Ming, however, cannot afford to buy her from her husband and mother-in-law, who meanwhile demand two hundred copper cash per day while Jia Ming houses her (chap. 25). Nevertheless, Jia Ming treats her like a family member. When Fenglin wants to visit her parents' grave, Jia Ming at first refuses to go but then agrees after she angrily accuses him of slighting her. He introduces her to his wife, who is "highly pleased" with Fenglin, who is quite skillful in "flattery"(chap. 28, 196).

One day, while they are in their room "passing their craving on either side of the gun" *(dui qiang guo yin,* chap. 28, 201), they receive a call from a rich Hanlin scholar from the north who has heard of her and desires her company. She initially declines, but Jia Ming urges her to go and thus earn some money to buy another supply of opium. When she returns, she announces that she intends to accept the Hanlin's offer to take her as concubine. The man is a nonsmoker, already has several concubines, and gives Fenglin a large amount of silver (chap. 29, 203). She persuades her husband and mother-in-law that since she is nearing thirty, she can't bring them income for many more years and that they would do better to sell her and use the money to buy new women. As for Jia Ming, he cannot compare in status to the Hanlin, but he warns her that she will not be accustomed to the northern environment and may not be able to smoke her opium there (chap. 29). She appears unwavering, however, and ignores his signs of growing upset and his accusations of disloyalty (perhaps all along, as the author may imply, intending to draw him into decisive action). Her husband weeps as he signs the contract giving her away; she pretends not to see. Also signing the contract are her husband's brother and mother and Fenglin's own brother and sister, all of whom have been wholly or partially dependent on her income. After presenting each other with mementoes, she and Jia Ming spend a final night alone reclining and smoking opium. "He was constantly sighing, while she did not utter a word for the whole night" (chap. 29, 207). When she leaves the next day, her mother-in-law weeps, Jia Ming curses Fenglin for not weeping, and Fenglin pretends not to hear him (p. 207). Angry at such lack of emotion, Jia Ming considers her to have "betrayed" him (chap. 29, 206). From his point of view, and compared with another more self-sacrificing and nonsmoking prostitute in *Dream of Moon and Romance*, Fenglin is disloyal and calculating, someone about whom he and another man gather and commiserate in a teahouse soon after she leaves him (chap. 30, 210).

If we briefly correlate the fictional scene here with the life of a real prostitute, two points seem evident. First, a woman in a situation like this is hard-pressed to escape the accusation that she has been calculating and heartless. The prostitute is defined as deceptive and in fact is because of her need to maneuver within her profession, from which she will do what she can to survive or escape. Second, a prostitute about to entrust herself to marriage is at great risk, having no guarantee that this next man will provide more security than the last. In terms of the story, Fenglin has already invested time and emotion with Jia Ming. She has been intense in demanding his loyalty and respect and in showing him her devotion. Besides chastising him for not wanting to visit her parents' grave, for example, or licking his eyes during his illness, she also demonstrates attachment when she jealously guards him from the intentions of another prostitute, Ailin, a heavy addict who has a "face that is all the look of opium" (chap. 27, 193).[54]

If opium heightens ambition and self-esteem but leaves one unable to follow through, as Zhang Changjia, Cocteau, De Quincey, and others say, then Jia Ming demonstrates opium inertia, but the prostitute Fenglin does not. Throughout her story, her addiction is continuous. During the opium prohibition, for example, Jia Ming takes a cure for addiction, which he urges on Fenglin, who nevertheless smokes secretly.[55] Earlier in the novel, when another prostitute says that Fenglin is lucky to have a certain fine-quality opium called *wanshougao*, "long-life extract," Fenglin replies: "You are joking. We're being buried alive by this thing"—and then lies down again to prepare more opium (chap. 7, 43).

How someone like Fenglin experiences the opium habit is briefly evoked in a song that another prostitute in *Dream of Moon and Romance* sings about the prostitute's craving and entrapment:

> Sister smothers, shut deeply in her room; up wells her craving, draining her of life, a truly living death. Always yawning and sneezing, her eyes red and watering. Her limbs listless, she feels her whole body go soft. Itchy throat, nauseous insides, as if about to give birth. She needs to buy some mud but she has no money; she'd like to scoop up some opium, close her doors, and pay the money later.

Smoking this dross severs me at the root. That lover of mine, he is so good to me, won't he scoop up a needleful and save my life. Then we'll live out the rest of our days sealed in our room. (chap. 7, 48)

In terms of opium use, this and other novels suggest three types of prostitutes: those who became addicted to the point of ruination (like Ailin or the figure in this song), those who kept their habit at a manageable level (like Fenglin), and those who viewed opium as something to be strictly avoided (like Qiuhen).[56] Prostitute-addicts like Fenglin need opium for themselves and for their customers, some of whom are smokers already, some of whom become smokers through visiting these women, and some of whom lose everything because of their involvement with opium and women. Although men in these novels devote everything to opium, even leading their families into destitution and renting or selling their wives and children, the women are not in a position to be so reckless. For women like Fenglin, opium smoking cannot be as central as it is for someone like Jia Ming or Zhang Changjia. However much they suffer from their addiction, Jia and Zhang at least have some basic ownership of themselves and ostensibly can choose whether or not to ruin themselves. For Fenglin, choice must be broken down into more minute layers, that is, tactics of survival. One circuitous route of escape that women rely on takes the form of prostitution. However undesirable, it can sometimes deliver them into relative comfort. As the example below will also show, they can reject one man and take chances with another, their experience in prostitution at least training them in the arts of being pleasing and persuasive. The addict-man, on the other hand, slumps into tears and anger as he watches the addict-woman go off to take care of herself.

Juhua, a woman smoker in *Precious Mirror of Boy Actresses* who also redeems herself out of prostitution, does so by becoming the concubine of the heavy opium smoker described above, Xi Shiyi. In contrast to Fenglin and Jia Ming's relationship, sex is a major part of the relationship between Juhua and Xi Shiyi, who is also avid about sex with boy prostitutes. *Precious Mirror of Boy Actresses* is mainly about the chaste love affair between Mei Ziyu, a sensitive and refined young upper-class man, and Qinyan, an equally sensitive and refined younger male actor of female operatic roles.[57] Xi Shiyi is merely the most bullying and profligate of a set of male characters who intrude, sometimes violently, on the lives of the two main male lovers, especially Qinyan. The author, Chen Sen, as I have shown, generally draws a clear line between the virtuous and refined characters and the profligate and villainous, especially in assigning sexual activity and opium smoking almost exclusively to the villainous. Although Chen Sen focuses primarily on relations between men, Fenglin in *Dream of Moon and Romance* and Juhua in *Precious Mirror of Boy Actresses* share the fate of the boy actors and boy prostitutes in *Precious Mirror of Boy Actresses*—forced by poverty and misfortune to become contractually bonded to people who earn a living by having them perform services for male customers. Juhua's opportunism gains her the same freedom as Fenglin's. But whereas Fenglin's narrative ends when she redeems herself, Juhua's begins when she becomes Xi Shiyi's new concubine.

Her background and her path into prostitution are as follows: Originally from Wuzhou in Guangxi, she at first marries a man who is "a good for nothing" but leaves him and forms a liaison with an official for several years. After he leaves for Beijing, she follows him and, failing to find him, "is forced to lean against the door and sell smiles" (chap. 18, 230–31). Eventually she meets Xi Shiyi in a brothel and cooks opium for him. As already translated above, she "takes several draws herself, then cuddling up to Xi Shiyi" helps him with several more pipes, after which they "become stirred and excited, then put out the lamp, close the door, and do the 'dream of Mt Wu.'" They then smoke more opium, eat, and drink, continuing this way for a week. After becoming "hotly" attached, Xi Shiyi pays a large sum of gold in order to formally set her up as his concubine at home (p. 232).

Juhua emblemizes the modest self-determination of the woman who is as much as possible her own go-between. She abandons her failure of a husband and pursues a long-term but nonconjugal relationship with a more successful man. When he disappears, she turns to "selling smiles" and contracts herself to a brothel. For her, prostitution is a temporary phase of opportunism that she leaves as soon as she enters it. As with the boy lovers in *Tower of Elegant View* and *Precious Mirror of Boy Actresses*, and as with prostitutes in *Dream of Moon and Romance*, opium the aphrodisiac is integral to her path of self-promotion. When other women in the brothel avoid Xi Shiyi because of his heavy accent and the strength of his imported opium, Juhua finds in him an opium master for whom she can become the perfect opium server. After she becomes his concubine, the most troublesome later development is the prospect of Xi Shiyi's losing the function of his penis to venereal disease (chap. 47, 11b).[58] The novelist completely ignores the possible effect of infection on Juhua. She merely becomes agitated when the man operating on Xi's penis tells him it will have to be reduced to "four inches" in length. Before she can stop herself—and just as Xi is in the middle of holding in his opium draw and unable to respond—she blurts out to the man to leave "five inches" instead. Later, just before Xi permanently ruins his penis while taking an overdose of aphrodisiac and having intercourse with a young boy, Xi and Juhua have a session of sex during which he jokes with her about the hugeness of her sexual appetite (chap. 58, 5b–6b, 745). She thus becomes the butt of satire in a more than usually male-oriented novel that now assigns her the role common to other beautiful female characters in fictional polygamies, above all Pan Jinlian in *Golden Lotus*: the jealous and insatiable woman who is forced to wait her turn with her sexually profligate husband.

Juhua's marriage nevertheless delivers her from prostitution into domestic comfort and allows her to maintain her opium habit. In contrast to the rich male addict, the opium server like Fenglin or Juhua is twice dependent: once, like the master, on opium, but once again on the master and his money. Added to this, the prostitute or boy lover must be concerned with their looks, age, and health. Fenglin and Juhua manage to "redeem themselves into virtue" before suffering the effects of ill health and age (about which Fenglin, almost thirty, is worried; chap. 29, 204), or before taking on the opium look: emaciation, yellowing of the skin, and blackening of the teeth—like an older, heavily made-up prostitute in *Souls from the Land of Darkness* (chap. 15, 166). In weighing the reality of these concerns about age and looks, one must recall that twenty was considered "old" for a prostitute, and that the effects of opium on a person's looks could take less than a year.[59]

The Daughter, Wife, or Mother

In contrast to the prostitute or the madam of a brothel, another type of woman, a kind of female wastrel, was pampered and self-centered in her opium habit—the unmarried daughter still residing in her parents' home. In the same category are wives and mothers who are also portrayed as having especially heavy addictions. As labeled in *The Vanity of Flourishing Life* and *Souls from the Land of Darkness*, these more privileged women are "spoiled" in their opium habit, accept only the best opium, and require comfortable surroundings in which to continue their life of smoking. Their opium escapism is similar to the wastrel son's except that since a man is more privileged and indulged to begin with, a woman's spoiled negligence of sober norms appears yet more self-centered and outrageous.

In marriage and motherhood, such a daughter encounters special problems: (1) her state of addiction makes it harder to have high expectations for the quality of the marriage match (an addicted son might have the same problem if he insists on marrying a woman from a well-placed family), and (2) the daughter must be concerned about her future supply of opium, especially if she moves into a poorer family or one in which opium is not smoked or is strongly prohibited. In *The Vanity of Flourishing Life*, the rich Zhou family seeks for their addicted daughter a son-in-law with both "wealth and rank" but only succeeds in finding a young man whose wealth is somewhat uncertain. Her father confides to her mother that they had better not be too demanding, since their daughter "has such a severe addiction to the Western extract" (chap. 25, 473). They hasten the marriage in order to avoid allowing the son-in-law's family too much time to learn about the daughter's "excessive addiction" (p. 474).

The daughter, however, gives up none of her high expectations. For her dowry, although a "Western-style bed" is more readily available, she demands a bed of very rare "red-sandalwood." After receiving an "imported American goose down quilt" and many other items of fabulous luxury, she arrives at the day of the wedding and readies herself to leave her parents' home by "smoking several large draws of Western extract," thereby "nourishing herself with plenty of energy" (p. 478). But after packing her various exquisitely appointed utensils, she suddenly discovers that no one has seen to her supply of opium. She refuses to leave until she has her favorite kind of "Gold Mountain Smoke," which would take many hours for someone to set out and purchase unless, as her father finally urges, her mother takes some of her own opium to give to her daughter as they await the next day for more to be delivered (p. 479). When it comes to the second daughter's marriage, the groom's mother learns about the daughter's addiction after it is too late to withdraw from the marriage. After numerous grievances and insults, the groom's parents finally arrive at the day of the wedding only to find the Zhou daughter refusing to kneel to them in the usual manner of bride to parents-in-law, the young woman "never having paid such obeisance to anyone else before" (p. 510). After more displays of insolence, the bride abruptly leaves before the celebrations are over and retreats to her room to smoke opium, making no effort to conceal what she is doing (p. 511).

A similar story unfolds in *Souls from the Land of Darkness* when a bride is likewise supplied with a specially processed opium to take to her new home.[60] When her husband later discovers her habit, the wife's servants encourage him to smoke as well, calling opium "the happiness extract," *huanxigao*, using the word *huanxi* with its connotation of sexual pleasure (chap. 9, 140).[61] The final part of the woman's story involves what Peng Yang'ou portrays as the consequences of opium smoking on a woman's fertility.[62] When the woman and her husband have no children after fifteen years of marriage, he decides to take a concubine, asserting that his wife is infertile. The wife protests that she is neither "stone maiden" *(shinü)* nor a person of uncertain sex *(cixiong ren,* lit., "female-male person"), and that her menstruation, regular when they first married, "is merely a little irregular lately, but it still comes every two or three months" (chap. 21, 193). Once he takes a concubine, the wife is jealous as she looks at herself with "her face of an opium demon, blackened teeth and parched lips, not fetching in the least" (chap. 21, 195). She tries to commit suicide by swallowing raw opium.[63] Finally, a doctor prescribes a cure for opium addiction that works on both her and her husband, although she is left drained and depressed and he has diarrhea in his clothing as he is judging cases in court a few days later (chap. 22, 201; chap. 23, 202).[64]

The prostitute-courtesan and especially her madam or pimp, if she has one, choose or reject men depending on their relative wealth. The daughter, wife, or mother stay within the conjugal family in which they display their own flair in serving their personal interests: delaying her departure for the groom's house on time, refusing to show respect to her parents-in-law, insisting on the best opium and the most luxurious items for the comfort of her new life exiled from home. She makes life center around herself as much as she can and continues her opium smoking unless her situation becomes impossible, when, as in the story just told, she takes opium to commit suicide. Her self-centeredness is particularly brazen in light of the customary expectation that women be subservient and accommodating, whether marrying into a new household or yielding to a husband who wants a concubine.

In the case of the woman just mentioned in *Souls from the Land of Darkness*, the final rage that leads to her attempted suicide stems from her effort to prevent her husband and the concubine from smoking opium together. Since he has taken the concubine based on the assumption that his wife's infertility was due to her addiction, the wife uses the same assumption to insist on removing the opium from the room her husband shares with the concubine: if he wants the concubine to have children, then why does he allow her to smoke opium (chap. 22, 198)?[65] After taking his opium away, the wife compromises with him by installing a bell he can ring to signal her to bring him his opium. The bell sounds one night, not because he intentionally rings it, but because he and his concubine shake the bed as they are having intercourse, which the wife then walks in on as she responds to the bell. This provokes the rage that leads to her attempted suicide, a kind of feminine version of the opium beggar's fate of being eaten by wild dogs.

NOTES

1. Nothing is known of the author's life. For a brief discussion, see Wu Runting 2000, 381–83. Opium also appears in late Qing drama, for example, Zhang Zufen (1845?–1894), *Zhaoyinju*, about the transformation of a firm hater of opium into an utter addict who sells son, daughter, and wife in order to maintain his addiction.

2. According to Su Zhiliang, 1910 production was down 75 percent from what it was in 1906 (1997, 215). See also Wong 2000 on opium suppression in this period.

3. See Yu Ende 1934, 113–48; Su Zhiliang 1997, 180–247.

4. There is also a story (by Wu Jianren), a play (by Xu Fumin), and a movie (director Zhang Shichuan) with the same title, *Heiji yuanhun*. The movie appeared in Shanghai in 1916. Adapted from the play, it is about a miser who forces his overly generous son to become an opium addict in order to pacify him and prevent him from being so generous. Some plot elements appear in both the play and Peng's novel, for example, a child mistakenly swallowing opium and dying; underlings in the rich household mismanaging and appropriating family wealth. See Cheng Jihu 1963, 23–28; Leyda 1972, 17–18.

5. This is a doctrinaire novel by a fervent reformer named Zhan Xi. He wrote it in 1895 in response to a contest sponsored by a foreigner calling for a new fiction that would attack three evils: opium, foot binding, and the examination system.

6. Zhang Chunfan's late Qing *Heiyu* is another novel in which opium plays a large role, but I have so far failed to see it. See also *Shenlou waishi* and a discussion of it and other relevant works in A Ying 1957, 24–32; and *Henhai*, which Alexander Des Forges discusses (2000, 180–81). For a short essay on *Yaguan lou*, see A Ying 1985, pt. 2, 157.

7. See *Huyou zaji*, by Ge Yuanxu (1876); *Songnan mengyinglu*, by Huang Shiquan (1883); and *Huyou mengying*, by Chi Zhizheng (1893) (Ge Yuanxu 1989, 31, 110, 159–60); and Des Forges 2000, 167, 176, and passim. The same guidebooks also record the negative side of opium smoking.

8. One of the most interesting is a poem cited in *Huyou zaji* in imitation of Li Bo's "The Road to Shu Is Hard," Ge Yuanxu 1989, 47–48. See also poems on 48, 62, 65.

9. An exception is the central character Hong Shanqing in *Flowers of Shanghai* (*Haishanghua liezhuan*), a smoker like the author Han Bangqing himself, though not like Han Bangqing someone versed in classical letters. *Flowers of Shanghai* does not foreground or elevate opium, but neither does it particularly condemn it. Hong Shanqing is a businessman who makes a living from his ginseng store and his various transactions among male customers of Shanghai brothels. His smoking is a very minor part of his portrayal, almost escaping the reader's attention (see chap. 17).

10. See Des Forges 2000, 181, who makes the same point.

11. See Chen Pingyuan 1988, *Zhongguo xiaoshuo xushi moshide zhuanbian.*

12. But see the 1897 novel, *Haishang chentianying*, or the 1912 novel, *Yulihun.*

13. See Catherine Yeh's discussion of four such writers (1997).

14. This history can be further broken down, but that is a study still to be written. Substantial beginnings can be found in David Wang 1997; Wu Runting 2000.

15. De Quincey wrote that he first drank laudanum because of a painful case of rheumatism in the face. The man whom Robert Fortune once met in a boat said he smoked for his health (1852, 51). When a husband in *Souls from the Land of Darkness* learns that his new wife is an addict, her servants assert that she has an illness of the liver; opium is for the sake of "pacifying the liver" (chap. 9, 140; chap. 19, 184).

16. See Edkins 1898, 5–30.

17. See Adshead 1966, 95, on opium smoking in late Qing Sichuan, where smoking was said to be the "correct thing to do." Moule says, "And now the plague has spread so widely as to have become fashionable instead of being a disgrace" (Moule 1891, 97). Missionary witnesses from the same period as Moule's book reported to the Royal Commission on Opium that they found opium use far more widespread then than in earlier decades. See, for example, Elwin, in United Kingdom 1894, 1:47; Turner, in United Kingdom 1894, 1:128–29.

18. If Peng had been writing a few decades later, he would have discovered that if opium can become fashionable, it can also become unfashionable. As Emily Hahn wrote in the late 1930s (not long after Chiang Kai-shek launched his New Life Movement), "The modern, Westernized Chinese of Shanghai frowned on smoking—not on moral grounds but because it was considered so lamentably old-fashioned" (Hahn 1970, 227). One Western fashion replaced another. To be modern meant to drink alcohol, as Hahn said, not to smoke opium. Her friends, on the other hand, were deliberately old-fashioned in their opium smoking, their traditional attire, and their tastes in reading, music, and painting.

19. The edition I use is from the rare book collection of the Beijing University Library and is unpaginated. These are numbers as counted according to the conventional pagination method of books in traditional binding, starting at 1a with each new chapter.

20. See, for example, *Souls*, chap. 19, 186, the story with the same title written by Wu Jianren, and the later play and movie also with the same title (in which the son is generous but not a spendthrift).

21. When a husband in *The Vanity of Flourishing Life* is worried about his wife's poor health, a friend of his recommends "Western extract," saying it will make her less prone to anger and will nourish her internal energy (chap. 10, 379).

22. On the adoption of the word "science" in the late Qing, see Wang Hui 1996, 14ff.

23. Which Cocteau, incidentally, found soothing to ride in while in the state of craving (Cocteau 1996, 29).

24. The text does not describe the precise way these eggshells were thus used.

25. As Moule wrote, "The Yamun officers told us that partly from the late habits formed by opium-smoking, and partly from the customs of the place, the court is open in the late evening for justice, and not in the daytime" (Moule 1891, 145).

26. See poem by Fan Yuanwei in Zhang Changling 1983, 1008–9.

27. Moule 1891, 98; several witnesses before the Royal Commission on Opium also reported these findings, e.g., United Kingdom 1894, 1:30, 43, and 45.

28. In his testimony to the Royal Commission on Opium, the missionary George Graham Brown, who spent six years in Lanzhou, mentioned the practice of eating crude opium in the form of little balls in order to relieve craving when one had no time to smoke (United Kingdom 1894, 1:45). Opium addicts also used anti-opium pills to relieve craving when smoking was impossible. These pills were a major tool in the treatments that foreign and Chinese physicians administered to patients attempting withdrawal, but–to the distress of medical missionaries–were also subject to unintended use (Howard 1998, 157–58).

29. The desperate addict, as William Burroughs later writes, "will crawl through a sewer and beg to buy" (Burroughs 1960, 16).

30. A long description of inept opium smoking (with the pipe brought too close to the flame and the vent hole clogging up) can also be found in *Shenlou waishi* (pre-1895), cited in A Ying 1957, 28–29.

31. See below under "Extortion and Conniving" for a further explanation of the "lawyer."

32. See Jones and Kuhn, who describe them as playing a significant role in nineteenth-century local government, although they were never afforded any "legitimate place" (1978, 112–13).

33. See *Precious Mirror*, chaps. 34–35, for another case of the theft of opium, the victim being Wei Pincai.

34. On opium suppression after the Treaty of Nanking, see Howard 1998, 112–17.

35. See Su Zhiliang 1997, for more precise estimations of the progressively higher figures and the patterns they project.

36. See United Kingdom 1894, 5, appendix XXVI, passim.

37. See Spence 1992, 238, citing United Kingdom 1894, 1:15–17, 1:113.

38. United Kingdom 1894, 1:14. Legge (1815–1897) was at the end of his career, referring back to the last several decades in China.

39. See Wang 1997, 73–81.

40. He saves her by prying open her mouth and putting his tongue inside to recover several bits of opium as yet unswallowed (chap. 20, 143). She had had an argument with her madam, whose interest was for Aiqing to see more customers, whereas Aiqing only wanted to see Yixiang, whom she eventually succeeds in marrying.

41. Miss Geraldine Guinness and William Lockhart, witnesses before the Royal Commission on Opium, reported that it was common for women to use opium to commit suicide (United Kingdom 1894, 1:7, 114).

42. *The Trace of Flowers and Moon* contains two more references. Qiuhen's lover has a poem of his own on the scourge of opium (chap. 20, 165), and someone writes a memorial to the emperor which contains a passing condemnation of opium (chap. 46, 383).

43. See Spence 1992, 238–39.

44. For more details, see McMahon 1995, chap. 13. See also Wang 1997, 156–71, and Altenburger 2000.

45. Exceptions exist: such women smoke in the earlier *Dream of the Red Chamber*; see chap. 101, where Baochai hands Wang Xifeng a tobacco pipe. Though not of the upper class, the cultured courtesan Qiuhen in *The Trace of Flowers and Moon* smokes tobacco, as she does when pondering a strange dream about her lover, who unknown to her has just died (chap. 44, 370).

46. On tobacco in terms of health and pollution, see McMahon 1995, 279–82.

47. On the masculine aspects of this purity, see McMahon 1995, 269–72.

48. Moule writes: "Shanghai is unfortunately notorious for opium-smoking. In one of the streets of the French settlement, the largest opium shop in all China is to be found. It may rather be called an opium hotel, to which all classes of the Chinese community resort to learn with fatal facility the delusion of this fascinating vice, and to return after two or three visits fast bound in its well-nigh inextricable toil. Women are to be found here as well as men; and this is but the head-quarters of a system which poisons and disgraces the streets and by-paths of the settlements and city alike" (Moule 1891, 93). For the type of den to which Moule possibly refers, see the so-called flower-smoke rooms, *huayanjian*, in *Flowers of Shanghai* (1892).

49. The qualification of "old," of course, may mean from the twenties on in the case of prostitutes. See Liang Gongchen 1960, 3.2.10ab.

50. See Jaschok 1988, 14, 45–47. Ida Pruitt's interviews with Ning Lao T'ai-t'ai tell of the sale of a daughter by Ning's opium-addicted husband. Ning Lao T'ai-t'ai does not seem to have been an opium smoker herself.

51. For brief mentions of opium among prostitutes in that period, see Wang Shunu 1988, 275–76; Yu Jiao 1988, 372; and part 4 of Shen Fu, *Fusheng liuji*.

52. On *Dream of Moon and Romance*, see Hanan 1998.

53. The husband in such a situation would pawn his wife but retain ownership over her. He might search for such deals in opium dens, where he and his mother might go when seeking information about where to purchase a girl to train in the art of entertaining men.

54. When Jia Ming invites Ailin to smoke, Ailin lies on top of him, bringing her face up to his and tickling him. Then they play for a while until Fenglin pushes Ailin aside, sits astride Jia Ming, grabs his ear, and angrily makes him a long weeping speech about his disloyalty (chap. 27, 193–94). She rams her head against his and rolls around in a lengthy outburst of emotion.

55. The recipe for the cure includes ginseng and a solution of opium ash (chap. 25, 180–81).

56. In *Flowers of Shanghai* (1892), the prostitute Zhang Huizhen refers to another, Shen Xiaohong, who smokes but supposedly does not ruin herself (but she actually does). Zhang says that if she herself smoked, she could not do business (chap. 24, 201).

57 On *Precious Mirror*, see Wang 1997, 60–76; Starr 1999; and McMahon 2002.

58. When *a* or *b* follows the page number, this refers to the traditionally bound edition, which is unexpurgated.

59. Numerous novels depict prostitutes who look heavily addicted, like Ailin in *Dream of Moon and Romance.* The effect of opium on looks was also related to diet and health. Prostitutes of the lower ranks were particularly vulnerable to disease. A passage from the novel *Haishang fanhua meng* (1903) has a man who is told that his face shows no remarkable signs of addiction. He then takes out a photo to demonstrate that a year before he was "brimming with youth and health" (chap. 22, 240–41). In a few months he has gone from an addiction of a few pipefuls of opium to one in which he needs one *liang* per day (ten mace), a level that was considered high.

60. She similarly delays leaving her home for her in-laws' while she "slowly passes her craving" and smokes an extra amount of opium (chap. 9, 138). Some delay may have been common, whether or not the bride smoked opium. Reverend Arthur Moule reports performing a marriage between two Chinese Christians, but, after "enjoin[ing] punctuality" and setting the time for 11 A.M., found himself forced to wait until nightfall before the bride finally arose from bed. "They informed me that this bed-ridden affectation was considered etiquette and true decorum on the part of the bride" (1891, 127–28).

61. "If the kind groom will smoke this opium he will be sure to add pleasure on top of pleasure, and will have a most delightful time with his bride" (chap. 9, 140).

62. A prior part of her story emerges from the mouth of the old man "Knows Everything" referred to previously, who goes from one opium den to another supplying information to people who offer him opium. As her brother hears from the old man, she and her husband interest the husband's mother in opium, the husband is caught smoking opium while taking his prefectural exams, and his prohibitionist father finally dies of anger (chap. 19).

63. See also Berridge and Edwards 1981, 80–81.

64. Reputed cures for opium addiction had been common for many decades by the time of this novel. Such malfunction of the intestinal tract was common among addicts, as well as those who were suddenly deprived of opium or who tried to quit all at once.

65. In the argument between the wife and the concubine, the concubine protests that she prepares the pipe but doesn't smoke it. The wife says she has seen the concubine with the pipe in her mouth and the opium already partly smoked. The concubine replies that she was only checking to see whether or not the pipe was blocked.

Chapter Seven

"Why the Chinese Smoked Opium"

SMOKING OPIUM IN ORDER TO REMAIN CHINESE

What would Zhang Changjia say about the women in these novels? He only describes men who voluntarily, even euphorically, deliver themselves into the state of unchoice that opium gives them. Curious about opium pleasure, men discover a historically unprecedented type of hermetic withdrawal, which had always been a refuge men were allowed to indulge in. As Zhang describes them, certain men first smoke opium to enjoy it along with women, but then replace one pleasure with another as they go into solo addiction and become lovesick with opium. Having replaced all other pleasures, especially sex with women, the man whom Zhang portrays becomes the abandoned lover after all, a likeness of the teased and abandoned woman who is a literary figure in countless poems by male writers from early times on.

How do we evaluate the female addict vis-à-vis the male? Based on the material in the previous chapters, let us return to the large issues having to do with the comparison between different smokers of opium, in particular in terms of whether they are the lovesick male or the headstrong female, or whether it is a matter of the laborer or rich merchant, the refined solo addict like Zhang or the profligate like Xi Shiyi. Each has specific reasons for smoking and particular ways of using opium. Their individual situations are on the other side of a divide from the grand question I have been asking about why "the Chinese" took up opium smoking. This question is impossibly generalizing because of its implication that the Chinese are a collective, as if they are of one mind and have one project, which is an incredible proposition. Similarly, in comparing male and female addicts, how can we assume that all women or all men are of the same mind? The gap between the individual and the collective enters the picture in all such questions and is something I will briefly address before answering the questions. My point is to reemphasize from a series of angles the central idea of this book—that the individual Chinese opium smoker is also the global smoker of opium and that opium is, as I have said, the bridge par excellence between the "Westerners" and the "Chinese" from the end of the eighteenth century on.

The fascination with such questions centers for us the confrontation between the two cultural entities called "East" and "West," and likewise forces the issue itself about why opium has assumed such global importance ever since the British began selling it to the Chinese. Of central importance is how and by whom such questions are asked. In such a giant confrontation, everything one side does is potentially questionable both from its own and its other's perspective. Perspective is also gaze, in the Lacanian sense, that is, the way one sees oneself being seen, the way one assumes subjectivity within the gaze of the other. When one subject looks at another, the other is always gazing back at the subject, but never from a point that the subject can see. As Lacan says, "You never look at me from the place at which I see you" (Lacan 1981, 103). Yet one assumes roles deriving from how one conceives the relation with that other and from how one comes to be symbolically marked in that relationship. The basic questions about subjectivity that the confrontation of "East" and "West" forces into articulation are ones such as: Why have we always acted this way and should we continue? Why don't they act this way and why do they act as they do?

The reason opium was so fascinating as a culturally symbolic marker has to do with what I refer to as opium insatiability: opium supersedes all other pleasures, diversions, and necessities. Zhang Changjia's preface writer speaks of the smoker's obliviousness to all ancient and venerable wisdom. Just as that wisdom is shown to be useless, Zhang signals that the appearance of opium parallels that of Europeans and Americans in China. They bring their Christianity which, he says, is bound to transform China while Confucianism cannot possibly transform the foreigners. Opium thus appears against this backdrop of utter transformation, which includes divorce from any sort of paradigmatic order of law or pleasure. In the face of such staggering possibilities, how does one change and yet retain enough of one's identity at the same time? Or does one completely throw out the so-called old identity and take on the new, assuming that the new has the answer and will deliver fulfillment? The question about why the Chinese smoked opium can also be worded as, How does one remain Chinese while undergoing Westernization? The answer that I explore in this concluding chapter is, By smoking opium.

THE UGLY FEMALE ADDICT

Let me first generalize some differences between male and female addiction. Besides summing up the observations about male and female opium smokers in the last two chapters, these generalizations will allow us to arrive at conclusions about individual and collective use of opium. Then I will (1) construe the issue of opium smoking in terms of cultural perspective, that is, ask why the Chinese smoked opium from a "Western" and then from a "Chinese" perspective, and (2) posit a kind of global consensus of addicts in their dialogue with those who have advanced the rationales for creating "drug-free" nations starting in the early twentieth century.

In the eyes of sober society, the apparent libidinal autonomy of the addict is one of the most offensive sights. As already noted, this narcissistic withdrawal is particularly offensive in a woman because of the strong expectations regarding female self-effacement. Proof of such expectations is clear from the example of the male profligate like Xi Shiyi, for whom larger-than-life excess is his motto of being. A lifestyle like his is generally unavailable to a woman. Even men who are less excessive than he nevertheless share with Xi the expectation that they deserve the devoted attention of female and other male subordinates. For Jia Ming in *Dream of Moon and Romance*, for example, genital sexuality becomes less compelling as the hermetic life of reclining and smoking opium with a devoted prostitute fixes him in a state of Zhang Changjia–like lovesickness.[1] However less excessive he may be than Xi Shiyi, Jia Ming assumes that he deserves the woman's attention. He thus takes up a fetal position of opium inertia and enjoys himself being attended to—even to the point of cuckolding himself to another man.

Female addicts, though generally adhering to the customs of female sequestration, nevertheless suspend other requirements of feminine decency and submission. Instead of doping them or making them useless, opium charges them with a certainty of their basic demands, including the demands of their addiction to opium. In charging them with that certainty, opium makes them in some guises equal or superior to their male counterparts. Hence, for example, Fenglin's switch to another man or the headstrong bride's refusal to bow to her parents-in-law.

If we interpret such behavior metaphorically, then we should say, in Avital Ronell's words, that the woman's drug use in these cases amounts to "feminine incorporations of a phallic flux" (Ronell 1992, 103). The wastrel woman ingests an energy of defiant strength and certainty, reminding us now of the addict–libidinal autonomist–in relation to normal society or of self-sufficient China in relation to the progressive and outgoing West. Even in advanced stages of opium ugliness and dependence, she presents the image of ugliness as if in subversion of the nice way a woman is supposed to look. Then she may withdraw for good to her opium chamber, become the prostitute who sells sex for opium money, or perhaps procure other women who do the prostitution for her. To be sure, her phallic strength is not properly channeled or focused. It is a quintessential representation of the collective addict's unnatural alteration of the physical and social self. Although virtuous in terms of social status, the addicted daughter, wife, and mother merge with the prostitute in their departure from the way of the normatively virtuous woman. In short, the addicted woman has found a new way to become a shrew, just as the addicted man has found a new way to become a wastrel.

Still, whether speaking of male or female, it is not simply a matter of reversal of roles. The image of the emasculated Xi Shiyi and especially Jia Ming might suggest such a reversal in contrast to the self-certain female addict. But man emasculated and woman phallicized imply neither gender equalization nor victory by the woman. Neither addict is any longer a normatively gendered or socialized person anyway. Opium and other drugs introduce a new type of identity, something that looms larger than the specific case of the individual smoker. That identity, moreover, is one that lawmakers have tried to stamp out in draconic and paranoid ways. Paranoia names the alarm about the potential deformation of the usual social and sexual reproductive cycles. Men too sensuous and women too lascivious threaten a dissolution of social productivity because of both their deficiency (uselessness to society) and their excess.

Zhang Changjia wrote that opium outdoes money in insatiability, that is, in its power to bring about insatiability. Similarly, David Lenson has written that drugs make the user much "too lascivious . . . to sustain the pieties of the free market."[2] This is like saying that the drug economy is too capitalistic, the Chinese opium smoker too sensual, or the female addict and prostitute too masculine and rapacious. Drug consumerism in general threatens to crowd out and pervert the more guarded consumerism of safer commodities, which permit old hierarchies and divisions to stay in place. Again, opium sensuality creates new forms of wastrels and shrews, who open up monstrous and ugly forms of enjoyment previously thought to have only a mythical existence in some tabooed primordial or fantastical time (ancient orgies, alien cultures). When these monsters appear, the symbolic order that has been known until now becomes threatened as hollow and vacant. Instead of, Why do they indulge in such monstrous pleasure? the question now becomes, What were we enjoying until now that we thought was so good, when this exponentially greater form of enjoyment came along?

OPIUM SUICIDE

As already noted, the gap between individual and collective use of opium makes asking why "the Chinese" smoked opium an impossibly generalizing question. A figure of the female opium user that helps frame this issue is the woman who commits suicide by swallowing raw opium. The story of how this "everywoman" arrives at the point of suicide by opium will allow us to make further comparisons between male and female addicts, while at the same time—borrowing the psychoanalytic notions of hysteria and desubjectivization—allowing us to interpret the individual woman's opium suicide as a symbol of suicide in a composite, collective sense. Female suicide by opium emblemizes opium use at the collective level as an act of abandoning one's placement in the social-symbolic order.

A common ground exists between individual smokers and the collective mass of Chinese smokers: One's fate as a smoker depends on where one stands vis-à-vis social predators in general. For example, male addicts like Zhang Changjia and Han Bangqing, the author of *Flowers of Shanghai*, present the image of the opium smoker who avoids self-ruination by maintaining independence from the predators who take advantage of more vulnerable or more gullible smokers.[3] However fantasized a figure like Xi Shiyi may be, he is an example of the predator himself, who in his case ends in ruination. The grotesque hyperbole of his portrayal has to do with author Chen Sen's desire to vilify and deliver poetic justice to ugly, vulgar men like Xi who prey on beautiful young boys like Qinyan. Xi's opium addiction is an inherent feature of this vilification. One of the main forms of Xi Shiyi's predation is precisely his commandeering of sexual partners. Women and especially boys are immensely appealing sexual companions. He smokes thirty "draws" of opium in anticipation of a long awaited and acutely desired meeting with Qinyan, the most beautiful boy actress in Beijing. Qinyan shuns Xi with the most visceral scorn and disgust, regardless of how dangerous it is for him to do so (chap. 36). Xi is characteristically prone to towering rage, which he exhibits when he is thus rejected. No one may reject him; no one may insult his appearance and manner. He further reacts by continuing to harass Qinyan and making it unsafe for him to reside in the relatively unprotected environs of Cao Changqing's home.

In the case of female addicts, higher-class ones, whether daughters, wives, or mothers, can live like men of their class. That is, they can achieve a mode of stability while addicted to opium as long as they observe basic precautions. As women, they are unlikely to act as unrestrainedly as Xi Shiyi, but little else stops them from being as predatory as he if they are so inclined. A prostitute smokes opium as part of her living. She is usually owned or rented by those who run the brothels, and she is under persistent pressure to attract customers. As victimized as she may be, she also learns to manipulate customers to her advantage. Ones like Ailin flirt audaciously with a customer in order to steal him from another prostitute (*Dream of Moon and Romance*, chap. 27). Sometimes a woman is fortunate enough to find a man to buy her out of prostitution. She can become especially powerful if as a young woman she becomes the concubine of an older man who then favors her over all other members of his family. If such a woman starts out being sold by poor parents into indentured status and eventually into prostitution and then concubinage, she may later become one who herself for her own reasons profits from the sale of daughters or even sons.[4] The money she earns may in part contribute to the maintenance of her opium habit, which she enjoys along with gambling, watching opera, or other types of entertainment and pleasure.

The woman who has made it to the top—for example, the one who has become the favorite of an old man—in effect interprets her role as outdoing all potential rivals and predators. The daring of female addicts illustrates this tendency, even in the case of women who are not well established as the old man's favorite. Hence the headstrong bride who scorns her in-laws, the jealous prostitute who grabs the man's ear and rages at him for his flirtation with another woman,[5] or the jealous wife who takes away her husband's opium and attempts to control his relationship with his new concubine.[6]

In the three cases just mentioned, shades of desperation appear as women strive to realize their demands. Something unusual happens with the most desperate women (like the one who tries to control the new concubine), who use opium in a way that is far more characteristic of women than men: swallowing it raw for the sake of committing suicide. Many women who did not smoke opium nevertheless resorted to it in this way, thus establishing an effective anti-use of opium subverting the normal ways of taking opium for its euphoria or relief from pain and illness.

A brief detour into psychoanalysis can give an account of this feminine use of opium in the act of suicide. In the simplest terms, the woman is deprived of choice and forced to accept roles and positions that are dictated to her by others, for example, fathers, husbands, mothers, rival women, and so forth. But in the broadest terms, it is the symbolic order that dictates how she must behave and where she must be placed. All subjects, male or female, are subject to these dictates, but since the master dictating the positions of subjectivity is typically masculine, the opposing position is therefore characteristically feminine. The Lacanian psychoanalytic term for the position of such a subject is that of the hysteric, the one who reacts to this dictation with bewilderment and screams in objection to the way she is expected to be. "Hysteria" is the word for the trauma experienced by the subject who reacts with horror at being reduced in this way to the other's object.

The ultimate gesture of hystericization is the act of committing suicide, which is the final resistance to forced placement in the network of the social-symbolic order. Again, male or female subjects can react with hysteria, which is a fundamental mode of subjectivity in that there is always a portion of their being that does not or cannot accord with the plans of the symbolic order. We can say that some irreducible excess always resists complete symbolization. For anyone (including groups of people united by a common set of features), this lack of accord is worse at certain times than at others. But my point is that hysteria, especially as expressed in the act of suicide, is an essentially feminine mode of subjectivity.[7] The fact that stereotype and fictional portrayal have women, not men, typically committing suicide by ingesting raw opium is the concrete sign of this. Although it is not necessary to be female to engage in what can be qualified as feminine gestures, certain markers tell us that women were more prone to such desperate gestures.

Another concept that is useful in this context is desubjectivization, which we can use to describe what the hysteric, in her final desperation, engages in. Suicide is the purest act of desubjectivization. It is the purest act of a self-contained assumption of subjective fate.[8] The desubjectivized subject is one who attempts to evade and reject the intersubjective circuit of mutual definition. Even an attempted suicide is a form of refusal of that subjectivization. It tends to have the effect of arresting the attention and even the behavior of the other in whose grip the subject feels entrapped. The attempted suicide is successful if it wins recognition for the subject based on a new set of conditions and demands. (Desubjectivization is also conceivable as a gesture that seeks mastery itself, especially since we cannot necessarily presume complete innocence on the part of the hysteric or complete sovereignty on the part of the master.)

It should by now be clear that my goal is to link the individual and collective use of opium via hysteria and desubjectivization. With these ideas in mind, let us revisit the question about why so many Chinese smoked opium by considering who asks the question and why. Since the West is the dominant culture, we must address the implications of this question as asked by Westerners in their assumption of cultural superiority or, in some cases, as asked by Westerners attempting to defuse the assumption of superiority (e.g., Claude Farrère). Then it will be possible to hypothesize a "hysterical" Chinese reason for smoking opium in the face of the advancing Western outsider.

THE "CHINA EFFECT"

In examining a Westerner who asks why Chinese smoked opium, I propose that we posit an expert on what he or she called the "China effect." After many years residing in and/or studying about China, the expert came to know what China was about, summing it up under this hypothetical rubric. The China effect was both the state the Chinese were in—the way they were—and the possible effect of that state on the outsider. The summation of expert opinion took the following allegorical form (by allegorical here I mean, in shorthand, impressionistic terms, using words in an essentialistic way): China was the opium addict, sottish, sedate, antediluvian, loose-robed, reclining, euphoric. China was a mystery that had to be solved, a closed country that had to be opened, a heathen place that had to be Christianized, a backward place that had to be modernized, a country of liars who had to be outwitted or else taught the value of truth. Finally, China was intractable; it was mysterious and outrageously anomalous. And opium addiction epitomized the state of being of China.

In asking why so many Chinese became addicted, this expert is in effect asking why China will not open up to "us." Why do they insist on being so opposite to us in every way? Why do they not want the good things we have to give them?

Some experts, as we know, did not find China so intractable and were not so firm in their assumption of superiority. The sinophile like Robert Fortune, who found boy actresses pleasing, discovered great and even exquisite pleasures in China. His enthusiasms were walking in the country talking with farmers, collecting porcelains, visiting antique collectors and connoisseurs, and collecting specimens of plants, especially flowers and trees he had never seen before and was eager to introduce to other plant lovers in England. We might gather that China was an exciting expansion of the world for him, as it may have been for the cross-dressers Scarth and Medhurst, and for the numerous others who could get published simply because they took an interesting walk in China. For them, China induced a type of euphoria and was even a cure and an escape. Probably more accurately, they were both the sober, superior expert and the sometime euphoric sinophile. As the former, they viewed China as a place to be transformed. But as sinophile they seemed addicted to the China effect. They enjoyed being among the "always cheerful" Chinese, as many travelers labeled them. For individuals like William C. Hunter, the joy was rattan mats on summer nights and the large and easy profits he spoke of in *The 'Fan Kwae' at Canton*. Being in China promised them an expansive and commanding view over China, just as expressed in their trope, "monarch of all I survey."

Such experts occasionally engaged in self-critique and a critique of Western culture, including Euro-Western transgressions in places like China. They, and even others not so sympathetic to China, might have experienced the feeling of being doubted and unwanted by the Chinese. The native struck them as being immensely distant. For those who were filled with such feelings of lack, China was a wholeness that would never let them in as long as they continued to be themselves. China was someone who wouldn't love them. As Joseph Edkins said at the end of his career in his address to the North China Branch of the Royal Asiatic Society in·Shanghai in 1902: "We wished to know what makes the Chinese hate us and how far they love us" (1903–1904, iv). Eager to be accepted, the outsider like Edkins wanted to know how to make the Chinese love him. Take away their opium and their other sins and perhaps they will love us. Spend half of your life in China and try to learn their language and culture as well as they know it. Dress like the Chinese or try smoking opium.

The diplomat Samuel Wells Williams wrote in his diary that the Chinese were "among the most craven of people, cruel and selfish as heathenism can make them, and we must be backed by force if we wish them to listen to reason" (Williams 1911, 64–65). But in July 1859 during a short residence in Beijing, he realized "the contrast on this hot day between our close-fitting woollen dresses and the flowing silk robes of the Chinese . . . who were cool and free while we were hot and constrained" (p. 179). Maybe the Chinese were good at hiding their suffering of the heat, but Williams granted them the superiority of silk over wool. At the same time, for him it was out of the question to change into silk robes. That would be an unacceptable crossing of categories, like switching from alcohol to opium. For Williams, dressing Chinese would be like dressing as a woman; and for a man to dress as a woman would in his view be tagged as foolish and wayward. Cross-dressing Europeans were playing games and pretending, in other words; the cross-dressing Chinese were taking serious steps to improve themselves.

Zhang Changjia wrote of opium and the crossing of categories. Opium smokers were awake in the night and asleep in the day; they reclined like things instead of standing like humans. Some decades later Claude Farrère wrote of another crossing of categories, namely, his brotherhood with Chinese smokers: "Opium, in reality, is a fatherland, a religion, a strong and jealous tie between men. And I can better feel a brother to the Asiatics smoking in Foochow Road than I can to certain inferior Frenchmen now vegetating at Paris, where I was born" (Farrère 1931, 145). He added that Europeans and Asiatics are "reduced to a level" by opium. Here the normally denigrating meaning of reduction is exchanged for one that takes reduction as a release. All differences are effaced, "and other strange new beings are born into the world, the smokers, who, properly speaking, have ceased to be men" (p. 146). In other words, first he merges in brotherhood with Chinese smokers, who are superior to nonsmoking Frenchmen vegetating in Paris. Then, with the European and Asiatic differences effaced, he and his fellow smokers become new beings altogether, ceasing to be men.

However different this is from the situation with Zhang Changjia, smokers have again skipped categories. With Farrère in particular, the insularity of the sober and upright European has sprung a leak as he discovers that he is one with the Chinese after all—regardless of how a Chinese man or woman might have viewed his presence. Opium did in fact produce a confusion and rearrangement of categories. Farrère in effect proved to the more insular fellow Westerner that drugs like opium were dangerous and uncanny, and they interfered with the maintenance and reproduction of proper categories of European and Asiatic, man and nonman. (Opium-smoking white women, of course, were even stronger proof of the evils of opium.)

The "China effect" can also be referred to as a doubling effect. Avital Ronell writes, "Like any good parasite, drugs travel both inside and outside of the boundaries of a narcissistically defended politics. They double for the values with which they are at odds, thus haunting and reproducing the capital market, creating visionary expansions, producing a lexicon of body control and a private property of self" (Ronell 1992, 50–51). The "narcissistically

defended" entities include the civilizing and modernizing enterprise of Westerners in China, the very profitable foreign opium trade (especially as exon-
erated by the Royal Commission on Opium), and the traditional privileges
of the male wastrel. What "doubling" refers to here is the haunting effect of
entities or systems that function outside of but parallel to the narcissistic center. The doubling is also parasitic, both living off the core and also thriving
independently. Examples of doubling are the Chinese domestic market in
opium, which doubles for that of Britain and overtakes the foreign import in
quantity and value; the wastrel daughter who acts suspiciously like the
wastrel son, then after her marriage keeps him guessing for years whether
she is fertile or not, meanwhile insisting on her favorite kind of opium in her
luxuriously furnished room.

THE CONSENSUS OF ADDICTS

Now let us examine the question of why Chinese smoked opium not as
asked by the Western observer and participant, but as hypothetically an-
swered by the mass of Chinese smokers. Who this mass is and where it supposedly speaks from are also questions that need addressing, however pre-
cariously. The answers I give must be seen as arriving retrospectively and
reconstructively. They are readings that derive from the hypothesized dialogue of Chinese versus Western identity, and are rather like abstractions of
the explicit, documentable statements that I have dealt with in earlier chapters. Actions and situations will be read as having collective meanings that
are beyond what individual subjects think in all their separate and idiosyn-
cratic ways.

My answers begin with the notion that the Chinese smoked opium in order to establish beyond a shadow of doubt that they would perform the
"opening up" of their country in their own fashion at their own speed. They
would, moreover, use opium or other Western medicines, products, or teach-
ings in the fashion they deemed desirable and suitable for them. They might
not follow the original instructions precisely, as is especially clear in the case
of the Christianity of the Taiping Rebellion. The original instructions as presented by the American preacher, for example, would expand into vastly
different tangents than the preacher ever imagined. The uses and appearances of whatever things traveled from one place to another would be overlapped and superimposed, and would sometimes become unrecognizable.

Another way to construe the service that opium ended up performing for
the Chinese is to see it as radically displacing both the past and the West,
rendering them both irrelevant, and in doing so giving birth to "other
strange new beings" of newer categories or noncategories, consumers, that
is, of opium. We may also conjecture that these strange new beings are ones

who smoke opium as a way of being Chinese while becoming Westernized. What better way to be Chinese while becoming Westernized than to consume the ultimate "Western drug" that was also the quintessential Chinese drug? If one could go to a Christian school without being Christian, one could also smoke opium without being Christian or, since one was smoking "Western extract," be "Christian" by smoking opium. Furthermore, to smoke opium was one way of inhabiting the foreign invasion; opium euphoria was one way of establishing one's own status, if not invincibility, within that invasion. Smokers were one of China's armies, besides the armies of the imperial government, Taiping rebels, bandit leaders, Boxers, warlords, "antlike" masses, intellectuals, novelists, and so forth. But the smokers' methods of attack were to use suffusion and seduction, if "attack" is even the right word here. Opium smokers did not have a Bible, a manifesto, or a plan of reconstruction, nor did they go about preaching, converting, or fighting revolutions.

If we look again at Westerners who warned about the "China effect," then opium addiction to them represents an absolute defiance of discipline, since opium takes the smoker farther away from the possibility of discipline than any other intoxicant. To them, the seeming undiscipline of opium is as defiant and destabilizing as rebellion, strike, or alternate sexuality. The most destabilizing aspect of opium, in fact, is the way it threatens to relativize the transfer of loyalties from one god, boss, substance, or goal to another. After opium, what is holy, sacred, or taboo; what is evil, healthy, or profitable?

The battle against addicts is one place where opium smokers may indeed be viewed as forming an army of resistance. The perspective of such a battle psycho-politicizes addicts by assuming that they are in consensus, even though smokers lack canons, anthems, or charismatic leaders. The paranoia that envisions such consensus creates that consensus by default, then. Paranoia, on the one hand, and the mass state of addiction, on the other, arrive to us as a result of the disjunctive encounter between the Euro-West and China. Both the phenomenon and the idea of addiction have arisen in the context of this intercourse and have done so in ways that have everything to do with the disjuncture and asymmetry that define this intercourse. The consensus of smokers is something that evolves and transforms from the in-between of this encounter. At the same time, neither culture can be thought of as an organic whole anymore, nor are their metaphysical foundations any longer isolatable—except if one insists too much. This compelled insistence to remain whole or pure gets at what gives rise to the fiction of the addict's godlessness and adultery. For someone who has to choose to be Confucian or Christian, it may be better to smoke opium under the rock Zhang Changjia wrote about, and to take craving farther than it has ever been taken in order to show that whatever is currently outside the rock is nothing next to that craving.

Yet another way to allegorize opium is as a cure for times when other choices become unviable. Here a kind of consensus exists among addicts and former addicts. These are times of imbalance between cultures, imbalances that involve both the disproportion of power and wealth, but also the equally fundamental and related question of the transfer of loyalties, which has always been imperfect. The "Occident" and the "Orient" are never fully intertranslatable, as Homi Bhabha has shown at great length.[9] No perfectly loyal translation or conversion is possible, and thus no completely uniform consensus.

The transfer of loyalties can also be expressed as contamination, whether by human outsiders or more intangible forces like demons, disease, madness, perversion, or powerful drugs. In this paranoid sense again, loyalties and boundaries of purity and contamination represent that by which each cultural entity defines itself against and in exclusion of the other. The opium high is a form of disloyalty and heresy that, like interracial marriage, tends to defy or confuse that exclusivist loyalty and challenge it to redefine itself. Such defiances sometimes incur repressive reactions, but it is also true that they sometimes find accommodation and acceptance, though often only in limbo-like realms of illegality or special tolerance.

THE CLEAN SLATE OF THE "DRUG-FREE NATION"

If opium addicts proved by means of their mass numbers that opium smoking was somehow necessary or fitting, they were unsuccessful in driving home their point as far as governments were concerned. We may now see drug users in general as forming a type of global unity, regardless of individual disparities. When the People's Republic of China in the early 1950s registered all opium addicts, outlawed all opium-related activities, and in 1953 declared itself a "drug-free nation," it went farther than most Western nations at that time or since to prohibit and eradicate drugs. But regardless of the methods of enforcement, China and the United States, whether "socialist" or "capitalist," have been alike in having governments that reserve the right to control these particular types of consciousness. That is, both nations reserve the right to control the states of body and mind and thus channel their productivity. The two may not agree precisely why opium is bad. In China opium represented parasitic foreign domination of a weak nation. In Britain and the United States, opium represented potential invasion and emasculation by alien masses. Those reasons, moreover, applied in former times. Later propaganda wars against drugs—many of which are synthetics that never existed before—have had to vary the same basic rationale while adding new ones.

Whatever the rationales are or were for outlawing dangerous drugs, they began taking shape in the context of this confrontation of cultures. How the confrontation drew a clean slate for both Britain and China can be articulated in terms of two things that were said about opium in the late Qing: (1) that parents relied on opium to keep wayward offspring under control and (2) that foreigners used opium to subdue and dominate China. The note in common between these two is the manipulative use of opium to pacify someone else. "Manipulative use" also connotes the dichotomy between the one who knowingly distributes opium and the one who is supposed to fall for it. The idea of opium pacification, moreover, suggests fighting a war without the usual weapons and carnage. The idea is to engage in massive seduction and then await the hoped-for results.

The second statement—that Britain used opium to soften and dominate China—was repeatedly aired during the hearings of the Royal Commission on Opium, and it drew two main types of reaction. The first, expressed by statesman Thomas F. Wade, denied that the British deliberately addicted the Chinese (United Kingdom 1894, 1:87). Chinese were already smoking opium before the British arrived, these witnesses would say. Some might add that the Chinese by predisposition had a "love of sensuous dreamy pleasure," as Reverend George Owen stated (United Kingdom 1894, 5:237). The second type of reaction was expressed by Polhill Turner, who reported that the Chinese even called native-grown opium "foreign smoke" (what I have translated as "Western-seas smoke"), for "that is the stigma put upon us" (where "us" refers to the English; United Kingdom 1894, 1:129). Many missionaries asserted that this stigma was the reason for Christianity's failure to succeed in China. Although statistics are impossible to come by, the general impression is that statesmen and merchants were less anti-opium than missionaries, of whom I find virtually all to be "anti-opium."

That parents used opium to pacify potentially wayward sons was proverbial in late Qing China, as I have discussed in chapters 1 and 6. Whatever connection with reality it may have had, this trope by its very existence and wide circulation broadcasted ready acceptance of the idea of using opium to manipulate others. Thus, one presumes, it would have been easy to link this trope with the idea that the British tried to soften China when they so knowingly and impudently sold the Chinese a substance prohibited by imperial decree.

Thomas Wade and others like him denied British complicity in such a plot. He was annoyed at other British—the "anti-opiumists"—who spoke openly of British culpability (United Kingdom 1894, 1:87–88). It was a case of betrayal by one's own and it was an insulting defamation of British face. He went on, moreover, to declare that opium was not such a serious problem, and that abuse was the exception rather than the rule.

In the end the Chinese were neither purely passive and innocent victims, nor were the British and other foreigners so consciously and diabolically conniving. Still, the eventual outlawing of opium and other "dangerous drugs" amounted to the excision of a problem that was easier to define and reduce than the much bigger and amorphous problem of British culpability— especially culpability in importing opium to China as part of a scheme to create "free markets." That is, it was easier to get rid of opium than to address, for example, the problem of how Britain could "make up for," so to speak, its culpability. It was easier to blame opium for stalling and perverting modern progress. Opium thus eventually drew to itself an array of negative and reductive images: it uses were mainly abuses, it was predominant among undesirable people whom it made more undesirable, and it was conducive to crime and exploitation. We might say that opium then became a conveniently disposable infection whose elimination would supposedly yield a state of health, renewability, and removal of guilt. Those who made money using any means they could would find other goods to sell besides opium, which had become too embarrassing a thing to deal with. With opium gone, the obvious complicity of the British and other nationalities could continue to be obfuscated and minimized.

OPIUM AS WILD BEAST

How, meanwhile, did opium addicts of whatever nationality represent themselves and what they were doing? What is their response, if we can put it this way, to those who for so long had been trying to outlaw them? The addicts responded that they were busy realizing a new experience of craving thirst. This was what was new: the depth of sadness that could be reached between opium euphoria and craving. Cocteau: "The craving penetrates everywhere. Resistance is useless. At first a malaise, then things become worse. Imagine a silence equivalent to the crying of thousands of children whose mothers do not return to give them the breast" (Cocteau 1996, 57). Zhang Changjia: "Three times awakening, three times cocooned, / every day, every night forever. / Life is either smoking or waking from dream; / it is like thirst, then like starvation" (no. 61). The problem was whether this experience could be put to use. Cocteau writes that through opium "we get an idea of that other speed of plants" (Cocteau 1996, 92). More to the point:

> Opium, which changes our speeds, procures for us a very clear awareness of worlds which are superimposed on each other, which interpenetrate each other, but do not even suspect each other's existence. (p. 88)

The superimposition of worlds allowed by the "immobile speed" (p. 88) of opium is similar to the crossing of categories between humans and things that Zhang Changjia writes of. It is also the superimposition of Chinese, British, Japanese, French, Indian, American, Eurasian, and so forth. As

Cocteau also writes, however, although "opium enables one to give form to the unformed . . . it prevents, alas, the communication of this privilege to anyone else" (p. 87).

Zhang Changjia, like Cocteau, wrote about opium as if there were important things to say about it. He did not render his words in a sober and transparent fashion, however. What use would that have been? He used an allusive, classical Chinese, wrote thoughts digressively with no central thread leading from beginning to end, and interspersed his digressions with poetic statements and lines of poetry, in a way very similar to Cocteau in *Opium: The Illustrated Diary of His Cure* (1930), Avital Ronell in *Crack Wars* (1992), or Dale Pendell in *Pharmako/Poeia* (1995; an herbal and literary guide to psychoactive plants). He would have been hard put to argue for the utility of smoking opium except for citing the common excuse that opium cured numerous ailments and prevented one from getting others. He and his friends consoled themselves one day for their exemption from "pestilence" (e.g., cholera, malaria, dysentery). As they mused, the god of pestilence only attacked nonsmokers, figuring that smokers already suffered enough (no. 25). Despite their suffering, smokers were in charge of their health in a new way and managed thereby to steal themselves from the clutches of at least one of the gods. We can draw a parallel between the acceptance of this suffering and the deliverance from another, on the one hand, and the choices one had to make between bigger things such as being Chinese or Western, on the other. Each such choice entailed the acceptance of some sufferings and the rejection of others. Addiction, no matter how excruciating, at least provided the addict with its own form of objective certainty in such things as method of consumption, amounts of dosage, and intervals of craving and relief.

Besides pestilence, smokers stole from another god, the god of money, and they did so in a way that was equally careless and possibly ended them in destitution. Zhang Changjia wrote of the rise of the opium demon and the fall of the god of money (no. 15). No one loves money as much as opium, he said. No one quits smoking because of love of money. The fall of the god of money means the end of the wise and pious use of money. The formula is that if a person gives offerings to the god of money, the god will help that person become rich or at least not go poor. But now a tremendous change in the scale of expenditure has occurred. Slowly but surely people smoke themselves into destitution, treating money wastefully and disrespectfully because they no longer care about such things as saving, investing, and deferring. Money no longer appeals to or enthralls them. Ever higher profits are like what Claude Farrère says of sex: an "inexplicable bit of clowning" (Farrère 1931, 202). The fall of the god of money in turn coincides with the fall of Confucianism, where Confucianism can be defined as the elite counterpart to the religion of the money god. The fall of the money god and Confucianism in turn means the rise of something else—the opium demon, alias the Western drug, which is delivered by foreign ships manned by Euro-Americans who overwhelm China with their industrial capitalism and Christianity.

Zhang Changjia leaves off at this brief reference to foreign incursion and returns, so to speak, to his main message of generally distinguishing good smokers from bad and otherwise meditating on the exitless world of opium smoking. Meanwhile the new ways of exitless life–however they are tagged (e.g., "modern" or "Westernized")–continue developing beyond Zhang Changjia's life through the fall of the Qing, the formation of a republic and then of socialism. How can we not avoid seeing Chinese socialism in part as an alternative form of opium bliss and refusal of Western hegemony, precisely in line with its draconian eradication of opium?

The issue is one of approach, again to use one of Cocteau's ideas, which Dale Pendell's *Pharmako/Poeia* also quotes: "The danger is smoking as a defense against some moral disequilibrium. Then it is difficult to approach the drug in the way it must be approached, as wild beasts should be approached–without fear."[10]

Those who wish to eradicate opium are like the ones who send a posse to kill the tiger that ate a child or to kill the Indians who scalped a white. The danger of smoking opium as a defense against some moral disequilibrium, if I read Cocteau sensibly, lies in resorting to opium as if it had mythic powers to resolve moral dilemmas or psychic imbalance, as if it could magically transform and repair the ego. The dialectical obverse of this use of opium is the fear that opium will turn humans into nonhumans or antihumans. Wild beasts, addicts, and Orientals are alike feared as antihumans, negations of humans. Hybrid mixes of wild and civilized are equally alien.

The harm or good that comes from associating with opium has to do with how one approaches it. The wrong approach, whatever that may be, violates the wild beast which is opium (wild like the tiger or the Indian). The nineteenth-century doctor Duncan MacPherson was also getting at this point when he said in a single paragraph at the end of his chapter on opium:

> There is no disease in which opium may not be employed; nor do we know of any substance which can supply its place. Yet here we find its use abused, like many others of the choicest gifts of Providence. (MacPherson 1842, 249)

Dale Pendell echoes Duncan MacPherson in a myth he tells about the First Doctor, a "wise and compassionate" woman, to whom the gods first presented opium, saying to her:

> After food, this is our greatest gift. Use it wisely and unselfishly. It is never wrong to ease the suffering of those who do not know the secret. But remember, for yourself, who are a doctor, this plant shall ever be a poison. (Pendell 1995, 117)

A poison is something that can only be used wisely and is prone to be used unwisely. Opium may be an addiction, but so are steamships, guns, oil, or cars. All these potential objects of abuse need not be looked upon as enemies, weapons, or gods, but as allies and relatives. They are neither too nice nor too other. They are poisons, chanting a beguiling message.

Opium both introduces a new kind of pleasure and reintroduces or reopens the view onto a deep kind of pleasure that always existed but is usually well hidden. The role of conventional order is precisely to keep that pulsating, unbridled pleasure hidden and off-limits. Perhaps it is the extreme irregularity of those nineteenth-century times in China that gave a thing like opium a better chance than usual to display its effects. Those effects have always been there, but finally, at this time of modernizing and leveling cultural boundaries, exerted themselves more broadly than ever on the boundaries of sexual and social identity. In the face of such shocking luxury, Western and Chinese prohibitionists eventually overcame their mutual alienation to join in outlawing opium at the beginning of the twentieth century. In so doing, they were in effect creating a new type of global uniformity while leaving each other just enough room to maintain their basic but distinct cultural integrities. Hence the potential of drugs to generate both global "identity crisis," as I said at the beginning of this book, and global unity.

Meanwhile we now seem lodged at the point where the illegal drug industry has established itself as a permanent marginal economy that continues to straddle and confuse the divide between legal and illegal, real money and laundered money, consumable and unconsumable, and developed and underdeveloped. Marginal connotes parodical: that which apes the real thing, tossing back and forth the question of whether the margin or the center is really the grotesque one.

NOTES

1. Male addicts typically experience a decrease in libido. See "Opium Talk," nos. 28, 30. In an example from Qing fiction, a male smoker in *Precious Mirror of Boy Actresses* cannot get an erection with a young man who fondles his penis. "It was as if he was in the middle of an opium craving, listless with head dangling despondently" (chap. 47, 17b).

2. Lenson 1995, 177. He also says in regard to cocaine: "Instead of money's measuring power, which both limits and suggests limitlessness, cocaine represents desire that at least temporarily overrides money's limiting aspect and permits the illusion of infinite consumption, infinite profit, or infinite expenditure" (p. 175). Cocaine trade and consumption are a "dangerous simulacrum" and "an embarrassing parody of the free market economy" (p. 176). These statements are from a chapter entitled "Blow Money: Cocaine, Currency, and Consumerism." Avital Ronell likewise refers to drugs' ability to parody the capital market (Ronell 1992, 50–51).

3. Han Bangqing's Hong Shanqing is such a smoker, as was perhaps Han himself. Since we do not have many details about either Zhang or Han, they may have suffered more than we know. But it is clear nevertheless that many smokers, refined or otherwise, lived relatively stable lives.

4. See the examples of such women in Jaschok 1988.

5. See passage in *Dream of Moon and Romance*, chap. 27, 193–94.

6. See *Souls from the Land of Darkness*, chap. 22.

7. On masculine and feminine modes of subjectivity and the femininity of hysteria in general, see Zizek 1997, 131, 137; Zizek 1998; Copjec 1995, chap. 8.

8. Self-contained subjectivity, so to speak, "desubjectivizes" the self from the normal order of things. I have borrowed the term "desubjectivization" from Zizek. See Zizek 1997, 66; 1998, 107–8. Using different terms, Paola Zamperini studies the act of female suicide and its role not as surrender but as assertion and as a gesture of independence (2001).

9. In numerous articles, but see, for example, Bhabha 1994, 224–26.

10. Pendell 1995, 117; Cocteau 1996, 59.

Appendix

Yanhua, "Opium Talk"

by Zhang Changjia of Jinshan County, Jiangsu Province

PREFACE

The darkness settles silently as the sleepless sea creature lights the lone lamp. Suffering the melancholy of distant parting, he is like a dreaming mite that grieves over the vast cosmos, with nowhere to bury his worries. Alone he embraces a wounded heart, having lost all hope of finding a sympathetic companion. Wishing to dispel this solitary frustration, he happens upon a marvelous book. With untrammeled talent, the author Mr. Zhang Changjia[1] weaves thoughts serene and profound! With nothing to his name, he sings golden-jeweled songs. He handles his pen as if riding the wind, while evoking the air of an antique bronze. Long lost in a deep obsession, he regrets having entered such a labyrinthine way. But he has made a testament of his unique understanding and has turned it into a philosophical treatise. He couches serious ideas in his banter and feigns humor while composing rigorous words. After reading it over and again, I am filled with admiration.

The beginning of the story can be traced back to Canton, where the poppy was first introduced. The Great Wall of China has gone to ruin! What use is it to lament over the gross blundering empire? The disaster spread everywhere as the poison flowed into the hinterlands. It was like flood, conflagration, and rampaging armies all at once, making no discrimination between rich and poor, high or low. It has been thus because fate must run its course, and even with heavenly intent it would be difficult to undo. Those fallen into this obsession will ever utterly waste themselves. They can never turn back even after repeated defeat. Like moths flying into a flame they gladly burn themselves to a crisp. They're like horses galloping toward a precipice with no one to pull back on their reins. Heroes drown themselves in the depths of a mere length of pipe. The Buddha of Mercy pities them as they devote themselves to the burning lamp. People cite venerable words to warn them but have no canons to lend them support. They admonish them with powerful logic, but however to the point, they never make headway.

But here you are whose passion is to linger in fragrant virtue. Words blossom from your writing brush. Not afraid to express yourself with biting tongue, you merely wish to take your own experience to articulate the truth. I retreat before you. You talk of everything under the sun in a torrent of words. You show me your work. I open it and find the words rushing as through a deep gorge.

Since we both abide in the realm of the orchid's aroma, I have dared to submit my humble views. I joined with the Master of the Hall of the Tuoluo Buddha of Western Zhejiang to admire this marvelous text and make an offering of some of my opinions. My goal has not been to improve it, as if I dared try, but perhaps to make it more piercing in its radiance.

The proofing is expert; the critical marks are just right. Copied in the style of fly-head characters, it is an eternal treasure of esoterica. Yet it is not just for our own sake that we have done this. We also wish to offer the work to those of similar tastes.

Alas! Rapacious rats swarm in the outskirts, having long since seized the vital centers. The moaning swans fill the wilds, their innards about to wither and dry. No one advances a cure or generates new energy. None blames himself for being cowardly and weak. Instead everyone talks glibly of making the nation wealthy and strong. Those good at patching cracks stir up an energy of the moment but last only as long as an opium high. Those with great plans compete to their last breath, no different in this from the fast ascent of the opium rush.

People cling to false hopes of improvement and can't stop even if they try. The habits of those who govern are fixed and unchangeable. Even they know they are wrong but still proceed in their error. What finally is today's greatest addiction? How can it only be opium?

High summer 1878, prefaced by Mr. Most Uninhibited of the Cloudlands at his abode in Shanghai, the City on the Sea, in the deep shade of the willows.

Poems in dedication:

> (1) Happy to put pen to paper, not fearing frustration,
> on a clean mat with a bright lamp amid the night sounds.
> Wafting the smoke of wisdom from his very throat,
> he is his own kingdom of thought.
> Void marvelous truth will flesh forth,
> roiling wild waves splash from his tongue.
> Whirling words come down which you, sir, remember,
> every one of them as full of joy as of bitterness.
> Hua Mengyu of Nanhui.

(2) Reclining on a couch,
greatly fond of the opium clouds and
the fragrant colors and sonorous taste.
Noticing the flame tiny as a star,
I trim the wick before it goes out,
as we talk in low voices freely confessing our hidden feelings.
I try to pull away, but it still pulls me back.
About to leave, but once again I return.
Nine times nine, the immortal drug is fired to perfection.
Hungering for it,
as the pellet is just now ready,
in one breath I am instant clarity.

Your pen criss-crosses with many colors,
yet another strand of feeling wafts in circles of clarity.
I sigh for 100 years of unreality,
life floating like a dream,
China resting on a high pillow,
sleeping soundly, hard to awaken.[2]
What need is there to free oneself,
nothing wrong with deep fascination,
for it is the tall golden body of Buddha that shows us this plant.
Describing it
gets at the wisdom within,
and lives out the joy of life.
Chen Shenghua of Shanghai.

(3) Another universe,
not a single hindrance or concern,
all day lying on the couch,
the taste of sleep country,
letting the person be completely free.
How many are the old comrades from the land of immortals,
who, having chanced to lose their footing, all go searching in the opium clouds.
The Buddha from the West,
opening the blossom of the poppy,
supplies us steadily to this day.

Mr. Zhang is wise in his ways;
and speaks from his own experience,
having long reflected upon his sunken state.
He set himself to writing and showed me;
it is enough to prove that his feelings are not shallow.
It has managed to ruin generations of heroes,
which in vain one regrets, the past is all dust.
From this day on,
through morning bells and evening drums,

it won't be difficult to arouse myself from spring dreams.
Sun Fanmin of Guwan.

(4) Limitless is the longing,
the taste of ease is forever.
Before the lamp hidden fragrance seeps from the golden poppy.
A guest arrives, the opium clouds become our fixation,
old hands we are in this land.

Marvelous words fall like flowers from heaven,
clear talk is fragrant as jade flakes.
We leave it up to you in your sagacity to unravel.
Awaken scores of spring dreams,
the chance is now.
Zhu Liu of Quantang.

YANHUA

1. *Apian* is also written *yapian.* In the *Bencao*[3] it is called *afurong.* Today it is simply called *yan,* smoke, or *dayan,* the great smoke, or *wuyan,* the black smoke, or else it is called *yangyan,* Western-sea smoke. A look at the character for *yan* reveals that it is made up of three characters, *huo* (fire), *xi* (west), and *tu* (earth). Clearly when the character was created it already foretold the present day of opium: fire (bringing) earth (from the) west.[4] It is said that at the time of the invention of writing heaven rained millet and demons wept at night. This old saying is quite applicable in the present instance too.

2. Opium comes from India, the land of Buddhism, which legend says is where the Buddhist paradise can be found. Many people seek that paradise, but few ever find it. The reason for this has to do with the fact that it is so difficult to traverse the miles of rough terrain and unbearable weather. No one can stand it.

Ever since opium has spread so widely, those who have entered its realm achieve nothing short of the same Buddhist paradise. My opinion about this is that the Buddha pitied this multitude and therefore spent millions so that the opium lamp could reach every part of China. Thus all of the teeming millions can enjoy enlightenment. The law of Buddha is boundless. The truth of this is clearer than ever now.

3. When young men of privilege *(zidi)* first smoke opium, in the beginning it is a matter of the thrill of "fishing and hunting" for courtesans. They smoke for pleasure but the pleasure of smoking is still not their main goal.

Later they seek a bright and tranquil room and the most exquisite utensils. They give their thoughts to nothing else. This is one transformation.

Then they wish for a place that is hidden and secluded where no one can discover them. In this stage of retirement from the world, they no longer make the effort to seek refinement. This is one more transformation.

Next, they want good opium with clean ashes. They must have thorough enjoyment. Now they reveal all signs of their preoccupation and couldn't care less about keeping it hidden from others. This is yet another transformation.

Next, smoking day after day gives rise to the problem of expenses, making them seek cheaper prices in order to maintain their daily supply. Appearances are now out of the question altogether. Thus another transformation.

Following this their addiction is heavy, their bodies weak, and they fall into extreme poverty. They resort to taking loans in order to relieve their ever present urge. Even if the price is high, they don't dare bargain down. This is another transformation.

Finally they haven't even a fraction of a cent to their name. No one will loan them anything. They wish they could break their addiction but can't bear the pain of it. So they put on an air of carefree idleness and go searching out former acquaintances, hoping for some kind of handout, no matter how demeaning the reception might be. This is another transformation.

At last they forgo all sense of conscience and turn into the ugliest of creatures. This is their lowest level.

4. In smoking opium there are stages of gradual entry. In the beginning is the situation in which when one doesn't smoke it, it is fragrant, but when one does smoke it, it is not.

The next stage is that of when not smoking it, it is not without fragrance, and for sure when one does smoke it, it has a fragrance.

Next comes the point at which it is only fragrant when one smokes it.

Finally, whether one is smoking it or not: no fragrance. This is the end.[5]

5. When people first start smoking opium they are filled with firm determination: "Other people have no control over themselves and thus sink into it. But I am intelligent enough not to end up that way!" Then when they are on the verge of sinking into it, they adopt a new approach and say, "Forswear the meat cleaver and instantly become a Buddha! I have the discipline to control it!" But later on when they know too well that there is no going back they say, "In the end I have the fortitude to stick to a moderate dose and to avoid falling into a state of complete fascination and oblivion!" When they land straight into the most unbearable suffering and it is too late for regrets, they finally say with amazement, "That one mistake can lead to such an end!" But how long is a human life after all? It is over now!

6. In recent times young men of privilege play at getting the secret knack of things. They aren't fearless of getting addicted but all the same love smoking opium. They insist, "Wait until I'm on the verge and then I'll stop." What I am trying to say is that if you're afraid of getting addicted, why smoke at all? If you want to quit, why wait until you are on the verge? In general,

when you're on the verge of addiction, you are already in a situation in which you are proceeding step by step into the highest states of ecstasy. It is just like water rushing downstream in a torrent. The flow is so fast who could stop it? At this point, only someone who can hold back waves can avoid the fate of drowning. Such people are rare indeed.

7. There are families who love their sons and thus under no circumstances allow them to smoke. In these cases absolutely no opium smoking apparatus is let into the house. Then there are sons who are good to their parents but not to the point of denying themselves opium. In these cases opium apparatus is inevitably let into the house. I have often seen people who upon learning that their son occasionally smokes will react with horror and will scold him harshly. But then when he becomes fully addicted, they merely admonish him gently or perhaps ask him to just lighten his addiction. Then when he has reached happy and reckless abandon, they proceed to tell him not to "associate with friends outside the home" and they say that they would "rather him stay inside and try to smoke a little more sparingly." Alas, isn't this a case of parental training that never follows through? Opium is an obsession that can't be allowed to take root. Once it does, then it realizes itself in a grip that only gets tighter. Whoever tells him to smoke at home and be "a little more sparing" is already at the stage of absolute hopelessness.

8. Anyone who reaches a point of no return will inevitably be filled with thoughts of repentance and salvation. But the obsession of smoking opium imposes a degree of bondage so ensnaring that you can't be saved. Fathers and brothers exhort the addict to quit, brothers fight and split up because of it, husbands and wives clash, friends cut you off. People reach the extreme of going out with stomachs barely full and bodies improperly clothed, with hunger and cold pressing on them all at once, their eyes watering and their noses running. With such people it isn't that they were unaware of the dangers and accidentally fell into the trap. They probably knew from the start what would happen and committed their mistake quite consciously. This is what it is all about to become so ensnared that you can't be saved.

9. I remember during my youth that whenever young men of privilege wished to amuse and enjoy themselves they would have a drinking party. This to them was the greatest pleasure in life. But later on they came to realize that smoking opium was even better. The most extreme among them would abandon themselves to opium and never touch liquor again. This makes me think of those nowadays who try to succeed by means of examination learning. They start with the canons of the sages and biographies of the virtuous. Next they intone the words of the great old essayists. Later they take the dregs of the present times, the so-called model essays, which they croon and recite, and spend their lives mouthing complete babble. I would like to know whether they remember even half a line of the so-called canons of the sages, biographies of the virtuous, and the essays of the old masters?

They think this is a way of gradually entering the realm of bliss. I say it is degrading yourself day by day.

10. There is a vast gulf between those who smoke and those who do not. The question is how to keep oneself in check. The answer: prudence in upbringing!

11. If you want to tell whether a smoker is addicted or not, just look at whether he neatens his utensils before or after he smokes. Those who neaten up after smoking are definitely already addicted. Neatening up first and then smoking is a sign of one not yet addicted. Only those who have been through these things understand what I mean.

12. I once knew of two smokers, one who smoked constantly, often going at it with abandon. The other was restricted to the home and never allowed to indulge. A few years later the one who went at it with abandon was still not deeply addicted. But the one who never indulged had already become deeply addicted. Thus the old saying: "Life is easier for the prostitute who gets married than for the nun who returns to the world."

13. Those who pursue higher learning are always saying "advance" but in fact retreat in ever increasing numbers. As for those who smoke opium, they are always saying "retreat," but in fact advance further every day. For this reason it is impossible for the way of Confucius to take effect in the foreign lands. Christianity, however, is surely on its way to transforming the ancient land of China. The fate of the times has made it thus.

14. Smoking opium is like a girl binding her feet. Tightening by a degree brings one more degree of pain. Loosen it a bit and she feels that much relief.

15. Opium is contractive in nature and thus capable of making people put all other things aside. In material essence opium is soft and thus capable of taming all other fires.

Keeping this in mind, look at the rich young wastrels who fly about acting brashly and impulsively. There is no evil they will not commit. Fortunately they take up opium and thus chance upon a medicine that is made precisely for those whom nothing else can save.

All people enjoy the pleasures of hearing, seeing, tasting, and smelling. Opium clearly is a pleasure of the mouth. Now the lowly people of the world all wish to fulfill their basic desires. When they get to such an extreme of desire that they can't suppress it, all they have to do is reflect a bit and they will see before their eyes a certain thing, the one that combines the round with the square, that is, money,[6] which is slowly but surely fluttering out the window. At this point they will come to a shocking realization. With this realization they will understand that all other desires must retreat in the face of the need for money.

If we take the mouth's fondness for food and transfer it to opium, then we will never find anyone who quits smoking out of a love *(ai)* of money. It is clear that love of food is not as strong as love of money, and that love of money is not as strong as love of opium. It thus follows that the rise of the opium demon has led to the fall of the god of money *(qianshen)*.

16. The ancient Master Cheng Lian's "Tune of Narcissus" was said to be capable of making listeners feel transported. I would say that opium too has this property. In general, when my opium craving first stirs, my mind's eye can see nothing but sad clouds and gloomy mist, bitter rain and desolate wind. After I have smoked to the point of passionate ecstasy, I feel free and uninhibited and my eyes are sparkling with fresh energy. At this point wherever I look I see nothing but auspicious visions. It is like the bright sun at the start of day.

The Creator of things cannot control the abnormal events of the world.

The Lord of Heaven cannot manipulate the moods of this person.

What is this black smoke that so vexes you, sir?

When Yi Di made wine, Yu drank it and enjoyed its sweetness. When Yi Ya cooked fine dishes, Duke Huan of the kingdom of Qi ate them and slept soundly until the next morning.[7] How shallow were these pleasures! Looking back from today's perspective, all the tantalizing things from ancient times on absolutely pale before opium.

17. Everyone has their pleasures to pass away the months and years. Some are transfixed with flowers, some sink into wine. There are those who abandon themselves to bamboo shoots, and those who love to gamble. In excess these things are enough in themselves to cause one to waste time and ruin one's livelihood, to offend against morals and harm one's health. If you don't blame people for these pleasures but instead only blame opium, is that not a narrow view of things?

What's more, pleasures and desires come in endless arrays but opium in itself encompasses them all. With it you can become completely carefree and content. It allows you to retire from the world. In one bed, on a single mat, you can sleep with it, take nourishment from it, and perform all ablutions in it. Meanwhile you are in another world and have no need to inquire about what is going on outside your door. Like Hongjing living in his tower, Zhongshu lowering his curtain, Shaowen roaming in his sleep, or Damo meditating while facing the wall. Sink into it, soak it up, to the end of your life. Isn't this the best way to banish sorrow, the crowning way to arrest desire? Alas! Without such a person with whom will I find solace?

18. Once the Western lamp is lit, it shines in all directions. Those whose eyes it meets come like moths flying into a flame. Once the Western smoke starts burning, its fragrance spreads all around. Those whose noses it enters arrive like maggots converging on rotten meat.

19. In their early stages opium smokers take after Mozi. The seasoned smoker takes after Yangzi. By this I mean that new smokers enjoy company, not solitude. They usually invite friends over, those of the same interests as themselves, and everyone smokes together. They'll even gladly mingle with

strangers and people of lower classes. If this is not an example of Mozi's "universal love" then what is it?

But the seasoned smoker, he likes solitude, not company. He usually hides himself away and shuts out noise. He sleeps alone in his own room. He scorns company with even the closest relatives and the most respectable people. If this is not a case of Yangzi-like self-serving, then what is it?

The true sage among smokers is one who associates with those he should associate with but does not overdo it, and he distances himself from those he should be distant from but does not become aloof. Such a person is rare.

20. I once knew an old man who was an adept at the art of nourishing life *(yangsheng)*. He still looked youthful at age seventy. When I asked him his method, he said, "You need just two things for nourishing life and nothing else: opium and sex." I thought this was nonsense, but he said otherwise. "Anything that is good for you," he explained, "becomes harmful if you abuse it. Likewise, with whatever is harmful, as long as you understand its true nature, then it can bring benefit. With opium there are those who smoke it all the time and completely reverse day and night. The way I take it is to smoke once after every meal. I never fail in this rhythm and I never exceed the same amount. Opium is something that enhances the flow of energy for me. Now with sex, there are those who do it all night, which wreaks utter havoc on the vital essences. My method is each time to have two beauties as my companions, but never to go to excess nor to allow ejaculation.[8] Sex is thus something that I use to nourish my vital essence. This is how I have reached old age while still looking young."

This man's example was a great wonder to me.

21. Truly, opium is something that the world cannot do without. Its ability to rouse the spirit, stir energy, solidify seminal essence, and cure dysentery, plus all its other swift and marvelous effects—absolutely none of the herbal drugs can outdo it. But people constantly revile it as an evil thing. Why? Because those who take it do not control themselves.

Now ginseng is a great tonic. If tried for only a day it is useless. But few are those who can take it in excess and avoid death.

Those nowadays who smoke opium can't get enough if they only smoke it once. After two times they must smoke it yet again. After smoking it yet again, they must smoke it all the time. You may wish to pursue it in a way that is not dangerous, but how can you?

Thus a Westerner once said: "In our country opium is a medical drug that we only use sparingly. In China people take it as if it were food and consume it daily in several meals." It is clear that it is not opium that harms people but people who harm themselves from opium.

22. Those who take tonic drugs get stronger the more they take. Those who take poison die. Opium is said to be beneficial, but why then after taking it for a long time do you become thin and emaciated? If you say it is

harmful, why is it that it fills you with such pleasure that your body feels weightless and you brim with energy? Seven times released, seven times caught again;[9] three times dormant, three times awakening.[10] Since ancient times there has never been such a marvelous drug.

23. Because humans are endowed with a wholeness of vital energy, they conform with the orientation of heaven and earth, and thus stand upright. Things, however, are endowed with an off-center form of energy, conform with the orientation of resting sideways and wending through, and thus lie on their sides. Although humans sometimes lie down, most of the time they are upright. Although things sometimes stand up like humans, most of the time they lie down. In general: different categories, different tendencies.

Opium is a kind of thing that can throw human nature into chaos and cause it to cross categories. Take a look at those trapped by it. Night and day they recline, feeling supremely peaceful and content. Occasionally there is something they have no choice but to get up and do, and they feel in every bone of their body that they are not meant for this. When they return to their old nest, though, they again have a feeling of their proper place. In these cases, then, the times of lying sideways exceed the times of standing upright. Are they humans, or are they things?

There is no way to know the answer to this.

24. Those who are good at reading the stars say: Heaven is like the shell of the egg, earth is like the yolk. The sun, moon, and stars revolve around the shell. Thus what is above and below as well as the four directions take turns alternating day and night. As for humans, they arise in the morning and sleep at night. This is the usual way. Nowadays those who smoke opium never get to sleep until the middle of the night nor do they arise until the middle of the day. Why is it that in waking and sleeping like this they are so different from others? It is probably because these people should have been born at a place in the extreme west. By this logic it would be just right for them to get up at the dawn of that place and to sleep when it got dark there. It's simply a mistake in the Registry of Destiny administered by the King of the Underworld. Why fault the smokers?

25. In a gathering of friendly smokers I once heard someone passing on the words of a soothsayer who said: "The Underworld compilers of the Registry of Victims of Pestilence granted an exemption to opium smokers. What this means is that opium smokers have already gone through more than enough suffering and so can be allowed some compensation." My jest in reply was: "But then it becomes such that one has to smoke opium by way of avoiding pestilence." Those present clapped delightedly upon hearing this.

26. Rest becomes impossible for the addict. Sleep becomes a small rest, death a big rest.

27. Smokers who wish to smoke only after the onset of craving are still at a stage of mild illness. Those who wish to smoke before the onset of craving,

however, are already deeply ill. In other words, in the case of someone who smokes when craving begins, once the craving is over, its traces can be left behind. For the one who smokes before craving comes on, although the craving is out of the way, the "yearning of the heart" [*xinyin*] never leaves. There are techniques for curing the craving, but not for curing the "yearning of the heart."

28. Many say that opium is beneficial to the affairs of the bedchamber, but I disagree. In fact it is quite the opposite. For opium can only bring about a contraction of vital essence. It cannot stimulate arousal. The contraction of vital essence, one would presume, increases staying power. But lacking arousal and having no way to drum it up leaves you such that even if you force yourself to go through with the act, you'll hardly feel any stimulation. I recall the time before I began smoking opium. My desires were at their height. Each time I went to bed I was full of ardor and lust. In later times if I smoked and then had sex, my sense of enjoyment mysteriously disappeared. Afterwards as I became increasingly addicted I began to lose my ability to become aroused. But I have still found one thing to be true. Whenever my craving is just approaching but still hasn't quite arrived, I feel a slight sense of a throb. Which proves that smoking opium is an effective way of curbing desire. As far as preserving vital essence and firing the inner fluids is concerned, these are idle fancies.

29. I once asked someone which malady was worse, opium or sex. He said that sex was worse. I disagreed. For people who go to excess in their likes, we give them the title of "fiend." Opium and sex are always the worst cases. If we put the two side by side and compare them, then we find opium fiends and sex fiends everywhere we look. But in a random selection of ten people you'll find seven or eight who are addicts, but hardly as many who are sex fiends. My conclusion then is that opium causes more harm than sex. How is this? Sex to begin with is one of the five principal human relationships. Opium, however, is something that came from somewhere utterly outside China.

30. Appetites are of two kinds, those that are inborn and those that are acquired. The appetites for food and sex are purely inborn. Nothing in them is acquired. Opium, on the other hand, is purely acquired, with nothing in it that is inborn. In general the appetites for food and sex require no learning and take effect without any need to go to extremes. Opium, however, is such that once you enter its realm you can't leave it for a second. But those who haven't yet dipped themselves into it will not have the slightest yearning for it. Thus the two kinds of appetites are opposite, and in fact not only opposite but mutually antagonistic. How is this so?

In general with opium it is a matter of sleeping and rising, that is, alternating between the cycles of opium high and opium craving. When I was thoroughly immersed in it and fully in its grip, food became for me a matter of filling my belly and being over with it. Sex was simply a case of going through the motions. I had no other aspirations. Later, however, I had a complete change of mind as I began to wonder how I had gone to such an extent of reversing priorities. I then made plans to gradually distance myself from opium with the ultimate goal of quitting it altogether. Although I was unable to cut loose completely, I nevertheless succeeded in rekindling my appetites for food and sex. I was like a hungry horse galloping to its trough. Still, my opium addiction was irreversible. I'd entered a bitter sea and left the shore too far behind. I'll never stop regretting that I ever took one puff of opium. Let this be a warning to all.

31. The strongest things in the world are good weapons and explosives. With the right luck, most people can avoid their harms. The tenderest things in the world are desire for women and opium addiction. Once entering their realms, even the most valiant hero will rarely escape. Still, can it be that the strength of desire for women and opium addiction so surpasses that of weapons and explosives? Indeed, I've never seen anyone who after falling in with these two fails to feel the profoundest anger and contempt, but those who can break with them are as few as can be.

32. When contributions are solicited for military needs, only the rich are expected to give. The poor can't be involved and are not considered stingy for not giving.

When sick people take medicine, they expect that it will take time for them to get well. If for as long as they live they never go poor, they are not considered wasteful.

On the other hand, if your household hasn't saved up enough grain and must therefore demand it daily from others, or if you have a slight illness but end up before half your life is over spending great amounts of money because of it, then you would not fail to wail and weep, saying that these are the most unbearable sufferings.

As for opium, in function it is like a leaky wine vessel and in nature like a wasting illness. Yet at this juncture those who wail and weep are in fact few. Is this not strange?

33. The proverb says: "If you drink wine, in three years you'll have no money. If you don't drink wine, in three years you'll also have no money." It is the same way with opium. In general those who smoke opium construct their whole life around it. As a result, in their expenditures they scrimp when they should spend, emptying their homes of anything that is unrelated to opium. They are stingy when they should be generous, thus depriving their bodies of all other pleasures. They are selfish when they should be magnanimous, thus eliminating social ties outside of those involving opium.

As for what they take in, they are always engaging in things they should have no part of, and end up forcing their way in all that they do. They take what they shouldn't take, and end up thinking they can get away with taking anything. They plot for things they shouldn't plot for and end up with everyone foisting plots on them.

If the smoker is poor, he'll surely be able to maintain himself. But if he is rich, then if his addiction is very strong, he will certainly cater himself lavishly. Or he may be lazy in his addiction and smoke less often. Either way, he will spend all he has bit by bit until he finally arrives at the level of those with no money.

34. Smoking opium not only squanders money but also wastes time. Let us hypothesize someone who lets himself go broke. He will make the excuse that he had no money to begin with. He stops striving for success, giving the excuse that he has no time to put into striving anyway.

If you apply these examples to someone who smokes opium, it won't merely be a matter of him squandering money but of him happily asking to squander it even further. It won't merely be a matter of wasting time, but of going to extremes of prolonging the process. He will exhaust his wealth and eat up his time, but feel no rancor or regret because of it.

From this I conclude that opium has a profound attraction for which all the beautiful palace women and the solicitous attentions of wives and concubines are no match. Outsiders can't possibly appreciate this. If this weren't so, then why is it that among so many rich misers and poor petty laborers, opium smokers are everywhere you look? From this you should also be able to get the general picture.[11]

35. There are hundreds of millions of people throughout the land, all smoking opium daily, each spending a good four hours a day. Two people together spend eight hours, three people spend twelve hours. Twelve hours a day is certainly nothing that young wastrels would consider worth saving and worrying over. But take one or two poor fellows who have eight mouths to feed and who rely solely on the labor of their hands. They should be ashamed enough for getting themselves into a state in which they abandon work and squander time. If they proceed to spend day after day in happy and rowdy company, they then become guilty of starving their wives and families.

I have said it before: in this business solitude is better than company. These are the reasons why.

36. When Western steamships are sufficiently fired up, they are keen and invincible and can sail a thousand miles in one journey. But when the fire is extinguished, the ship rests in complete silence, all night long surrendering its ability to move. If you want it to go the next day, you must fire it up again. The more fired, the more it can move. Upon reaching full potential, it is ready again for another journey of moving without stopping.

It is the same with opium smokers. When their craving comes on, their bodies feel shriveled and listless, their joints all stiff. They must rely on opium to fire themselves up. At the beginning of firing up, they wriggle like worms. A little more fired up and they begin to flow like a great river. Fired up for a good while, they brim and burst with energy, and quickened in every limb they steam forth with indomitable heat. By the middle of the night they have even more energy to spare.

Everywhere they look they try to make something out of nothing, seeking ever higher levels of refinement. Perhaps they chance upon someone else's accomplishment, which makes them recall the happiness at once having done that something themselves. They almost want to claim the other person's accomplishment as their own. Nothing exceeds the rush of inspiration at such times.

But alas it can't last. In the turn of an instant there is the "malady of the snake's tail," that is, the inevitable tapering off. It's just like making flowers bloom in winter. As soon as they bloom they begin to wither. In the end it isn't as good as the beauty of the seasonal thaw arriving of its own, the whole earth turning to spring, and trees and plants blooming in all their glory.

37. Opium is the opposite of food. Food wants thriving, opium wants decline. When one is young and robust, one thrives. When one gets old, one declines. The older one gets the less one eats but the more often one smokes. When one is strong and healthy, one thrives. When one gets ill, one declines. The sicker one gets, the more distant one gets from food, but the more intimate one gets with opium.

38. In prehistoric times humans ate their food uncooked and enjoyed healthy life spans of several hundred years. After Suiren[12] drilled wood to make fire, life spans gradually decreased in length. When that method was superseded by the use of flint, humans became even more violent and life spans were further rushed.

Still, food in those times was all boiled, pots and clay steamers serving as containers. There was still an attention to healthy living. In recent times, however, once tobacco became popular, all everyone did was to consume fire, searing their lungs and harming their vital essence. If tobacco is this harmful, then opium must be worse by far.

39. Why is it that opium smokers are always thin and anemic and their mouths always dry? In general, one's energy has definite limits. Nourish it and it is ready for action; stimulate it and it rises. Things have always been this way. Compare this with the nation's use of military. Training in times of peace is a way of maintaining resources so that they will be effective when needed. But putting an army to constant use will rarely fail to run it into the ground. Is one's energy then something one can so harmlessly keep stimulating? Restrain yourself then! Be prudent!

40. My younger brother has by nature always been honest and upright. Pointing to my opium utensils, he once said to me angrily, "What do you get from it that makes you so transfixed?"

I replied, "It's the taste of it. What's more, it's a matter of attachment [*qing*]."

My brother said, "The world's most delicious delicacies offer their own pleasures that one can enjoy all the same. As for attachment, flowers and beautiful women are where it should take hold. Why not transfer your attention to these things?"

I was silent and unable to come up with an answer. Is it really for the sake of taste? or attachment? Even I am incapable of knowing myself here.

However, if we look among all the strongest attractions in the world and ask which one absolutely cannot be replaced, it is probably true that the power of women over men is the strongest.

41. With the appearance of opium countless reputations have been ruined, countless minds have been wrecked. Even the most valiant of heroes fall into the trap, the wisest of wise are all the same taken in.

The following example illustrates my point: take a destitute man who tries to use every scheme possible to coax a wealthy man to visit him. Even if he lays out precious treasures or provides the most beautiful music, and goes himself to welcome him, even doing him the honor of repeated visits as if to a man of great distinction—none of this would work.

But if he whispered in the other's ear that there was someone just arrived from Canton who had a fresh supply of opium specially prepared by means of the most refined processing and would he be interested in going to have a try? Then even if it were the most wretched hovel, the rich man would fly there in an instant. Once such magic words are said, they outdo all the spurious tricks and strategies that masters can bestow on their disciples.

42. Our thankfulness for opium and our hatred of it are both easy to understand. When we are at the point of extreme craving and want to smoke but can't, or try to endure the craving but can't, the suffering is impossible to describe. Just give us a few tokes, though, and, there, now we feel that thankfulness. The general Han Xin would have starved had not the old woman given him food; the roving strategist Fan Ju would have frozen to death unless Xu Jia gave him clothing. The examples of these two, however famous, represent nothing compared with this kind of relief.[13]

But if we have opium whenever we want it, we begin to take it for granted. So let's say that the day comes when we're sick of it and decide to quit. Then we will experience the most unforgettable hatred of it.

Thus I say that ever since the rise of opium, our lives have been thrown into endless chaos.

43. Some people compare opium to sex. In my opinion they are not the same. Sex has to do with nature, opium with habit. When humans are young, they know nothing about sex. After developing an awareness of it, they follow a natural course of becoming attracted to one another.

As for opium, those who have not entered its realm will never in their whole lives acquire a love for it. It is only after lengthy immersion in it that one develops a condition of chronic illness. Thus abstention can only occur before taking it up.

44. Day after day people nourish their vital energy, their blood, and their flesh and bones. In this they resemble plants and trees. An internal illness can be likened to insects creating havoc from within. External harms are like axes and machetes chopping away from without.

One who smokes opium over a long period of time becomes as if covered by a huge stone: rain and dew can't get in to provide nourishment, and the plant has no way to sprout and grow. There is only fatigue and emaciation.

All we need do is look at someone who suddenly quits smoking. In not even a month the complexion has gradually enriched itself and the body has begun to fill in. Isn't this like taking the stone away and watching the plant burst into growth? This example gives us a good mirror of ourselves.

45. Everyone is endowed with a measure of virtuous energy. As soon as one takes up opium smoking, however, a perverse energy begins to invade, bit by bit chasing the virtuous energy away. After enough time has passed, the perverse energy is the only one in action. As a result, if one suddenly quits opium and deprives the perverse energy of opium as well, how can one not fall into great peril?

The virtuous energy is like the upright minister, the perverse energy like the petty sycophant. In the imperial court, as long as there are no sycophants, the upright ministers will persevere and can be relied on to maintain lengthy peace and enduring control.

Even when petty people invade the court, the regime will not necessarily collapse as a result. For if there is an enlightened ruler, he can step forth and make a show of vigor. He dismisses the crafty sycophants and recalls the worthy elders. Reform is then something foreseeable. But if there is no such plan and instead one just lets things go to ruin, then when affairs have gotten to a point of no return, one can no longer suddenly decide to come up with a plan and expect change for the better. For at that time it will be like the end of the Tang dynasty, when sycophants like this usurped power and laid the realm open to enemy invasion.

Thus those who wish to quit opium must take care to consider the method they will use in order to quit.

46. There are those who in desiring to quit go to doctors for a remedy. The doctor says: "How did you become so ill?" You answer: "Little by little I came to like it until it completely took over. Then it was another bit by bit that I increased my dosage until I arrived at such a great capacity."

The doctor replies, "You will succeed in quitting if you reverse this sequence. From today on, why not reduce your amount little by little until you can do with a very small portion, then gradually abstain from it until you can completely do without it. It is simply a matter of the worthy and virtuous gentleman willing himself to quit. What other way is there? Even the most effective drugs cannot outdo this single bit of sincere intent. For it is no easy thing to quit opium after becoming deeply addicted to it."

I have a way. Although it doesn't lead to complete abstention, at least it keeps you from smoking ever increasing amounts. All you need do is wait until the urge to smoke is at its extreme before letting yourself smoke. If you can just manage to get by, then you will learn what the appropriate dosage is and stop there.

In addition, you must rise immediately after you finish. You must put the lamp out right away. If you follow these rules then there will only be decrease, no increase.

But think carefully about the words "rise immediately" and "put the lamp out right away." These are words of eternal truth! Because all too often smokers finish their pipe and stay tossing and turning on the couch, moaning and groaning as the lamp glimmers away. They feel the greatest reluctance to part with their cherished friend. This then is the crux of their peril.

47. Once the masses of smokers have entered the opium realm and acquired their taste for the drug, they discover that all their perils are concentrated within it, and that they are in an utterly incurable condition. Now I'm saying that not only those who revel in it can't be saved, but neither can those who go to great lengths to sever their attachment. Even those people have such a long way to go that there never seems to be an end to it.

Why is this? He who abstains for one day must put his heart into it for that whole day. If he abstains for one year, he must put his heart into it for that whole year. Even if he has abstained for a very long time, he can never for an instant let his heart stray from the task.

Still, I ask, how can one quit and keep away from it for good? Only by means of the constant and unwavering effort of forcing oneself to resist it.

But in fact no one is in the least capable of such effort. For this reason we always see people who quit and go back to it over and again. There has never yet been one who quit once and for all and never went back to it.

48. It is easier for a woman to achieve glory by martyring herself than to gain honor by practicing chastity. This is because martyrdom arises from an instantaneous impulse of innate goodness—she cuts off her arm or scars her face and with that single gesture establishes herself for all eternity.

The chaste widow, however, must endure the spring air and autumn moon, the birds chirping and the flowers blossoming. These shapes and sounds impinge upon her from everywhere.

It's as if a wealthy and charming youth were always about to pass by as she looked expectantly out her door. She thinks back on the lonely lamp with its tiny flame, her bedcovers as cold as ice, day in and day out. At this point how can she resist longing for the old days again?

Those who wish to quit opium must be seen in this light.

49. I know of two people from the same village. One never smoked opium until seventy and then took it up; the other was a smoker all his life but quit at seventy. If neither had lived so long but instead had died in midlife, then it would be like the difference people of old saw between the fortunes of the Duke of Zhou, who at first failed but then was successful in governing and thus commemorated for the ages, and Wang Mang, who was at first successful but then failed and was vilified for eternity.[14]

50. No matter what the pleasure may be, people always come to a point at which they lose interest in it. Take food and sex. The desire for them is innate, but when we get old and ill we don't care for them anymore. It is the same with other objects of desire. Opium stands apart, however, because as long as we're even barely alive, we'll still want it. There is absolutely no giving it up in midstream—the day will never come. The most precious treasures won't lure you away. Even bizarre calamity won't make you give it up because of poverty. Indeed there has never been such a bewitching thing in all human time.

Still some say that addiction merely ties you up. What is so hard about untying yourself?

If you truly wish to "untie" yourself, however, the pain in fact will be worse than the severest illness. Weeks will go by before the pain goes away. No one in the end is willing to test themselves in this. In my opinion, there is a great force involved here. Take a look at someone who has not yet become addicted, and someone who has actually quit. The former is not ignorant of the warnings of others before him, while the latter—the one who has quit—is not ignorant of the troubles that are yet to follow.[15] Take a sharp knife and cut a silk thread with it. Nothing could be easier. So why is it that people follow failure with failure and remain forever unable to abandon opium?

For this reason I say: it is because with opium there is no arriving at a point of loss of interest.

51. I have playfully composed a list of ten prescriptions for quitting opium.

(1) Sex: once one enters this labyrinth, home and nation topple. How could such an insignificant thing as opium addiction outdo this?

(2) Gambling: the desire for profit becomes an obsession. One thinks only about winning and losing. People keep at it without respite, going night and day, spending minute after minute, cent after cent, without the slightest interruption.

(3) Conversation: when interest is aroused to a passion, one's heart bursts with joy—other pleasures can wait.

(4) Reading: even amid the noises of the city, one's attention is transfixed. Having caught the rabbit, forget about the trap.

(5) Travel: famous mountains and great rivers make one feel transported. In a broad and open place petty worries suddenly vanish.

(6) Wine: in the state of drunkenness lies another paradise in which I spend all day intoxicated. Lord Alcohol allows me to switch to an alternate realm.

(7) Making oneself busy: exhausted to death rushing off to yet another engagement, one doesn't even have time to eat or sleep, and so even less time for anything else.

(8) Sleep: in extreme boredom escape to sweet darkness.

(9) Destitution: the old saying has it that hunger and cold lead one to steal. If one can still steal, one is still not at the point of dire straits. A person in truly dire straits has gone all the way to the point of no longer being able to steal. Then finally one is forced to quit.

(10) Death: all phenomena end in emptiness. Consciousness turns to nothingness. One can no longer be touched by earthly dust. All opium smokers arrive at this point and thus meet their end.

52. Weapons are evil instruments that sage kings used only when they were forced to. For today's opium utensils the word "gun" is taken to refer to the smoking shaft, while "bottom of the sea" designates the opening of the mouthpiece, and "gate of struggle" the opening of the bowl. Such names indicate the formidability of opium. But people become numbed to this fact by habit of frequency and end up applying dangerous instruments directly to their own bodies. That one can be fully conscious and still make such a mistake is thus easier to believe.

53. When a smoker tips the bowl over the flame, it is called "shooting the fire." When one leans toward the fire at a slight distance, it is called "keeping the fire distant." When people formerly used lamps with oil cups, it was called "horizontal fire." Today we use a Western lamp, which is called "vertical fire."

If we reflect upon these expressions, "keeping distant" would seem superior to "shooting," "horizontal" superior to "vertical." But compared with the standard of ancient times when people ate uncooked food, then we are off by a great distance. By comparison, the minute differences of distant and close, horizontal and vertical are also insignificant.

54. The high and low of using things changes according to situation and place. If we take the example of ancient rulers, for luxury some used jade cups and ivory chopsticks. Out of frugality some lived in thatched houses and had steps made of earth. The difference between these extremes is tremendous.

With the opium utensils of today it is quite different, however. For the barrel both high and low use nothing more than bamboo. Even if you had rhinoceros or elephant ivory, neither would be suitable for the task. For the bowl both high and low use nothing more than clay. Even if you had the finest jade it would not be the right material. As for the tweezers, iron is all that either high or low users need. Gold and silver, however fine they may be, would not do the job. In the use of all three of these things, regardless of social rank, unequal people become equal users.

55. When Tang emperor Taizong met with new graduates of the highest degree, he said, "All the heroes in the world come within my compass." These words are prophetic of what later happened with opium.

56. I once saw a poem that had the following lines:

> You associate with me, but I still will be myself.[16]
> Being haggard because of you in fact shames me.[17]

I think the words "associate with me" and "haggard because of you" can be transferred and dedicated to opium.

57. When I took the first puff of opium, I felt no pleasure. But after ten more tokes, I began to feel the richness of its taste. Each time I smoked, I wanted more. I once read these words in a collection of poems:

> At first so sharp it stabbed my throat.
> Later, its richness released, I always craved for more.

This is worthy of being applied to opium too.

58. Chen Yuquan of Zhapu (in Zhejiang Province) had four seven-line poems called "Intoning upon Opium." One of them had these fine lines:

> Its marvelous effect is no second to the cinnabar elixir.
> In famine I would willingly put it before food.

My friend He Qiushi of Lou County also had a poem with a pair of couplets that I remember well:

> Foreign ships from afar deliver their tribute of mud.
> From such earthly flames we turn into immortals

and

> Morning and night the taste of lovesickness.
> Rain and wind to sleep the day through.

Compared with works of the past, these lines are even more natural and transcendent.

59. An old friend, Xia Guanfu, was good at both poetry and painting, his elegance approaching the manner of the ancients. He detested opium. He once wrote the following on an opium pipe for a friend:

> All night love thoughts join in one breath.
> Burning through lamp oil, who can equal you?

I know, sir, you have abandoned lofty ambition,
happily taking up the company of your opium clouds.

Hearing this is like being clubbed on the head and berated. It strikes fear in me!

60. Wang Meiyin tells of his teacher Ruan Yiyuan who composed a *ci* lyric called "Singing of the Western Drug":

On a short divan beside a lone lamp,
the pillow lies sideways across the quilt.
The cloudy smoke supplies nourishment;
spring flourishes under the plum flower canopy.
Sobering us from drink it dissipates our troubles;
the sound of our smoking is like the wind.
The feeling is sweet and free.
What, pray, is the extent of your capacity?
No less than the great general of Huaiyin![18]

61. There was once a scholar who fell into such extreme poverty that he resorted to selling opium in order to support himself. On his door he put the following couplets:

Three times awakening, three times cocooned,
every day, every night forever.
Life is either smoking or waking from dream;
it is like thirst, then like starvation.

This is quite like it is.

62. I sent a letter to a friend in which I wrote, "For every happy occasion, I have a room full of orchid guests. Fortunate to have such good friends, I have us gather side by side as we talk of old times. This is the good side of opium.

Endlessly caressing the lamp, scorching the lungs, exhausting the spirit, despairing all day and night, squandering time and ruining one's livelihood: this is the harm of opium."

Today I have a short formula to give him: "No need to refrain from it, but you can't always be at it either."

63. I once wrote a rhyme prose on opium that I had inscribed on an opium pipe for a friend. In it there was the following set of couplets:

If you go to the land of black sweetness,
  call out to it to be your go-between for summoning sleep.
If you meet it in the tower of painted women,
  then let it be your ambassador for visiting the flowers.

Mr. Xu Songyu liked these lines a great deal, saying that they showed true experience. But as I look at these lines today, I see them as nothing more than superficial words.

64. Of the things in the world that must go horizontal, like the so-called union of fertile essences spoken of in the *Book of Changes*, there is, we were sure, one and only one such thing. Little did we know that lately there has been added one more thing. For this reason I have written a poem on opium which includes these lines:

> In the horizontal lies yet another true pleasure;
> the dream of the love couch is no longer alone.

65. There is an old saying: "Plain cotton warms me. A vegetable root is fragrant food. Poetry is delicious forever." I parodied this in order to make fun of the opium smoker: "The cold cage is narrow.[19] The big mud[20] is fragrant. The opium pipe is delicious forever." Those present at the table laughed so hard that their food flew out of their mouths.

POSTSCRIPT

Cai Erkang of Shanghai adds his inscription: The harm of opium is something that anyone can describe. But they sit formally in all seriousness speaking with grave words, and we typically reach a point long before they finish when we are sick of their preaching. This work contains subtle satire within its humor, hints of deep emotion beyond the writing brush. The author speaks with great eloquence and marvelous depth. Readers will be enlightened before they know it. Clearly, scratching an itch through one's boot is no match for getting at the real thing.

I wish that all who have become obsessed with opium would copy this out in entirety and take it as their set of maxims.

NOTES

1. Here called by his style name, Junsheng.
2. Note in the original: "China but rests on a high pillow, the lamp passing around to everyone" is originally from a poem by Ding Shishui of Nanhui.
3. The sixteenth-century work on herbal medicine by Li Shizhen (1518–1593). Listed under *afurong*, opium at this time is already known as *apian* and *yapian*. Its two main uses are as a cure for various forms of dysentery and as an aphrodisiac. See Li Shizhen 1982, 1495–96.
4. *Tu*, earth or dirt, is another term used to refer to opium.

5. "Fragrance" stands for *wei*, which also means flavor, interest, or pleasure. Thus the last line, for instance, could be translated as "Finally, not smoking it is certainly no pleasure, but so is smoking it."

6. In imperial times money at the lowest denomination took the form of copper cash that was round with a square hole in the middle.

7. See *Zhanguo ce, Sibu congkan* 7.7a (Shanghai: Shangwu, 1920–1922), in which Yi Di's wine, Yi Ya's food, and other pleasures are said to be of such enticing quality that rulers lose their kingdoms because of them.

8. My interpretation of *liti*, literally, leaving the body, relies on the concept of ejaculation retention as taught in the traditional Chinese ars erotica, which does not use this expression.

9. This saying is from military terminology and represents a strategy used, for example, by Zhu Geliang in the novel *Sanguo yanyi* (Romance of the Three Kingdoms), meaning to soften and subdue someone by repeatedly catching but then purposely, and as if generously, releasing him.

10. In this saying, as silk worms grow, they "sleep" and then wake to eat again three (or four) times before making their cocoons. This expression appears again in nos. 30 and 61 and describes the condition in which the smoker either smokes and gets high or "awakens" from being high. One doesn't do without the other; there is either being up or being down, nothing else.

11. I interpret this to mean that rich misers supposedly have enough money to indulge in sexual entertainment, but they choose to spend money on opium instead and nothing else. Poor laborers (like the person in item 33 who lives in poverty and is able to maintain himself) are single addicted men who work menial jobs ("petty laborers"). If they weren't so fixed on earning just enough money for their daily supply of opium, they could supposedly find more lucrative jobs and earn enough to support wife and children.

12. A mythical inventor of fire.

13. See *Shiji* j. 92 and j. 79.

14. For clarity I have added the words "and thus commemorated for the ages" and "and was vilified for eternity," which do not appear in the original.

15. The one not yet addicted has seen addiction in others; the one who has quit knows how difficult it is to keep on quitting.

16. See chapter 5 above and *Shishuo xinyu* 9:35 (Xu Zhen'ou 1984, 284) for the original source of these lines.

17. See the Tang dynasty story "Yingying zhuan." These lines occur in a poem by Yingying at the end of the story after she and her lover have separated.

18. That is, General Han Xin of the early Han dynasty, who said that the more troops there were under his command the better.

19. "Cold cage," *lenglong*, refers to a special technique of the cooking process that produced what was prized as an especially mellow and fragrant type of opium. See Li Xiuzhang, 1988, 57.

20. Here again the word *tu*.

List of Characters

A Ying 阿英

afurong 阿芙蓉

ai 愛

Ailin 愛林

Aiqing 愛卿

An Ji 安驥

An Xuehai 安學海

apian 阿片

Bai Xiao 百曉

baitu 白土

Baochai 寶釵

Beidongyuan bilu 北東園筆錄

Bencao gangmu 本草綱目

Bencao gangmu shiyi 本草綱目拾遺

Cai Erkang 蔡爾康

Cao Changqing 曹長慶

Chen Sen 陳森

Chen Shenghua 陳笙華

Chi Zhicheng 池志澂

chishangle yin 吃上了癮

chiyan 吃煙

chou 抽

chui 吹

cixiongren 雌雄人

congliang 從良

datu 大土

dayan 大煙

dengyin 燈癮

doumen 斗門

du 毒

duiqiang guoyin 對槍過癮

dupin 毒品

Ernü yingxiong zhuan 兒女英雄傳

Ershi zai fanhuameng 二十載繁華夢

Fan Yuanwei 范元偉

fangui (fankwae) 番鬼

Fenglin 鳳林

Fengyuemeng 風月夢

Fusheng liuji 浮生六記

gao 膏

Ge Yuanxu 葛元煦

Gong Zizhen 龔自珍

guoyin 過癮

haidi 海底

Haidong zhaji 海東扎記

Haishang chentianying 海上塵天影

Haishang fanhuameng 海上繁華夢

Haishanghua liezhuan 海上花列傳

Han Bangqing 韓邦慶

hanjian 漢奸

Hanshang mengren 邗上蒙人

He Shutian 何書田

Heiji yuanhun 黑籍冤魂

heitu 黑土

Heiyu 黑獄

Henhai 恨海

Hong Shanqing 洪善卿

Hou Liaozhai zhiyi 後聊齋志異

Hua Guangsu 華光宿

Hualiu shenqing zhuan 花柳深情傳

Huan Wen 桓文

Huang Shiquan 黃式權

Huang Xiaopei 黃小配

Huang Yupu 黃玉圃

huanxigao 歡喜膏

huayanjian 花煙間

Huayuehen 花月痕

huo 火

Huyou mengying 滬遊夢影

Huyou zaji 滬遊雜記

Jia Ming 賈銘

Jiumi liangfang 救迷良方

Juhua 菊花

kang 炕

kexue 科學

kuaixie 快蟹

lenglong 冷籠

Li Shizhen 李時珍

liang 兩

Liang Gongchen 梁恭辰

Liang Qichao 梁啓超

Lin Zexu 林則徐

liti 離體

Lu Shu 陸書

Lu Xun 魯迅

mantuoluohua 曼陀羅花

Meng'an zazhu 夢庵雜著

miantiaoyan 麵條煙

miantiaoyan 棉條煙

minang 米囊

na tu　納土

palong 扒龍

Pan Jinlian 潘金蓮

Pan Qiguan (Pwan Keiqua) 潘啓官

pao 泡

Peng Yang'ou 彭養鷗

Pinhua baojian 品花寶鑑

Qian Zheng 錢徵

qiang 槍

qianshen 錢神

Qingloumeng 青樓夢

Qingshiduo 清詩鐸

Qinyan 琴言

Qiuhen 秋痕

Shen Fu 沈復

Shen Xiaohong 沈小紅

Shenbao 申報

shengyan 生煙

shengyi 生意

Shenlou waishi 蜃樓外史

shi ge yapian dayin 是個鴉片大癮

shihua 詩話

shimao 時髦

shinü 石女

Shishuo xinyu 世説新語

Songnan mengying lu 淞南夢影錄

songshi 訟師

su hu wei yin 俗呼爲癮

Sun Jiazhen 孫家振

ta shi ge chiyan de 他是個吃煙的

Taihai shichalu 台海使槎錄

Taiwanfu zhi 台灣府志

tan jin shuo gu 談今説古

tieqiu 鐵球

tongxin zhi yan, qi xiu ru lan 同心之言，其臭如蘭

tongyangxi 童養媳

tun pao 吞泡

tuo yin 脱癮

wanshougao 萬壽膏

Wang Tao 王韜

Wang Xi 王璽

Wang Xifeng 王熙鳳

Wang Yao 王瑤

Wei Pincai 魏聘才

Wei Zi'an 魏子安

Wen Kang 文康

wo guoguo yinle 我過過癮了

Wu Jianren 吳趼人

Wu Lian 吳廉

Wu Rui'an 吳瑞菴

wuduguo 無毒國

wuhui 烏喙

wulai 無賴

wushisan 五石散

wuyan 烏煙

xi 西

xi 吸

Xi Shiyi 奚十一

Xiamen zhi 廈門志

xianggong 相公

xiangsitu 相思土

xiangsiwei 相思味

xiaotu 小土

xiaozhao 小照

Xieyu congtan sanji 屑玉叢譚三集

Ximen Qing 西門慶

xinyin 心癮

xiu 嗅

Xu Fumin 許復民

Yaguanlou 雅觀樓

yan busi, zhu buluan 煙不死主不亂

yang 洋

yanggao 洋膏

yan'gaotang 煙膏湯

yangjinhua 洋金花

yangren 洋人

yangsheng 養生

yanguan 煙館

yangui 煙鬼

yangyan 洋煙

yangyao 洋藥

Yanhua 煙話

yannu 煙奴

yanpao 煙泡

yanyin 煙癮

yanyin laile 煙癮來了

yapian 鴉片

yin 引

yin 隱

yin 癮

yin fa 癮發

Yin Hao 殷浩

yin xu guo ge shifen zu 癮須過個十分足

yingsu 罌粟

Yingying zhuan 鶯鶯傳

yiqing 移情

Yixiang 把香

you shi sheng lan 有室生蘭

you wei 有味

Yu Da 俞達

Yu Ende 于恩德

Yu Jiao 俞蛟

Yu Jiaxi 余嘉錫

yu shanren ju, ru ru zhilan zhi shi 與善人居，如入芝蘭之室

Yuan Yi 袁翼

Yue Jun 樂鈞

Yulihun 玉梨魂

Zhan Xi 詹熙

Zhang Changjia (Junsheng) 張昌甲（雋生）

Zhang Chunfan 張春帆

Zhang Huizhen 張蕙貞

Zhang Shichuan 張石川

Zhang Yingchang 張應昌

Zhao Xuemin 趙學敏

Zhaoyinju 招隱居

Zhapu 乍浦

Zheng Zhenbiao 鄭振彪

Zhong Zufen 鐘祖芬

zidi 子弟

zuidaole 醉倒了

zuo hun shengyi 做葷生意

Bibliography

CHINESE AND JAPANESE SOURCES

A Ying, ed. 1957. *Yapian zhanzheng wenxue ji.* Beijing: Guji chubanshe.

——. 1985. *Xiaoshuo xiantan sizhong.* Shanghai: Guji chubanshe.

Chen Pingyuan. 1988. *Zhongguo xiaoshuo xushi moshide zhuanbian.* Shanghai: Renmin chubanshe, 1988.

Chen Sen. N.d. *Pinhua baojian.* Gest Library, Princeton University.

——. 1986. *Pinhua baojian.* Taibei: Guiguan tushu gongsi.

Chen Xiuqian. 1986. "Apian shilue." *Zhonghua yishi zazhi* 4: 238.

Cheng Jihu, ed. 1963. *Zhongguo dianying fazhanshi.* Beijing: Zhongguo dianying chubanshe.

Gao Heng. 1979. *Zhouyi dazhuan jinzhu.* Jinan: Qilu shushe.

Ge Yuanxu et al. 1989. *Huyou zaji, Songnan mengying lu,* and *Huyou mengying.* Shanghai: Shanghai guji chubanshe, 1989.

Han Bangqing. 1997. *Haishanghua liezhuan.* Hainan: Hainan chubanshe.

Hanshang Mengren. 1990. *Fengyue meng.* Beijing: Beijing daxue chubanshe.

He Shutian. 1984. *He Shutian yizhu sizhong.* Shanghai: Xuelin chubanshe.

Huang Xiaopei. [1960] 1982. *Ershi zai fanhuameng.* In *WanQing wenxue congchao; xiaoshuo sanjuan,* edited by A Ying, 313–568. Beijing: Zhonghua shuju.

Li Ling. 1993. *Zhongguo fangshu kao.* Beijing: Renmin Zhongguo chubanshe.

——. 1997. "Yao du yijia." *Dushu* 3: 77–84.

Li Shizhen. 1982. *Bencao gangmu.* Beijing: Renmin weisheng chubanshe.

Li Xiuzhang. 1988. "Guangdongbang fanmai yapian de yi lin ban zhao." In *Jiu Shanghaide yan du chang,* edited by Shanghaishi wenshiguan, 56–64. Shanghai: Baijia chubanshe.

Liang Gongchen. 1960. *Beidongyuan bilu.* Taibei: Xinxing shuju.

Liu Mingxiu. 1983. *Taiwan tochi to ahen mondai.* Tokyo: Yamakawa shuppansha.

Mao Haijian. 1995. "Sanyuanli kang Ying shishi bianzheng." *Lishi yanjiu* 1: 145–55.

Peng Yang'ou. [1960] 1982. *Heiji yuanhun.* In *WanQing wenxue congchao; xiaoshuo sanjuan,* edited by A Ying, 107–212. Beijing: Zhonghua shuju.

Shanghaishi wenshiguan, ed. 1988. *Jiu Shanghaide yan du chang.* Shanghai: Baijia chubanshe.

Su Zhiliang. 1997. *Zhongguo dupinshi.* Shanghai: Shanghai renmin chubanshe.

Sun Jiazhen. 1993. *Haishang fanhua meng.* Changchun: Shidai wenyi chubanshe. Also published under the title *Hualiu meng.*

Wang Shunu. [1933] 1988. *Zhongguo changji shi.* Shanghai: Sanlian shudian.

Wei Zi'an. 1981. *Huayue hen.* Fuzhou: Fujian renmin chubanshe.

Wen Kang. 1989. *Ernü yingxiong zhuan.* Jinan: Qilu shushe.

Wu Jianren. 1986. "Heiji yuanhun." In *Wu Jianren xiaoshuo xuan,* 439–50. Zhengzhou: Zhongzhou guji chubanshe.

Wu Runting. 2000. *Zhongguo jindai xiaoshuo yanbianshi.* Jinan: Shandong renmin chubanshe.

Xu Zhen'ou. 1984. *Shishuo xinyu jiaoqian.* Beijing: Zhonghua shuju.

Yaguan lou. N.d. Beijing University Library. Hand-copied edition.

Yu Da. 1990. *Qinglou meng.* Beijing: Beijing daxue chubanshe.

Yu Ende. 1934. *Zhongguo jinyan faling bianqianshi.* Shanghai: Zhonghua shuju.

Yu Jiao, Fang Nansheng et al., eds. 1988. *Meng'an zazhu.* Beijing: Wenhua yishu chubanshe.

Yu Wenyi. 1984. *Xu xiu Taiwan fu zhi.* Taiwan datong shuju.

Zhan Xi. 1992. *Hualiu shenqing zhuan.* Beijing: Beijing shifan daxue chubanshe.

Zhang Changjia. 1957. *Yanhua.* In *Yapian zhanzheng wenxue ji,* edited by A Ying, 765–79. Beijing: Guji chubanshe.

——. N.d. *Yanhua.* In *Xieyu congtan, sanji.* Shanghai Shenbaoguan. Shanghai Municipal Library.

Zhang Changling, ed. *Qingshiduo.* 1983. Beijing: Zhonghua shuju.

Zhang Hailin. 1993. *Wang Tao pingzhuan.* Nanjing: Nanjing daxue chubanshe.

Zhao, Xuemin. [1963] 1983. *Bencao gangmu shiyi.* Beijing: Renmin weisheng chubanshe.

Zhou Kai. 1984. *Xiamen zhi.* Taibei: Taiwan datong shuju.

WESTERN LANGUAGE SOURCES

Adshead, S. A. M. 1966. "The Opium Trade in Szechuan, 1801–1911." *Journal of Southeast Asian History* 7, no. 2: 93–99.

Allen, Nathan. 1853. *The Opium Trade in India and China.* Lowell, Mass.: James P. Walker.

Altenburger, Roland. 2000. "The Sword or the Needle; the Female Knight-errant (*xia*) in Traditional Chinese Fiction." Habilitationsschrift, University of Zurich.

Baumler, Alan. 2000. "Opium Control versus Opium Suppression: The Origins of the 1935 Six-Year Plan to Eliminate Opium and Drugs." In *Opium Regimes,* edited by Timothy Brook and Bob Wakabayashi, 270–91. Berkeley: University of California Press.

Bello, David. 2000. "Opium in Xinjiang and Beyond." In *Opium Regimes,* edited by Timothy Brook and Bob Wakabayashi, 127–51. Berkeley: University of California Press.

Berman, Marshall. 1982. *All That Is Solid Melts into Air: The Experience of Modernity.* New York: Simon & Schuster.

Berridge, Virginia. 1978. "East End Opium Dens and Narcotic Use in Britain." *London Journal* 4, no. 1: 3–28.

Berridge, Virginia, and Griffith Edwards. 1981. *Opium and the People: Opiate Use in Nineteenth-Century England.* London: Allen Lane; New York: St. Martin's.

Bhabha, Homi. 1992. "Postcolonial Authority and Postmodern Guilt." In *Cultural Studies*, edited by Lawrence Grossberg, Cary Nelson, and Paula A. Treichler, 56–68. London: Routledge.

——. 1994. *The Location of Culture.* London: Routledge.

Bingham, J. Elliot, Commander. 1843. *Narrative of the Expedition to China from the Commencement of the War to Its Termination in 1842.* 2 vols. London: Henry Colburn.

Blofeld, John. 1989. *City of Lingering Splendour.* Boston: Shambhala.

Blue, Gregory. 2000. "Opium for China: The British Connection." In *Opium Regimes*, edited by Timothy Brook and Bob Wakabayashi, 31–54. Berkeley: University of California Press.

Booth, Martin. 1998. *Opium: A History.* New York: St. Martin's.

Brook, Timothy, and Bob Tadashi Wakabayashi, eds. 2000. *Opium Regimes: China, Britain, and Japan, 1839–1952.* Berkeley: University of California Press.

Broomhall, B. 1882. *The Truth about Opium Smoking.* London: Hodder & Stoughton.

Burroughs, William. 1960. "Deposition: Testimony Concerning a Sickness." *Evergreen Review* 4, no. 11: 15–23.

——. 1967. "Kicking Drugs: A Very Personal Story." *Harper's* 235 (1967): 39–42.

——. 1983. *Junky.* Harmondsworth, U.K.: Penguin. Originally published in 1953.

Chang, Hsin-pao. [1964] 1970. *Commissioner Lin and the Opium War.* New York: Norton.

Chinese Repository. 1832–1851. Edited by E. C. Bridgman and S. Wells Williams. Vols. 1–20. Macao or Canton.

Chow, Rey. 1991. *Women and Chinese Modernity.* Minneapolis: University of Minnesota Press.

Cocteau, Jean. [1930] 1996. *Opium: The Illustrated Diary of His Cure.* Translated by Margaret Crosland. London: Peter Owen.

Cohen, Paul. 1978. "Christian Missions and Their Impact to 1900." In *The Cambridge History of China*, edited by Denis Twitchett and John K. Fairbank, 10, 1:543–90. Cambridge: Cambridge University Press.

Collis, Maurice. 1947. *Foreign Mud.* New York: Knopf.

Cooke, George Wingrove. 1858. *China: Being "The Times" Special Correspondence from China in the Years 1857–58.* London: Routledge.

Copjec, Joan. 1995. *Read My Desire: Lacan against the Historicists.* Cambridge: MIT Press.

Courtwright, David T. 1982. *Dark Paradise: Opiate Addiction in America before 1940.* Cambridge: Harvard University Press.

——. 1989. *Addicts Who Survived: An Oral History of Narcotic Use in America, 1923–1965.* Knoxville: University of Tennessee Press.

Cunynghame, Captain Arthur. 1845. *The Opium War: Being Recollections of Service in China.* Philadelphia: G. B. Zieber.

Dally, Ann. 1996. "Anomalies and Mysteries in the 'War on Drugs.'" In *Drugs and Narcotics in History*, edited by Roy Porter and Mikulas Teich, 199–215. Cambridge: Cambridge University Press.

Deleuze, Gilles, and Felix Guattari. 1987. Translated by Brian Massumi. *A Thousand Plateaus.* Minneapolis: University of Minnesota Press.

De Quincey, Thomas. [1821] 1994. *Confessions of an English Opium Eater.* Hertsfordshire, U.K.: Wordsworth Editions.

Des Forges, Alexander. 2000. "Opium/Leisure/Shanghai: Urban Economies of Consumption." In *Opium Regimes,* edited by Timothy Brook and Bob Wakabayashi, 167–85. Berkeley: University of California Press.

Douglas, Mary. 1987a. "A Distinctive Anthropological Perspective." In *Constructive Drinking,* 3–15. Cambridge: Cambridge University Press.

Douglas, Mary, ed. 1987b. *Constructive Drinking: Perspectives on Drink from Anthropology.* Cambridge: Cambridge University Press.

Downing, Charles Toogood. [1838] 1972. *The Fan-Qui in China in 1836–7.* 3 vols. Shannon: Irish University Press.

Edkins, Joseph. 1898. *Opium: Historical Note, or the Poppy in China.* Shanghai: American Presbyterian Mission Press.

——. 1903–1904. "Proceedings." *Journal of the North China Branch of the Royal Asiatic Society* 35: i–xi.

Emboden, William A. 1979. *Narcotic Plants.* Rev. ed. New York: Macmillan.

Fairbank, John K. 1978. "The Creation of the Treaty System." In *The Cambridge History of China,* edited by Denis Twitchett and John K. Fairbank, 10, 1:213–63. Cambridge: Cambridge University Press.

Farrère, Claude. 1931. *Black Opium.* Translated by Samuel Putnam. New York: Issued privately by Robert C. Fairberg.

Fay, Peter Ward. 1975. *The Opium War, 1840–1842.* Chapel Hill: University of North Carolina Press.

Forbes, Lieutenant F. E. 1848. *Five Years in China: From 1842 to 1847, with an Account of the Occupation of the Islands of Labuan and Borneo by Her Majesty's Forces.* London: Richard Bentley.

Fortune, Robert. 1847. *Three Years' Wanderings in the Northern Provinces of China.* London: John Murray.

——. 1852. *A Journey to the Tea Countries of China.* London: John Murray.

——. 1857. *A Residence among the Chinese (1853–1856): Inland, on the Coast, and at Sea.* London: John Murray.

Gandhi, Leela. 1998. *Postcolonial Theory: a Critical Introduction.* New York: Columbia University Press.

Goodman, Jordan, Paul E. Lovejoy, and Andrew Sherratt. 1995. *Consuming Habits: Drugs in History and Anthropology.* London: Routledge.

Graves, Reverend R. H. 1895. *Forty Years in China.* Baltimore: Woodward.

Greenberg, Michael. 1951. *British Trade and the Opening of China, 1800–42.* Cambridge: Cambridge University Press.

Griffith, William. 1993. *Opium Poppy Garden: The Way of a Chinese Grower.* Berkeley: Ronin.

Gully, Robert, and Capt. Denham. 1844. *Journals Kept by Mr. Gully and Capt. Denham during a Captivity in China in the Year 1842.* London: Chapman & Hall.

Gutzlaff, Charles. 1834. *Journal of Three Voyages along the Coast of China in 1831, 1832, and 1833, with Notices of Siam, Corea, and the Loo-choo Islands.* London: Frederick Westley and A. H. Davis.

Hahn, Emily. 1970. "The Big Smoke." In *Times and Places*, 220–40. New York: Crowell.

Halcombe, Charles J.H. 1896. *The Mystic Flowery Land: A Personal Narrative*. London: Luzac.

Hanan, Patrick. 1998. "*Fengyue Meng* and the Courtesan Novel." *Harvard Journal of Asiatic Studies*, 58, no. 2: 345–72.

———. 2000. "The Missionary Novels of Nineteenth-Century China." *Harvard Journal of Asiatic Studies* 60, no. 2: 413–43.

Hao, Yen-p'ing. 1986. *The Commercial Revolution in Nineteenth-Century China: The Rise of Sino-Western Mercantile Capitalism*. Berkeley: University of California Press.

Hayter, Alethea. [1968] 1988. *Opium and the Romantic Imagination*. Wellingborough: Crucible.

Headland, Isaac Taylor. 1906. "Chinese Children's Games." *Journal of the North China Branch of the Royal Asiatic Society* 37 : 150–84.

Heath, Dwight. 1987. "A Decade of Development in the Anthropological Study of Alcohol Use, 1970–1980." In *Constructive Drinking*, edited by Mary Douglas, 16–69. Cambridge: Cambridge University.

Hedin, Sven. 1935. "The Chinese Government Expedition to Sinkiang, 1933–35." *Journal of the North China Branch of the Royal Asiatic Society* 66: 129–30.

Henderson, James, M.D. 1864. "The Medicine and Medical Practice of the Chinese." *Journal of the North China Branch of the Royal Asiatic Society* 1: 21–69.

Henriot, Christian. 1997. *Belles de Shanghai: Prostitution et sexualité en Chine aux XIXe–XXe siècles*. Paris: CNRS Éditions.

Hershatter, Gail. 1997. *Dangerous Pleasures: Prostitution and Modernity in Twentieth-Century Shanghai*. Berkeley: University of California Press.

Herviev, Jean-Michel, ed. 1989. *L'Esprit des drogues: La dépendance hors la loi?* Paris: Autrement Revue.

Hevia, James. 1992. "Leaving a Brand in China: Missionary Discourse in the Wake of the Boxer Movement." *Modern China* 18, no. 3: 304–22.

———. 1995a. *Cherishing Men from Afar: Qing Guest Ritual and the Macartney Embassy of 1793*. Durham: Duke University Press.

———. 1995b. "The Scandal of Inequality: *Koutou* as Signifier." *Positions* 3, no. 1: 97–118.

Hosie, Alexander. 1914. *On the Trail of the Opium Poppy*. London: George Philip.

Howard, Paul. 1998. "Opium Smoking in Late Qing China: Chinese and Western Responses to a Social Problem, 1858–1915." Ph.D. diss., University of Pennsylvania.

Hu, Ying. 1997. "Re-Configuring *Nei/Wai*: Writing the Woman Traveller in the Late Qing." *Late Imperial China* 18, no. 1: 72–99.

Hunter, William C. 1855. *Bits of Old China*. London: Kegan Paul, Trench.

———. 1882. *The "Fan Kwae" at Canton before Treaty Days, 1825–1844*. London: Kegan Paul, Trench.

Jack, Ian. 1963. *English Literature, 1815–1832*. London: Oxford University Press.

Jamieson, George. 1888. "Tenure of Land in China and the Condition of the Rural Population." *Journal of the North China Branch of the Royal Asiatic Society* 23: 59–174.

Jaschok, Maria. 1988. *Concubines and Bondservants: A Social History*. London: Zed.

Jocelyn, Lord. 1841. *Six Months with the Chinese Expedition*. London: John Murray.

Jones, Susan Mann, and Philip A. Kuhn. 1978. "Dynastic Decline and the Roots of Rebellion." In *The Cambridge History of China*, edited by Denis Twitchett and John Fairbank, 10, 1:107–62. Cambridge: Cambridge University Press.

Kane, Harry Hubbell. 1881. "American Opium Smokers." *Harpers Weekly*, September 24, 645–46.

——. [1882]. 1976. *Opium-smoking in America and China.* New York: Arno.

Klein, Richard. *Cigarettes Are Sublime.* 1993. Durham, N.C.: Duke University Press.

Ko, Dorothy. 1994. *Teachers of the Inner Chambers: Women and Culture in Seventeenth-Century China.* Stanford: Stanford University Press.

Kobayashi, Motohiro. 2000. "Drug Operations by Resident Japanese in Tianjin." In *Opium Regimes,* edited by Timothy Brook and Bob Wakabayashi, 152–66. Berkeley: University of California Press.

Kulp, Daniel H. 1932. "Chinese Anthropometrics: Studies in Chekiang and Kwangtung." *Journal of the North China Branch of the Royal Asiatic Society* 63: 100–117.

Lacan, Jacques. 1981. *The Four Fundamental Concepts of Psycho-Analysis.* New York: Norton.

Lamantia, Philip, and Antonin Artaud. 1959. *Narcotica.* San Francisco: Auerhahn.

La Motte, Ellen N. 1920. *The Opium Monopoly.* New York: Macmillan.

The Last Year in China to the Peace of Nanking. 1843. London: Longman, Brown, Green & Longmans.

Latimer, Dean, and Jeff Goldberg. 1981. *Flowers in the Blood: The Story of Opium.* New York: Franklin Watts.

Lee, James S. 1935. *The Underworld of the East.* London: Sampson Low, Marston.

Lenson, David. 1995. *On Drugs.* Minneapolis: University of Minnesota Press.

Lewin, Louis. 1931. Translated by P. H. A. Wirth. *Phantastica: Narcotic and Stimulating Drugs, Their Use and Abuse.* London: Kegan Paul, Trench, Trubner.

Leyda, Jay. 1972. *Dianying: Electric Shadows.* Cambridge: MIT Press.

Lindstrom, Lamont. 1987a. "Introduction: Relating with Drugs." In *Drugs in Western Pacific Societies,* 1–12. Lanham, Md.: University Press of America.

Lindstrom, Lamont, ed. 1987b. *Drugs in Western Pacific Societies: Relations of Substance.* Lanham, Md.: University Press of America.

Liu, Lydia. 1995. *Translingual Practice: Literature, National Culture, and Translated Modernity–China, 1900–1937.* Stanford: Stanford University Press.

Lodwick, Kathleen D. 1996. *Crusaders against Opium: Protestant Missionaries in China, 1874–1917.* Lexington: University Press of Kentucky.

Lowe, Lisa. 1991. *Critical Terrains: French and British Orientalisms.* Ithaca: Cornell University Press, 1991.

Lyotard, Jean Francois. 1982. *The Postmodern Explained to Children: Correspondence 1982-1985.* Edited by Julian Pefanis and Morgan Thomas. Sydney: Power Publications.

MacPherson, Duncan, M.D. 1842. *Two Years in China: Narrative of the Chinese Expedition.* London: Saunders & Otley, 1842.

Marshall, Mac. 1987. "An Overview of Drugs in Oceania." In *Drugs in Western Pacific Societies,* edited by Lamont Lindstrom, 13–49. Lanham, Md.: University Press of America.

Martin, William Alexander Parsons. 1896. *A Cycle of Cathay; or, China, South and North.* New York: F.H. Revell.

Mather, Richard, trans. 1976. *A New Account of Tales of the World.* Minneapolis: University of Minnesota Press.

McMahon, Keith. 1995. *Misers, Shrews, and Polygamists: Sexuality and Male/Female Relations in Eighteenth-Century Chinese Fiction.* Durham, N.C.: Duke University Press.

——. 2000. "Opium and Sexuality in Late Qing Fiction." *Nan Nü: Men, Women, and Gender in Early and Imperial China* 2, no. 1: 129–79.

——. 2002. "Sublime Love and the Ethics of Equality in a Homoerotic Novel of the Nineteenth Century, *Pinhua baojian.*" *Nan Nü: Men, Women, and Gender in Early and Imperial China* 4, no. 1: 1-40.

Medhurst, Walter H. 1850. *A Glance at the Interior of China, Obtained during a Journey through Silk and Green Tea Countries.* London: John Snow.

Merlin, Mark David. 1984. *On the Trail of the Ancient Opium Poppy.* Rutherford, N.J.: Fairleigh Dickinson University Press.

Mervin, Samuel. 1908. *Drugging a Nation: The Story of China and the Opium Curse.* New York: Fleming H. Revell.

Meyer, Kathryn. 1995. "Japan and the World Narcotics Traffic." In *Consuming Habits: Drugs in History and Anthropology,* edited by Jordan Goodman, Paul E. Lovejoy, and Andrew Sherratt, 186–205. London: Routledge.

Meyer, Kathryn, and Terry Parssinen. 1998. *Webs of Smoke: Smugglers, Warlords, Spies, and the History of the International Drug Trade.* Lanham, Md.: Rowman & Littlefield.

Milligan, Barry. 1995. *Pleasures and Pains: Opium and the Orient in Nineteenth-Century British Culture.* Charlottesville: University of Virginia Press.

Morse, Hosea Ballou. 1910. *The International Relations of the Chinese Empire.* Shanghai: n.p.

Moule, Arthur Evans. 1891. *New China and Old: Personal Recollections and Observations of Thirty Years.* London: Seeley.

Murray, Alexander. 1843. *Doings in China. Being the Personal Narrative of an Officer Engaged in the Late Chinese Expedition, from the Recapture of Chusan in 1841, to the Peace of Nankin in 1842.* London: R. Bentley.

Musto, David F., M.D. 1973. *The American Disease: Origins of Narcotics Control.* New Haven: Yale University Press.

Newman, R. K. 1995. "Opium Smoking in Late Imperial China: A Reconsideration." *Modern Asian Studies* 29, no. 4: 765–95.

Nichols, Francis H. 1902. *Through Hidden Shensi.* New York: Charles Scribners' Sons.

Owen, Stephen. 1996. *An Anthology of Chinese Literature.* New York: Norton.

Parker, E. H. 1884a. "A Journey in Chekiang." *Journal of the North China Branch of the Royal Asiatic Society* 19: 27–53.

——. 1884b. "A Journey in Fukien." *Journal of the North China Branch of the Royal Asiatic Society* 19: 54–74.

——. 1884c. "A Journey from Foochow to Wenchow, through Central Fukien." *Journal of the North China Branch of the Royal Asiatic Society* 19: 75–93.

Parssinen, Terry M. 1983. *Secret Passions, Secret Remedies: Narcotic Drugs in British Society, 1820–1930.* Philadelphia: Institute for the Study of Human Issues.

Pendell, Dale. 1995. *Pharmako/Poeia: Plant Powers, Poisons, and Herbcraft.* San Francisco: Mercury House.

Polachek, James. 1992. *The Inner Opium War.* Cambridge: Harvard University Press.

Porter, Roy, and Mikulas Teich. 1996. *Drugs and Narcotics in History.* Cambridge: Cambridge University Press.

Pomeranz, Kenneth. 1997. "'Traditional' Chinese Business Forms Revisited: Family, Firm, and Financing in the History of the Yutang Company of Jining, 1779–1956." *Late Imperial China* 18, no. 1: 1–38.

Pratt, Mary Louise. 1992. *Travel Writing and Transculturation.* London: Routledge.

Pruitt, Ida. [1945] 1967. *A Daughter of Han: The Autobiography of a Chinese Working Woman.* Stanford: Stanford University Press.

Rattray, David. 1992. "Roger Gilbert-Lecomte." In *How I Became One of the Invisible,* 189–214. New York: Semiotext(e).

Richards, Thomas. 1993. *The Imperial Archive: Knowledge and the Fantasy of Empire.* London: Verso.

Ronell, Avital. 1992. *Crack Wars: Literature, Addiction, Mania.* Lincoln: University of Nebraska Press.

Rudgley, Richard. 1993. *Essential Substances: A Cultural History of Intoxicants in Society.* New York: Kodansha International.

Rush, James R. 1990. *Opium to Java: Revenue Farming and Chinese Enterprise in Colonial Indonesia, 1860–1910.* Ithaca: Cornell University Press.

Said, Edward. [1978] 1979. *Orientalism.* New York: Vintage.

Scarth, John. 1860. *Twelve Years in China.* Edinburgh: Thomas Constable.

Scott, John Lee. 1841. *Narrative of a Recent Imprisonment in China after the Wreck of the Kite.* London: W. H. Dalton.

Sherratt, Andrew. 1995. "Alcohol and Its Alternatives: Symbol and Substance in Pre-Industrial Cultures." In *Consuming Habits,* edited by Jordan Goodman et al., 11–46. London: Routledge.

Sirr, Henry Charles. 1849. *China and the Chinese.* London: W. S. Orr.

Skvortzow. B. W. 1921. "Notes on the Agriculture, Botany, and Zoology of China." *Journal of the North China Branch of the Royal Asiatic Society* 52: 79–111.

Slack, Edward R., Jr. 2000. "The Nationalist Anti-Opium Association and the Guomindang State, 1924–1937." In *Opium Regimes,* edited by Timothy Brook and Bob Wakabayashi, 248–69. Berkeley: University of California Press.

Smith, Arthur H. *Chinese Characteristics.* 1894. New York: Fleming H. Revell.

Spence, Jonathan. "Opium." [1975] 1992. In *Chinese Roundabout,* 228–56. New York: Norton.

Starr, Chloe. 2000. "Shifting Boundaries: Gender in *Pinhua baojian.*" *Nan Nü: Men, Women, and Gender in Early and Imperial China* 1, no. 2: 268–302.

Stifler, Susan Reed. 1938. "The Language Students of the East India Company's Canton Factory." *Journal of the North China Branch of the Royal Asiatic Society* 69: 46–82.

Szasz, Thomas S. 1974. *Ceremonial Chemistry: The Ritual Persecution of Drugs, Addicts, and Pushers.* New York: Anchor Doubleday.

Tang, Xiaobing. 1996. *Global Space and the Nationalist Discourse of Modernity: the Historical Thinking of Liang Qichao.* Stanford: Stanford University Press.

Trocki, Carl. 1999. *Opium, Empire, and the Global Political Economy: A Study of the Asian Opium Trade, 1750–1950.* London: Routledge.

United Kingdom. 1894. Parliamentary Papers, Cd. 50, 51, 52. *Reports and Minutes of Evidence of the Royal Commission on Opium.*

———. 1895. Parliamentary Papers, Cd. 42. *Final Report of the Royal Commission on Opium.*

Von Glahn, Richard. 1996. *Fountain of Fortune: Money and Monetary Policy in China, 1000–1700.* Berkeley: University of California Press.

Wakabayashi, Bob Tadashi. 2000. "From Peril to Profit: Opium in Late-Edo to Meiji Eyes." In *Opium Regimes,* edited by Timothy Brook and Bob Wakabayashi, 55–75. Berkeley: University of California Press.

Wakeman, Frederic. 1966. *Strangers at the Gate: Social Disorder in South China, 1839–1861.* Berkeley: University of California Press.

Waley, Arthur. 1958. *The Opium War through Chinese Eyes.* New York: Macmillan.

Walker, William O., III. 1991. *Opium and Foreign Policy: The Anglo-American Search for Order in Asia, 1912–1954.* Chapel Hill: University of North Carolina Press.

Wang, David Der-wei. 1997. *Fin-de-siècle Splendor: Repressed Modernities of Late Qing Fiction, 1849–1911.* Stanford: Stanford University Press.

Wang Hui. 1996. "The Fate of 'Mr. Science' in China: The Concept of Science and Its Application in Modern Chinese Thought." *Positions* 3, no. 1: 1–68.

Watson, W. C. Haines. 1905. "Journey to Sungp'an." *Journal of the North China Branch of the Royal Asiatic Society* 36: 51–102.

Werner, E. T. C. 1926. "Obituary of E. H. Parker." *Journal of the North China Branch of the Royal Asiatic Society* 57: i–vi.

Williams, Frederick Wells, ed. 1911. "The Journal of S. Wells Williams, LL.D." *Journal of the North China Branch of the Royal Asiatic Society* 42: 3–232.

Williams, Samuel Wells. 1874. "Recollections of China Prior to 1840." *Journal of the North-China Branch of the Royal Asiatic Society* 8: 1–21.

———. *The Middle Kingdom.* [1847] 1895. New York: Charles Scribners' Sons.

Wong, J. Y. 1998. *Deadly Dreams: Opium, Imperialism, and the Arrow War (1856–1860) in China.* Cambridge: Cambridge University Press.

Wong, R. Bin. 2000. "Opium and Modern Chinese State-Making." In *Opium Regimes,* edited by Timothy Brook and Bob Wakabayashi, 189–211. Berkeley: University of California Press.

Woodhead, H. G. W. 1931. *The Truth about Opium in China.* Shanghai: *Shanghai Evening Post and Mercury.*

Wylie, Jerry, and Richard E. Fike. 1993. "Chinese Opium Smoking Techniques and Paraphernalia." In *Hidden Heritage: Historical Archaeology of the Overseas Chinese,* edited by Priscilla Wegars, 255–303. Amityville, N.Y.: Baywood.

Yeh, Catherine. 1997. "The Life-style of Four *Wenren* in Late Qing Shanghai." *Harvard Journal of Asiatic Studies* 57, no. 2: 419-70.

Zamperini, Paola. 2001. "Untamed Hearts: Eros and Suicide in Late Imperial Chinese Fiction." *Nan Nü: Men, Women, and Gender in Early and Imperial China* 3, no. 1: 77–104.

Zhou, Yongming. 1999. *Anti-Drug Crusades in Twentieth-Century China.* Lanham, Md.: Rowman & Littlefield.

———. 2000. "Nationalism, Identity, and State-Building: The Antidrug Crusade in the People's Republic, 1949–1952. In *Opium Regimes,* edited by Timothy Brook and Bob Wakabayashi, 380–403. Berkeley: University of California Press.

Zizek, Slavoj. 1993. *Tarrying with the Negative.* Durham, N.C.: Duke University Press.

———. 1997. *Looking Awry: An Introduction to Jacques Lacan through Popular Culture.* Cambridge: MIT Press.

———. 1998. "Four Discourses, Four Subjects." In *Cogito and the Unconscious,* edited by Slavoj Zizek, 74–113. Durham, N.C.: Duke University Press.

Index

A Ying, 18
Adams, Joseph Samuel, 88, 96, 97
addiction: definitions, 3, 24–25;
 meanings, 14, 19, 20–22, 24; seen as
 disease, 16–17, 24; structure of, 15;
 theories of, 16; variability of effects,
 20; as way of life, 28–29. *See also*
 opium addiction
Affairs of the Eastern Seas (Haidong zhaji),
 35, 36
alchemical drugs, 114–15, 117
alcohol: anthropological literature, 17;
 drinking by Chinese, 108, 114, 118,
 158; drinking by fictional characters,
 158; drinking by Westerners, 27, 45
alcohol, comparisons to opium: alcohol
 seen as worse, 78, 85; differences
 between Chinese and Westerners, 11,
 27, 56, 62, 72; differences in
 intoxication, 72, 76–77, 103n5; moral
 differences, 71, 72; similarities, 77,
 86; suitability to Westerners or
 Chinese, 45
Allen, Nathan, 72–74, 76, 82, 91, 92, 96
Allen, Young J., 106
Amoy, 91, 96, 120
Amoy Gazetteer (Xiamen zhi), 36
animals, opium consumption, 148
Anne, 38, 44n24
Anstruther, P., 67n45, 67n50

aphrodisiac, opium as, 9–10, 33, 114,
 166
Arrow War, 13, 29n9
Asia. *See* Orientalism; Southeast Asia

Bagnall, B., 99
Beale, Thomas, 65n33
beggars, 99, *100*
Beijing opera, boy actresses, 62, 153,
 160, 165. *See also Precious Mirror of
 Boy Actresses*
The Bell of Qing Poetry (Qingshiduo), 18,
 148
Berridge, Virginia, 72
Bhabha, Homi, 5, 6, 108, 125, 186
Bingham, J. Elliot, 49, 53–54, 56, 58,
 59, 77, 82, 84–85
Birdwood, Sir George, 87, 88–89
Bits of Old China (Hunter), 77, 78
blackmail, 154, 155
Black Opium (Farrère), 126
Book of Changes, 114
bound feet, 53–54, 64n20, 145
boys: actresses, 62, 153, 160, 165;
 prostitutes, 165–66. *See also Precious
 Mirror of Boy Actresses*
Bridgeman, Elijah C., 51
Britain: commercial relations with
 China, 8, 15, 29n6; debate on opium
 trade, 87; fiction, 15, 16, 40, 59, 69;

laudanum use, 6, 39, 170n15;
medical use of opium, 39, 82; opium
dens, 127, 129; opium smoking,
39–40, 75, 102; prohibition of
opium, 11, 12, 16–17, 69; role in
opium trade, 187–88; state control of
narcotics, 16–17; Tianjin Treaty, 8,
20. *See also* De Quincey, Thomas;
London, opium dens; Opium Wars;
Royal Commission on Opium;
Western-Chinese relations
British East India Company, 36, 44n19,
51
British Empire, 7–8, 16, 29n7, 29n9
Broomhall, Benjamin, 74–75, 87
brothels: fictional depictions, 162–67;
opium smoking in, 114, 132, 162–67.
See also prostitutes
Brown, George Graham, 171n28
Burma, 34
Burroughs, William, 3, 18, 26, 28, 29n5,
42, 103n7, 125

Cai Erkang, 106, 143
Canton, 51; extent of opium smoking,
77–78; Westerners residing in, 33,
45, 57–59
capitalism, 7–8, 12, 29n7, 178
chair-bearers. *See* coolies
Chang, Hsin-pao, 92–93
Chefoo Convention, 104n19
Chen Sen. *See Precious Mirror of Boy
Actresses*
Chen Shenghua, 115
Chiang Kai-shek, 41
children: effects of opium, 148–49;
involvement in opium smoking,
153–54; mothers and, 56. *See also*
boys
China: corruption, 25, 37, 44n19, 86;
cultural superiority, 11, 112;
economy, 13, 25, 29n10, 37–38, 39,
98; opening to West, 4, 7, 11, 15, 23,
188; population growth, 38;
Republic, 41, 140; suspicions of
Chinese with foreign friends, 129;
use of term, 22–23. *See also* opium,

domestic production; prohibition of
opium; Western-Chinese relations;
Western views of China
China effect, 181, 183–84, 185
Chinese Characteristics (Smith), 55
Chinese Communist Party: prohibition
of opium, 10–11, 41, 43, 186;
socialism, 135, 190
Chinese Repository, 45, 51, 70, 76,
100–101, 109
Chinese views of opium: as allegory for
ruin of China, 10–11, 140, 143–44; as
allegory for transformation of China,
105; association with West, 2, 6,
10–11, 108–9, 113, 146, 176; as cause
of Chinese problems, 37–38, 108–10,
139, 142, 187; contrast with Western
views, 6–7; debates on opium trade,
29n10, 38, 70; negative effects on
China, 23; negative views of addicts,
35–36; as parasitical activity, 12;
reasons for smoking, 6, 144–45,
175–76, 184–86; as response to
cultural void, 125; as sign of Chinese
backwardness, 145; as sign of
Chinese weakness, 99–100; smoking
to be Western, 185; as Western
strategy to dominate China, 36,
108–10, 126, 146. *See also* "Opium
Talk"
Christianity: association with opium, 6;
Chinese converts, 106, 173n60, 184;
difference from Confucianism, 125;
lack of success in China, 187;
transforming effect on China, 2, 4,
99, 105, 124, 127, 176. *See also*
missionaries; Taiping Rebellion
clothing, Chinese, worn by Westerners,
46, 51, 52, 129, 137n22, 182, 183
cocaine, 40, 134, 191n2
Cocteau, Jean, 3, 8; on addiction, 27,
116, 119, 124, 131, 188; addiction of,
18, 127, 131, 171n23; descriptions of
opium smoking, 147; homosexuality,
137n27; on opium, 26, 28, 29, 92,
101, 123, 125, 190; on opium in
Annam, 148; *Opium: The Illustrated*

Diary of His Cure, 41, 189; similarities
to Chinese addicts, 125
Cohen, Paul, 106
Coleridge, Samuel Taylor, 15, 18,
55–56, 69, 116, 126
Collection of Opium War Literature, 18
Collins, W. H., 75
colonialism: East-West dichotomies,
47–49; effects on colonized culture,
5–6; fear felt by colonizers, 6, 16;
opium seen as punishment for, 75;
opium's role, 2, 7–8. *See also*
Western-Chinese relations
Communists. *See* Chinese Communist
Party
concubines, 162, 163, 165, 166, 168,
169, 179. *See also* prostitutes
Confessions of an English Opium Eater (De
Quincey), 6, 69, 70, 72
Confucianism: decline of, 2, 105, 106,
127, 189; difference from
Christianity, 125
Confucius, grave of, 88
Cooke, George Wingrove, 86, 96–97
coolies, 4, 13, 25, 42, 96–97, 112, 132,
155
corruption, 25, 37, 44n19, 86
courtesans, 157. *See also* prostitutes
Cowper, William, 60, 66n43
cravings: descriptions of, 26, 188;
satisfying without smoking, 150–51,
171n28
crime, 66n40, 121, 153–55
cross-cultural comparisons: blurring of
boundaries, 129; framework,
125–26; of opium addiction, 27–28,
126–29, 131–32; similarities, 125
Cunynghame, Arthur, 38, 49, 54, 55,
59, 85

Darwin, Charles, 15
A Daughter of Han (Pruitt), 101, 162
Davis, John, 93, 104n27
de Banville, Théodore, 131
De Quincey, Thomas: addiction, 131,
170n15; on addicts, 124; on Asia, 55,
69; *Confessions of an English Opium*

Eater, 6, 69, 70, 72; demonization of
Orient, 1, 14, 15, 55–56; description
of euphoria, 28; laudanum use, 18;
readers, 7, 94; similarities to Chinese
addicts, 125; solitude, 6, 116, 127;
visions, 72, 126, 127
Derrida, Jacques, 14, 15
Dickens, Charles, 40, 93
diseases. *See* medical use of opium
Downing, Charles Toogood, 49, 53, 56,
57, 60
Dracula (Stoker), 16
drama, depictions of opium addiction,
169n1
Dream Hut Notebook (*Meng'an zazhu*; Yu),
21
Dream of Courtesan Chambers (*Qinglou
meng*), 156, 157
Dream of Moon and Romance (*Fengyue
meng*; Hanshang Mengren), 140;
descriptions of opium smoking, 144,
151, 177; extortion, 154–55; language
of opium smokers, 149, 150; opium
wastrels, 118; prostitutes smoking,
162–66, 179
Dream of the Red Chamber, 172n45
drugs: addictive, 19; alchemical,
114–15, 117; anthropological
literature, 17; consumption of, 19–20,
178; current political rhetoric, 8;
definitions, 19; doubling effect,
183–84; evolution of use, 17; market,
178, 183, 191; misuse of, 162;
positive views of, 87; prohibition
efforts, 41; state control of, 10, 16–17,
186; trafficking, 17; use in ancient
times, 114–15, 117; uses, 20; war on,
24, 185, 186

"Earth of Lovesickness" (*"Xiangsi tu"*;
Yuan), 122
East India Company, 36, 44n19, 51
Edkins, Joseph, 34; contacts with
Chinese, 53; *Opium: Historical Note*,
49, 89; research, 51–52, 91, 182;
travel in China, 88
Edwards, Griffith, 72

Elwin, A., 96, 97
erotic fiction, 9–10, 142
Ershi zai fanhua meng. See The Vanity of Flourishing Life
Europeans. *See* Britain; France; Westerners in China; Western views of China
extortion of opium addicts, 121, 153–55

The 'Fan Kwae' at Canton before Treaty Days (Hunter), 58, 77, 78–79, 182
The Fan-qui in China in 1836-7 (Downing), 53
Farrère, Claude: *Black Opium*, 126; on lack of sexual desire, 114, 189; opium smoking, 18, 116, 128, 129, 131; opium smoking with Chinese, 27, 183
female smokers: comparison to male smokers, 175, 176–81; daring of, 180; daughters, wives, and mothers, 167–69, 177–78, 179, 184; dependence, 167; differences from men, 132; effects of opium on fertility and children, 148–49, 168, 169; effects of opium smoking, 177–78; estimated numbers, 156; fictional depictions, 132, 150, 154, 157, 162–69; lack of autobiographical accounts, 132; ugliness, 177; wastrels, 177, 184; Westerners, 41, 113, 116, 120, 170n18. *See also* prostitutes
Fengyue meng. See Dream of Moon and Romance
fertility, effects of opium smoking, 148–49, 168, 169
fiction: short stories on opium smoking, 126. *See also* novels
films, 10, 139, 169n4
fire: association with alcohol, 76; image of, 108–9, 110–11, 112, 113, 127, 145; of opium lamp, 113
Flowers of Shanghai (*Haishanghua liezhuan*; Han), 140, 142, 170n9, 172n56, 179
food: lack of importance to addicts, 114; land taken from grain production for opium, 12, 98

fools, addicts as, 124–25
Fortune, Robert, 49; contacts with Chinese, 53; description of Chinese, 56, 61, 62; descriptions of addicts, 96; descriptions of opium smoking, 85–86, 92, 94; illustration of opium utensils, 85; life in China, 182; opium offered to, 97; robberies of, 66n40; travel in China, 52, 63
Forty Years in China (Graves), 45
France: colonies, 8; concessions in Shanghai, 22; opium addicts, 26; Tianjin Treaty, 8, 20. *See also* Cocteau, Jean
free intercourse, 45, 50–51, 57, 59–60, 61
Freud, Sigmund, 14

gender: drug use and, 17; effeminacy of opium addicts and Chinese, 3, 47, 66n41, 74; feminization of Zhang, 134; male primacy, 9; mixing of sexes in opium dens, 40, 59. *See also* boys; female smokers; male smokers; marriage
Gilbert-Lecomte, Roger, 18, 26, 41
A Glance at the Interior of China (Medhurst), 52
Golden Lotus, 166
Gong Zizhen, 18
government employees, opium addiction, 148
Graves, R. H., 45, 49, 72, 75, 76
Gully, Robert, 66n42, 80, 82
guns: of Europeans, 112–13; term used for opium pipes, 107, 112, 145
Guomindang. See Nationalist (*Guomindang*) government
Gutzlaff, Charles, 49, 50, 51, 52–53, 56

Hahn, Emily, 18, 27, 41, 113, 116, 120, 170n18
Haishang fanhua meng (Sun), 173n59
Haishanghua liezhuan. See Flowers of Shanghai
Halcombe, Charles J. H., 86
Han Bangqing. *See Flowers of Shanghai*

Hanshang Mengren. *See Dream of Moon and Romance*
Hayter, Alethea, 26
He Shutian, 22
Heiji yuanhun: story, play, and film, 169n4. *See also Souls from the Land of Darkness*
Heiyu (Zhang), 170n6
Henderson, James, 74, 77, 86
hermits, 21, 114–15, 175
heroin, 42
Hevia, James, 48
homosexuality, 16, 137n27
Hualiu shenqing zhuan. See Love among the Flower and Willow Girls
Huang Xiaopei. *See The Vanity of Flourishing Life*
Huang Yufu, 35
huanxigao (happiness extract), 168
Huayue hen. See The Trace of Flowers and Moon
Huc, Evariste Régis, Abbé, 52, 64n15
Hume, David, 63n8
Hunter, William C., 51; in China, 49, 57–58, 60, 77–79; Chinese sleeping methods, 56–57; contacts with Chinese, 66n35; descriptions of opium smoking, 77–79; Huc and, 64n15; on opium trade, 23, 79, 145; positive view of China, 182; view of Chinese, 54; visits home, 62

India: British rule, 29n9; medical use of opium, 82; opium production and trade, 7, 34, 37, 42, 70, 88; opium smoking, 88–89
Indonesia, 33, 34, 35, 36, 109
inertia, opium, 164, 177
insatiability, opium, 3, 35–36, 76, 176, 178

Japan, involvement in drug trade, 8, 17
Jaschok, Maria, 162
Java. *See* Indonesia
Jesuits, 52
Jiumi liangfang. See Remedies for Rescue from Oblivion

JNCBRAS. *See Journal of the North China Branch of the Royal Asiatic Society*
Jocelyn, Robert, Lord, 49, 71–72, 74, 86, 91, 92, 94
Journal of the North China Branch of the Royal Asiatic Society (JNCBRAS), 51–52, 53, 97–98

Kaempfer, Englebert, 35
Kane, Harry Hubbell, 18, 77, 86, 91, 92, 93, 132–33
Klein, Richard, 25, 26, 131

laborers: Chinese in United States, 13. *See also* coolies
Lacan, Jacques, 176
Lamantia, Philip, 18
lamps, opium, 113, 130
The Last Year in China to the Peace of Nanking, 60–61, 72, 76
laudanum: use by Westerners, 27, 39, 73–74, 116, 124, 127; use in Britain, 6, 39, 170n15
Lazarus, Henry, 80, 89, 107
Lee, James S., 18, 27, 80, 87, 116, 134, 135
Legge, James, 53, 88, 106, 156
Lenson, David, 20, 21, 178
Lewin, Louis, 42
Li Bo, 142, 170n8
Liang Qichao, 48, 112, 147
Lin Zexu, 29n10, 38, 70, 77, 79
Linnaeus, 15, 50, 56
liquor. *See* alcohol
Lockhart, William, 89, 107, 156
London, opium dens, 15, 16, 39, 40, 59, 75, 91
Love among the Flower and Willow Girls (*Hualiu shenqing zhuan*; Zhan), 140, 145, 148–49, 150–51, 169n5
lovesickness of opium smokers, 9, 122, 130–31, 132, 175
Lu Xun, 55
Lyotard, Jean-François, 48

Macao, 34, 45, 59
MacPherson, Duncan, 9, 49, *84*; on abuse of opium, 190; description of

bound feet, 64n20; descriptions of
    Chinese, 81–82; descriptions of
    opium smoking, 80–81, 82–83, 90,
    91, 93–94; opium smoking, 18
Malaysia, 33, 34
male smokers: effects of opium on
    fertility, 148–49; fates, 179; fictional
    depictions, 151–52, 177, 179;
    lovesickness, 9, 122, 130–31, 132,
    175; proportion of smokers, 129–30;
    self-love, 132–33; Western, 131–32.
    See also opium smokers
marriages: interracial, 59, 66n38, 186;
    wedding customs, 173n60; wives
    addicted to opium, 167–68. *See also*
    polygamists
Marx, Karl, 7
Medhurst, Walter, Sr., 49, 52, 53, 96,
    97, 106, 154, 182
medical use of opium, 16, 73; in China,
    33, 34, 103n10; as excuse of addicts,
    28, 94, 189; history, 28; by
    Westerners, 39, 80, 82–83, 103n10,
    170n15
medicine: arguments for prohibition of
    opium, 72; development of, 16, 40
men. *See* gender; male smokers
Meng'an zazhu. See Dream Hut Notebook
Merlin, Mark David, 28
Mervin, Samuel, 92, 97, 98
Mesny, William, 137n22
The Middle Kingdom (Williams), 91, 92
Milligan, Barry, 15, 59, 75, 127
Ming China: opium trade, 36;
    restrictions on foreigners, 33–34
missionaries, 49; Chinese converts, 106,
    173n60; Chinese views of, 89; efforts
    to suppress opium, 13, 88, 89–90,
    139, 187; Jesuits, 52; stigma of
    opium, 31n34, 187; tracts, 51, 53;
    views of opium smokers, 12; writers,
    49, 51
modernity, 48, 107
money, unimportance compared to
    opium, 2, 110, 178, 189–90
monstrosity, 15–16
Moore, Sir William, 89

morphine, 8, 40, 42, 134
Morrison, Robert, 49, 54–55, 63n9
Moule, Arthur Evans, 49, 56, 148,
    173n60
Murray, Alexander, 60, 94–95
The Mystery of Edwin Drood (Dickens),
    40, 93
*The Mystic Flowery Land: A Personal
    Narrative* (Halcombe), 86

Nanking Treaty (1842), 8, 38, 52
narcotics. *See* drugs
Narrative of the Expedition in China
    (Bingham), 53–54
nationalism: Chinese, 12, 41, 48,
    139–40, 145; relationship to
    modernization, 48; Western, 12, 48
Nationalist (*Guomindang*) government,
    41
New Life Movement, 41
Nichols, Francis H., 99
nightmares of opium addicts, 26, 94,
    126–27, 128
Ningbo, 67n45, 96–97, 148
nonsmokers: differences from smokers,
    155, 160–61; estimated numbers,
    156; fictional depictions, 156,
    157–58, 160–61; prostitutes, 172n56;
    social classes, 156
noodle, opium, 152
novels, British, 15, 16, 40, 59, 69
novels, Chinese: allegories of opium
    addiction, 9–11; anti-opium views,
    142; censorship of, 141; criminal
    activities, 153–55; daily life of opium
    smoking, 140–41, 147–48, 150–53;
    erotic elements, 9–10, 142; evolution
    in nineteenth century, 143; female
    smokers, 132, 150, 154, 157, 162–69;
    images of opium addicts, 101, 141,
    142, 148–49, 156–57; language of
    opium smokers, 149–50; late Qing,
    10, 141–43; nonsmoking characters,
    156, 157–58, 160–61; opium wastrel
    characters, 9, 10, 118, 119–20,
    142–43; polygamists, 166; readers,
    143; sexual heroes, 142; totalizing

allegory of opium, 143–45, 147–48, 149; virtuous characters, 142–43; widespread use of opium depicted in, 140, 157. *See also Precious Mirror of Boy Actresses; Souls from the Land of Darkness*

opera, Chinese. *See* Beijing opera, boy actresses

opium: arrival in China, 2; attraction, 27, 123–24; Chinese consumption, 39, 41; Chinese terms for, 6, 20, 31n34, 34, 108, 144, 168; distinctions from other drugs, 28; eating, 73–74, 80, 150, 171n28; history of use, 28; pellets, 150; processing, 34, 42; scholarship on, 13–14; taxation, 39, 41; as weapon, 132. *See also* Chinese views of opium; Western views of opium

opium, domestic production: distribution, 98; economic benefits, 13; enforcement of prohibition, 42; greater than imports, 37, 39, 132, 184; increase, 8; land taken from grain production, 12, 98; opium villages, 91, 98–99, 101; in twentieth century, 41

opium, use in West: autobiographical accounts, 18; in Britain, 39–40, 75, 102; cross-cultural comparisons, 27–28, 125–29, 131–32; debates on, 40; forms, 42; medical use, 39, 73–74, 82; opposition to, 40; reasons for smoking, 41; in United States, 13, 39, 40, 42, 77, 86. *See also* Cocteau, Jean; De Quincey, Thomas; laudanum; Western views of opium

opium addiction: causes, 24; costs, 96–97, 98; cross-cultural comparisons, 27–28, 125–29, 131–32; danger of, 90–91; descriptions in "Opium Talk," 29, 98, 121–23, 128; fictional depictions, 101, 141, 142, 148, 156–57; long–term effects, 95–97; mild or deep, 121–23; negative views, 25;

outsiders' views, 13, 14–15; as parasitical activity, 12; physical effects, 21, 36, 124, 173n64; poverty caused by, 98, 99, 100–101, 120, 121, 135, 189–90; psychological effects, 1, 3, 13; as response to cultural void, 125; spread of, 99–100, 144–45, 155–56; stages, 100–101, 117–18, 119–21, 122–23, 130, 175; totalizing allegory in novels, 143–45, 147–48, 149

opium addicts: appearance, 36, 89, 92, 96, 120, 121, 167, 173n59; autobiographical accounts, 18–19, 26, 27; cravings, 26, 150–51, 171n28, 188; distinction from other smokers, 116, 121; effeminacy, 3, 47, 74; extortion of, 121, 153–55; fictional portrayals in Britain, 16; as hermits, 21, 114, 115, 175; lack of identification with Christianity, 125; in local government offices, 148; nightmares, 26, 94, 126–27, 128; power of opium, 109–10, 113–14, 130, 135; satires of, 121, 124; as scandalous figures, 13, 14; sleeplessness, 128; solitude, 116–18, 120, 127, 130–31, 133, 153. *See also* wastrels, opium

opium blight, 100–101

opium dens: in Britain, 127, 129; descriptions in British novels, 15, 40, 59, 69; descriptions in Chinese novels, 152; "lawyers," 152, 154; locations, 152–53; in London, 15, 16, 39, 40, 59, 75, 91; prohibition of, 36; in United States, 27, 39, 40, 75, 127, 129; Westerners' descriptions of, 71–72, 74, 86, 91, 102n3, 172n48; women in, 162, 172n48

Opium: Historical Note (Edkins), 49, 89

opium poppies, 34

opium smokers: Chinese with Westerners, 27, 128–29, 183; coolies, 4, 13, 25, 42, 96–97, 112; cross-cultural similarities, 27–28; estimated numbers, 155–56; experiences described in "Opium Talk," 111, 113, 115, 116, 118, 128, 129, 141, 175; identities, 178; inventiveness, 146–47; language, 149–50; learning to smoke, 116–17, 151, 152; physical effects, 24; positive view of opium, 28; reasons for smoking, 6, 41, 144–45, 175–76, 181–86; social classes, 71, 106, 153, 156; Westerners in China, 70, 77, 89, 91, 128–29, 183. *See also* female smokers; male smokers; opium addicts

opium smoking: as aphrodisiac, 9–10, 33, 114, 166; approaches to, 190–91; category crossings, 183, 188–89; classic Chinese style, 42–43; compared to eating, 73–74, 80; crash, 81; daily life of, 13, 140–41, 147–48, 150–53; dosages, 91, 92–93; effects on perceptions, 81; effects on sexual desire, 114, 130, 131, 177; euphoria, 28, 72, 73, 76, 81, 141; fictional depictions, 140, 147–48; in groups, 35, 116–17, 127–28, 152–53; growth in China, 36, 37; history in China, 33–39, 40–41; immediate effects, 91, 94–95, 114; massive use, 95–98, 99–100, 101–2, 127–28, 143–45; mixed with tobacco, 33, 34, 35, 146; in 1930s, 41, 170n18; as pacifier, 144–45, 187; physical effects, 80–81, 123, 148–49; preparation, 93, 121; productiveness, 13, 23; proverb on, 145; racial differences in reactions, 73, 75; risks, 153; smell, 92; by soldiers, 94–95; in Southeast Asia, 33, 34–35, 36; techniques, 35, 42–43, 151–52; types of opium, 98, 120, 151; utensils, 35, 42, *85*, 93, 120, 146, 149; visions, 86; witnessed by Westerners, 71–72, 84–86, 90–91. *See also* pipes, opium

opium sots, 4, 6, 7, 101

"Opium Talk" (*Yanhua*; Zhang): category crossings, 183; context, 106; cravings described, 188; decline of China, 109–11; definition of

addiction, 3; description of addiction, 29, 98, 121–23, 128; effects of opium on China, 4, 23, 105; effects of opium on smokers, 21, 123; experiences of opium smoker, 111, 113, 115, 116, 118, 128, 129, 141, 175; fall of god of money, 2, 106, 108, 110, 178, 189–90; good and bad smokers, 118–19; groups of smokers, 117; harm caused by opium, 119; history of opium in China, 2, 108, 110–11, 176; importance of opium, 28, 105; language and style, 7, 106, 189; lovesickness, 9, 130–31, 175; male smokers, 130–31; meanings of addiction, 19; medical use of opium, 189; methods of quitting opium, 133–35; moderation techniques, 113, 122; opium fools, 124–25; opium wastrels, 116, 118–19, 145, 161–62; perspective of addict, 105, 107, 108, 109, 119; poetry included, 18, 112, 115, 122, 133, 145; power of opium, 109–10, 112, 114, 115, 130; publication, 106; significance of text, 18, 105; stages of addiction, 117–18, 119–21, 122–23, 130, 175; transformation of China, 4, 105, 106–7, 108–10, 112–13, 127, 176; utensils described, 112, 120

Opium: The Illustrated Diary of His Cure (Cocteau), 41, 189

opium trade: British monopoly, 8, 29n9, 44n19; Chinese merchants involved, 8, 23, 36, 57, 78; competition, 8; corruption in, 44n19; debates among Westerners, 40, 69, 70, 77, 86, 87, 90; debates in China, 29n10, 38, 70; decline, 69; defense of, 78–79; destructiveness, 25; economic impact, 37, 98; growth, 23, 70; history, 34; importance in Western-Chinese relations, 8, 36–37; Japanese involvement, 8, 17; legalization, 8, 20, 38–39; official opposition in China, 20; profits, 7–8, 23, 57, 79; role in capitalist

development, 29n7; role in global trade, 2, 3, 17; role in opening of China, 4, 7, 11, 15, 23, 188; in Southeast Asia, 34, 70, 109
The Opium Trade in India and China (Allen), 72–74
opium villages, 91, 98–99, 101
The Opium War (Cunynghame), 54, 55
Opium Wars (1839–1842), 60; accounts of participants, 49; British deaths, 82, 83; British goals, 11, 95; British strength, 25; British views of Chinese, 60; Chinese defeats, 38; criticism of, 77; effects on foreign access to China, 33; opium smoking by Chinese soldiers, 94–95; Westerners imprisoned, 67n45
The Opium War through Chinese Eyes (Waley), 18
opium wastrels. *See* wastrels, opium
orchid images, 117, 127, 136n11
orientalism, 47
Owen, George, 187

Parker, E. H., 66n38, 97–98
Pendell, Dale, 135, 189, 190
Peng Yang'ou, 8. *See also Souls from the Land of Darkness*
People's Republic of China (PRC). *See* Chinese Communist Party
Picasso, Pablo, 92
Piercy, George, 75
Pinhua baojian. See Precious Mirror of Boy Actresses
pipes, opium: evolution, 35, 42; fictional account of invention, 144, 146; "gun," term for, 107, 112, 145; illustration of, *85*; parts of, 112; seen as modern invention, 107; for travelers, 146–47
poetry: on opium, 18, 106, 112, 115, 122, 133, 141, 145, 148; sexual heroes, 142
Polachek, James, 37
polygamists, 9, 131, 142, 145, 166
poppies, opium, 34

poverty, caused by opium addiction, 98, 99, 100–101, 120, 121, 135, 189–90
PRC. *See* Chinese Communist Party
Precious Mirror of Boy Actresses (*Pinhua baojian*; Chen), 140; descriptions of opium smoking, 151–52; descriptions of sexual activity, 142; female smokers, 165–67; nonsmoking characters, 160–61; opium addicts, 151–52, 153–54, 177, 179
prohibition of opium: addicts' responses, 188; based on fear, 178, 190; in Britain, 11, 12, 16–17, 69; Chefoo Convention, 104n19; Chinese motives, 11–12; destruction of opium, 38; enforcement in China, 42, 97, 126, 133, 140, 153; medical arguments for, 72; movements in early-twentieth-century China, 10, 40–41, 139–40, 191; in 1950s China, 10–11, 41, 43, 186; official Chinese, 36, 37, 38, 96, 129, 155; rationales in West, 7, 12, 16–17, 47, 76, 91, 187–88; reformers' support of, 139–40, 145, 147; in United States, 12, 69, 186; Western supporters, 7, 70, 76
prostitutes: ages, 167; boys, 165–66; contacts with foreigners, 59, 66n38; deceptiveness, 164; extortion of, 154–55; fictional depictions, 144, 151–52, 165–66, 173n56, 173n59; nonsmokers, 172n56; opium smokers, 42, 132, 155, 162–66, 172n56, 173n59, 179–80; prohibition in 1950s, 10; sales of women, 162, 179; smoking with customers, 13, 114, 165
Protestant missionaries. *See* missionaries
Pruitt, Ida, 162

Qian Zheng, 106, 143
Qing China: censorship, 141; elite, 48, 106; nationalism, 41; poetry, 18; restrictions on foreigners, 33–34. *See also* novels, Chinese
Qingshiduo. See The Bell of Qing Poetry

quitting opium: difficulty, 125, 134; effects on former smoker, 123, 173n64; methods, 133–35, 164, 168, 172n55

races: differing reactions to opium, 73, 75; marriages between, 59, 66n38, 186; mixing in opium dens, 40; physical differences, 53. *See also* Western views of China
Rattray, David, 42
recluses. *See* hermits
Remedies for Rescue from Oblivion (Jiumi liangfang, He), 22
Report of the Royal Commission on Opium. See Royal Commission on Opium
Republic of China, 41, 140
A Residence among the Chinese (Fortune), 62
Richard, Timothy, 106
Richards, Thomas, 16
robberies, 66n40, 154
Ronell, Avital, 3, 13, 14–15, 24, 26, 177, 183–84, 189
Royal Asiatic Society, North China Branch, 182. *See also Journal of the North China Branch of the Royal Asiatic Society*
Royal Commission on Opium, 70, 87–90, 96, 102n3, 145, 156, 187
ruffians, 60
Russell and Co., 49, 58, 65n32, 78

Said, Edward, 47
Scarth, John: in China, 49, 182; descriptions of Chinese, 54, 61–62, 66n44, 70, 97; on opium smoking, 86; travel in China, 52, 63
scientists, 15–16, 53, 54, 91; explorers, 50; language, 80, 90, 94. *See also* Fortune, Robert
Scott, John Lee, 66n42, 67n45
Selby, T. G., 90
sexuality: effects of opium on desire, 114, 130, 131, 177; erotic fiction, 9–10, 142; fictional descriptions of activity, 141, 142; homosexuality, 16, 137n27

Shanghai: concessions, 22, 51; guidebooks, 18, 141; international meeting on opium, 40–41; opium dens, 22, 126, 128, 133, 141, 172n48; opium trade through, 38; opium utensils produced in, 120; publishing activity, 143; Westerners' descriptions of, 56. *See also* Hahn, Emily
Shanxi, 91, 98–99
Shaow-Tih, 58, 66n34
Shen Fu, 59
silver, 15, 37
Singapore, opium dens, 71–72, 91
sinophiles, 47, 61–62, 182
Six Months with the Chinese Expedition (Jocelyn), 71–72
Six Records of a Floating Life (Shen), 59
sleeping arrangements, 56–57
Smith, Arthur, 49, 55, 108
smokers. *See* opium smokers
socialism, Chinese, 135, 190
Souls from the Land of Darkness (Heiji yuanhun, Peng): blackmailers, 154; Chinese inventiveness, 146–47; descriptions of addiction and smoking, 122, 152; descriptions of opium dens, 152; destruction of opium, 38; female smokers, 150, 154, 167, 168, 169; harmful effects of opium, 149; history of opium in China, 139, 140, 143, 144, 146–47; invention of opium pipe, 144, 146; pan-addiction depicted, 143–45, 147, 148, 149; power of opium, 113–14; process of addiction, 116–17; prostitutes, 167; satires of addicts, 124; spread of opium smoking, 101, 139
Southeast Asia: opium smoking, 33, 34–35, 36; opium trade, 34, 70, 109
Spence, Jonathan, 12, 34, 98
Stoker, Bram, 16
straight consciousness, 19, 20
Su Zhiliang, 41, 98
subjectivity, 176, 180–81
suicide, 172n41, 178–79, 180–81
Sunqua, 100–101
Szasz, Thomas S., 26

Taiping Rebellion, 6, 37, 156, 157, 184
Taiwan: interracial marriages, 59;
    opium smoking, 35; trade, 34;
    Westerners imprisoned, 66n42
Taiwan Gazetteer (*Taiwan fuzhi*), 36
Tales of Romantic Heroes (*Ernü yingxiong
    zhuan*; Wen), 142, 156, 157–59
Tao Qian (Tao Yuanming), 114, 142
taxes, 12, 39, 41, 98
tea, 15, 62, 97
Tianjin Treaty (1858–1859), 8, 20
tobacco: introduction to China, 108,
    111; as metonym for opium, 158–59;
    mixed with opium, 33, 34, 35, 146;
    use in China, 97, 158–59, 172n45
Tower of Elegant View (*Yaguan lou*), 140,
    144, 149, 153, 166
The Trace of Flowers and Moon (*Huayue
    hen*; Wei), 142, 156, 157, 172n42,
    172n45
trade. *See* opium trade
travel writing: accounts of contacts with
    native women, 50–51, 58;
    descriptions of opium dens, 71–72,
    172n48; descriptions of opium
    smoking, 70–72, 91; by explorers,
    50; famous writers, 63n9; by
    Western visitors to China, 50–51, 56,
    99
treaty ports, 25, 38, 52, 106. *See also*
    Canton; Shanghai
The Truth about Opium Smoking
    (Broomhall), 74–75, 87
Turner, Polhill, 187
Twelve Years in China (Scarth), 52, 54

The Underworld of the East (Lee), 87
United States: Chinese laborers, 13;
    diplomats in China, 49, 65n27; drug
    laws, 12, 40, 69, 186; morphine
    addiction, 40; opium dens, 27, 39,
    40, 75, 127, 129; opium use, 39, 40,
    42, 77, 86; prohibition of opium, 12,
    69, 186; ships involved in opium
    trade, 38; Tianjin Treaty, 8, 20;
    views of opium smokers, 27. *See also*
    Western-Chinese relations

utensils, opium, 35, 42, *85*, 93, 120, 146,
    149. *See also* pipes, opium

The Vanity of Flourishing Life (*Ershi zai
    fanhua meng*; Huang), 140, 149,
    167–68, 171n21
villages. *See* opium villages
von Glahn, Richard, 37

Wade, Thomas F., 89, 187
Waley, Arthur, 18
Wang Tao, 53, 106, 107–8
Wang Xi, 34
Ward, Frederick Townsend, 66n38
wastrels, fictional, 142
wastrels, opium: Chinese view of, 6–7;
    descriptions in "Opium Talk," 116,
    118–19, 145, 161–62; descriptions of,
    101; female, 177, 184; in fiction, 9,
    10, 118, 119–20, 142–43; prostitutes
    and, 132
Watson, W. C. Haines, 98
Wei Zi'an. *See The Trace of Flowers and
    Moon*
Wen Kang. *See Tales of Romantic Heroes*
West: progress and modernity, 48; use
    of term, 22–23. *See also* colonialism
Western-Chinese relations: anti-Western
    views in China, 11–12; Chinese
    adaptations of Western products,
    184; Chinese reactions to Western
    invasion, 185, 190; commercial
    relations, 8, 15, 29n6, 37; cultural
    competition, 5–6, 11, 185, 186–87;
    opium as bridge, 23, 27, 129, 176;
    resistance to Western hegemony,
    190; role of opium, 2, 176; role of
    opium trade, 8, 36–37; seduction
    and estrangement allegory, 3–4;
    symbolic cross-cultural order, 5–7;
    transforming effect on China, 4, 105.
    See also Christianity; opium trade
Westerners in China: China specialists,
    49; Chinese terms for, 6; Chinese
    views of, 53, 56, 71; concessions in
    port cities, 51, 52; contacts sought
    by, 45–46, 59–60, 63; contacts with

Chinese, 53, 55, 57–59, 62, 63, 66n35, 128–29; cultural effects, 106; dressing as Chinese, 46, 51, 52, 129, 137n22, 182, 183; expertise, 62–63, 70, 181–83; free intercourse, 45, 46, 50–51, 57, 59–60, 61; love-hate relationship with Chinese, 52–53; as observers, 48–49, 53–55, 62–63, 70, 80, 90; opium smokers, 18, 70, 77, 80, 83, 87, 89, 91, 116, 128–29; opium smoking with Chinese, 27, 128–29, 183; reciprocity in relationships, 57, 61; research conducted, 51–52, 53, 62–63, 80, 91; restricted movement, 33–34, 45, 50, 52, 59–60; sailors, 59, 78; sense of superiority, 48–49; sinophiles, 47, 61–62, 182; views of each other, 22; violent contacts with Chinese, 59–61, 66n40, 66n44. *See also* missionaries; Opium Wars

Western views of China: as alien or other, 3, 15, 46, 47–48, 54–56; assumptions, 46; awe, 1–2; Chinese understandings of, 55; common humanity seen, 47, 56, 57, 61; conflation of opium smokers and Chinese, 7, 8, 11, 13, 15, 69, 74–75, 181; demonization of Orient, 1, 14; effeminacy of opium addicts and Chinese, 3, 47, 66n41, 74; fascination with bound feet of women, 53–54; in fiction, 15; generalizations about, 22; as inferior, 47–48, 50, 128; as lawless, 125–26; love-hate relationship, 52–53; as negativity, 55–56; as phlegmatic, 56; physical differences, 53; positive, 47, 56–57, 61–62, 99, 128, 182; remoteness from Chinese, 71; stereotypes, 4, 40, 45, 46, 47, 54–55; as weak, 57, 60–61, 65n27, 66n41, 95, 102

Western views of opium: assumption that Westerners did not smoke, 45, 83, 89, 107; of capitalists, 12; contrast with Chinese views, 6–7; dangers of addiction, 185; debates on, 69, 70, 187–88; descriptions of opium dens, 71–72, 74, 86, 91, 102n3, 172n48; descriptions of opium smoking, 45, 70–72, 80–81, 84–86, 87, 90–91, 93–94; explanations of smoking by Chinese, 181–84; as eyesore, 6; harmfulness, 71–77, 83, 88; massive use, 95–98; medical use, 39, 80, 82–83, 103n10, 170n15; medical view, 72–73; of missionaries, 12; negative, 7, 8, 187, 188; positive, 77–90; as punishment for colonialism, 75; seen as natural for Chinese, 4, 74–75; stereotypes of opium smokers, 4, 47; support of prohibition, 7; as threat, 10, 11, 12, 15, 102

Williams, Samuel Wells, 49, 51, 65n27, 91, 92, 93, 94, 182–83

women, Chinese: bound feet, 53–54, 64n20, 145; chastity, 54; contacts with foreigners, 54, 58–59, 66n35; descriptions of, 58, 66n35; hysteria, 180–81; marriages, 167–68, 173n60; marriages with Western men, 59, 66n38; motherhood, 56, 167; in opium dens, 162, 172n48; social expectations of, 177, 180; subjectivity, 180–81; suicides using opium, 172n41, 178–79, 180–81; tobacco smoking, 159, 172n45. *See also* concubines; female smokers; gender; prostitutes

women, Western: marriages with Chinese men, 59; in opium dens, 75; opium smokers, 41, 113, 116, 120, 170n18; prohibited from residing in Canton, 58

Wong, J. Y., 8

Wu Jianren, 169n4

wushisan (five mineral powder). *See* drugs, use in ancient times

Xi Shiyi (*Precious Mirror of Boy Actresses*), 151–52, 165–67, 177, 178, 179

Xiamen zhi. *See* *Amoy Gazetteer*

"Xiangsi tu" ("Earth of Lovesickness";
    Yuan), 122
Xu Fumin, 169n4

Yaguan lou. See Tower of Elegant View
yangyan (Western-sea smoke), 6, 31n34
yangyao (Western-seas medicine), 20, 144
Yanhua. See "Opium Talk"
yapian (opium), 20, 34, 108
Yen-p'ing Hao, 37
yin (addiction), 19, 21, 36, 114
Yu Ende, 34
Yu Jiao, 21, 36
Yuan Yi, 122

Zhan Xi. *See Love among the Flower and
    Willow Girls*
Zhang Changjia, 8; addiction, 115,
    179; family, 131; feminization of,
    134; opium smoking related to
    Western dominance of China,
    99–100; smoking with friends,
    117, 127; as spokesman for
    addicts, 115–16. *See also* "Opium
    Talk"
Zhang Chunfan, 170n6
Zhang Shichuan, 169n4
Zhang Zufen, 169n1
Zhaoyinju (Zhang), 169n1

About the Author

Keith McMahon is professor and chair of East Asian Languages and Cultures at the University of Kansas.

JACKSON LIBRARY - LANDER UNIV.

3 6289 00273832 3